D1598422

CLIMATE, AFFLUENCE, AND CULTURE

Everyone, everyday, everywhere has to use money to cope with climatic cold or heat to satisfy survival needs. This point of departure led to a decade of innovative research based on the tenet that climate and affluence influence each other's impact on culture. Evert Van de Vliert discovered survival cultures in poor countries with demanding cold or hot climates, self-expression cultures in rich countries with demanding cold or hot climates, and easygoing cultures in poor and rich countries with temperate climates. These findings have implications for the cultural consequences of global warming and local poverty. Climate protection and poverty reduction are used in combination to sketch four scenarios for shaping cultures, from which the world community has to make a principal and principled choice soon.

Evert Van de Vliert received his PhD from the Free University in Amsterdam in 1973 and held teacher and researcher positions at the same university, at the University of St. Andrews in Scotland, and at the Royal Military Academy in the Netherlands. He served as chairman of the Dutch Research Association of Social and Organizational Psychologists (1984–1989) and as research director of the Kurt Lewin Institute (1993–1996). He has published more than 200 journal articles, chapters, and books including *Complex Interpersonal Conflict Behaviour: Theoretical Frontiers* (1997). In 2005, he received the Lifetime Achievement Award of the International Association for Conflict Management. At present, he is professor emeritus of organizational and applied social psychology at the University of Groningen in The Netherlands and research professor of work and organizational psychology at the University of Bergen in Norway. His current research concentrates on cross-national comparisons, with an emphasis on the impact of cold, temperate, and hot climates on national and organizational cultures.

CULTURE AND PSYCHOLOGY

Series Editor: David Matsumoto, San Francisco State University

As an increasing number of social scientists come to recognize the pervasive influence of culture on individual human behavior, it has become imperative for culture to be included as an important variable in all aspects of psychological research, theory, and practice. *Culture and Psychology* is an evolving series of works that brings the study of culture and psychology into a single, unified concept.

Ute Schönpflug, *Cultural Transmission*
Evert Van de Vliert, *Climate, Affluence, and Culture*

Climate, Affluence, and Culture

Evert Van de Vliert

University of Groningen and University of Bergen

CAMBRIDGE UNIVERSITY PRESS
Cambridge, New York, Melbourne, Madrid, Cape Town, Singapore,
São Paulo, Delhi, Dubai, Tokyo

Cambridge University Press
32 Avenue of the Americas, New York, NY 10013-2473, USA

www.cambridge.org
Information on this title: www.cambridge.org/9780521517874

First published 2009

A catalog record for this publication is available from the British Library

Library of Congress Cataloging in Publication data
Vliert, Evert Van de.
Climate, affluence, and culture / Evert Van de Vliert.
p. cm. – (Culture and psychology)
Includes bibliographical references and index.
ISBN 978-0-521-51787-4 (hardback)
1. Human beings – Effect of climate on. 2. Environmental psychology.
3. Wealth. 4. Culture. I. Title. II. Series.
GF71.V65 2009
304.2′5-dc22   2008021908

ISBN 978-0-521-51787-4 Hardback

Transferred to digital printing 2010

CONTENTS

Acknowledgments   *page* ix

PART ONE: INTRODUCTION

1 Creators of Culture   3

PART TWO: CLIMATE, CASH, AND WORK

2 Climate Colors Life Satisfaction   31

3 Cash Compensates for Climate   57

4 Work Copes with Context   84

PART THREE: SURVIVAL, COOPERATION, AND ORGANIZATION

5 Survival, Self-Expression, and Easygoingness   113

6 Cooperation   137

7 Organization   165

PART FOUR: CONCLUSION

8 Bird's-Eye Views of Culture   197

Appendix: Climate Indices   225
References   233
Index   245

ACKNOWLEDGMENTS

Others are the motor of personal progress. In 1995, I gave an opening address at the combined annual conferences of the International Association for Conflict Management and the Ethnic Studies Network. The predominantly critical reactions to my presentation, entitled "Temperature, Culture, and Domestic Political Violence Worldwide," encouraged me to start what became a never-ending scientific expedition. Since then, a wide array of people have helped me to shape my ideas on a wide array of topics covering climate, affluence, and culture. Special thanks go to those colleagues who co-authored my publications on research conducted to crack climate-culture codes, to wit, Serge Daan, Ståle Einarsen, Martin Euwema, Geert Hofstede, Xu Huang, Sipke Huismans, Onne Janssen, Esther Kluwer, Robert Levine, Richard Lynn, Philip Parker, Shalom Schwartz, John Simister, Peter Smith, Henk Thierry, Gerben Van der Vegt, and Nico Van Yperen.

I am enormously grateful to Martin Euwema, Patricia Goldrick, Onne Janssen, David Matsumoto, and Evy De Koning for having taken the trouble to read the entire manuscript and to make many suggestions to improve it. Portions of the book have further benefited from the comments of Serge Daan, Douwe Draaisma, Xu Huang, Lourdes Munduate, Ab Van de Vliert, and Huadong Yang. Last but not least, related to Cambridge University Press, Patterson Lamb, David Matsumoto, Regina Paleski, Eric Schwartz, and two anonymous reviewers of my work were indispensably helpful in bringing this publication project to fruition. The finishing touches are all theirs to be proud of.

PART ONE

INTRODUCTION

1

Creators of Culture

We shape our environment, and then our environment shapes us.
Winston Churchill, undated

Animals face a variety of problems. In addition to attacks by predators, they often have to survive harsh climates and shortages of food and drink. They react instinctively with a corresponding variety of solutions. Salient responses to bitter winters, scorching summers, and lack of food and drink include winter sleep, summer sleep, and migration. Although humans face the same survival problems, they have not evolved these particular reaction patterns. In common with most animals, humans living near the poles do not sleep all day in dark winters, and those living near the equator do not to sleep all day in blistering-hot summers. And almost all humans are reluctant to migrate permanently or to follow flocks of birds in spring and fall on their way to more comfortable places for the oncoming winter or summer. Indeed, unlike our distant ancestors in hunting and gathering societies, we tend to stay where we are, and that seems convenient. But in a hardening climate we are in danger.

In harsh climates, humans must ceaselessly solve problems of extreme cold or heat, shrinking food and drink supplies, and lurking diseases. In response, they have invented a tool no animal action ever can compete with. Its miraculous power can solve a fantastic variety of climatic, nutritional, and health problems. What's more, its wondrous achievements are in no way tied to a specific ethnic group, a

particular geographic area, or a certain period in time. That tool is
money. As a rule, money can buy all the necessities of life, including
heat and cold, food and drink, cure and care. Slowly but surely, the
availability of money resources has become the essential solution for
the basic problem of human survival. Indeed, we have come to use
money as a kind of life preserver, and that seems convenient. But in
poverty-stricken circumstances we are in danger.

Both climate and cash, therefore, are of vital importance as
resources in supporting survival and a desirable quality of life.
Temperate climates offer the best of all worlds, with comfortable
outdoor temperatures, thriving plants and animals as living resources of enormous benefit, and relatively healthy living conditions.
Cold or hot climates, lacking the climatic resources of temperate
areas, endanger our lives and frustrate us. Money resources, however, can compensate for the lack of climatic resources, enabling us
to also survive and live happily in harsh climates. These ecological
matters of life and death are relevant to a proper understanding
of what we collectively value, believe, seek, avoid, and do: that is,
our culture.

Each society gives birth to a culture that includes everything that
has contributed to survival in the recent or remote past – tools such
as money, practices such as work, goals such as cooperation,
constructions such as organizations. And climate and cash rock
the cradle of culture. This should not be taken literally, of course.
Climate and cash are inanimate things; only *we* can bring them to
life. Or, to paraphrase Winston Churchill's pointed piece of wisdom,
"We shape our environment and, through it, we shape our culture."
This is an immense project. It takes a long time, multiple trials and
errors, and much competition and coordination to build and
rebuild culture in response to climate and cash. Hence, a crucial
part of this culture-building process is that we pass on what we have
learned from generation to generation in a nongenetic way (for a
thorough overview of how this works, see Whiten et al., 2003).

In short, we create our climatic and economic contexts, and these contexts then create our cultures. On this two-way street between contexts and cultures, a vast array of scholars moves from cultures toward climates and economies. My drive is in the opposite direction, from climates and economies toward cultures. I aim to contribute to a body of knowledge about the fit between given combinations of climate and cash and the cultures created in response to them. In this introductory chapter, the points of departure are sketched under the headings "Culture and Survival" and "Culture in Context." The chapter is summarized in a diagram. In combination with the propositions at the end of each of Chapters 2 to 7, this diagram forms the groundwork for an outline of several bird's-eye views of culture presented in Chapter 8. One of the views provided in that final chapter, a strategic view of the context-culture links found, sheds novel light on two huge threats humanity faces today: global warming and local poverty. If we can create global warming and local poverty, we can create cultures.

CULTURE AND SURVIVAL

Borrowing from leading cross-cultural psychologists (Hofstede, 2001; Schwartz, 2004; Smith et al., 2006; Triandis, 1995), I define societal culture as a rich complex of values and practices passed on and changed from generation to generation. Complex syndromes of culture have many origins and are developed further in numerous ways (Boyd & Richerson, 2005; Buss, 2004; Diamond, 2005; Nolan & Lenski, 1999). But the most fundamental explanations of culture have been rooted in two clearly distinguishable types of survival: genetic survival over time and climatic survival in a particular place.

On the one hand, culture has been traced back to human reproduction represented by, for example, the "selfish gene" (Dawkins, 1989), menstruation (Knight, 1991), son-daughter preferences (Kanazawa, 2006), and parental investment (Buss, 2004). On the other hand, through the ages, Hippocrates, Ibn Khaldun, Montesquieu, Quetelet, and Huntington, to mention but a handful of classic scientists, have all tried in vain to relate culture to climate. At the beginning of the 20th century, the proponents of the so-called geographical school also argued that climate matters for all sorts of psychosocial phenomena (for an overview, see Sorokin, 1928). But the geographical school, too, failed to demonstrate and clarify convincingly how climatic effects come about and link up to values and practices. As a result, genetic roots of culture have received much more attention than climatic roots of culture, which is unfortunate because climatic survival is more basic than genetic survival. Genetic survival is simply impossible without climatic survival.

This state of the science is unfortunate also because cold and heat are potentially important origins of culture for descriptive, explanatory, and strategic reasons. The descriptive reason is that thermal climates relate distinct cultures to stable differences in latitude and altitude. Scientifically, climate-based culture maps have to be taken as seriously as geographic maps and astronomic charts. The explanatory reason is that thermal climates relate distinct cultures to unobtrusive differences in atmospheric contexts. Climate is a more fundamental and more stable antecedent condition of culture than more proximate correlates of values and practices such as subsistence technology, urbanization, and democracy. The strategic reason is that knowledge about climatic anchors of culture may keep us from attempting to implement infeasible policies and procedures as a result of aiming to reach beyond contextual limits to globalization and planned cultural change (for details, see Van de Vliert, Einarsen, et al., 2008).

CULTURE IN CONTEXT

Animals instinctively select and change a specific natural environment as their habitat. Analogously, humans create a specific culture that optimizes successful existence in a given context. Perhaps it is

better to talk about several contexts. First are the climatic and economic contexts. In addition, the contexts of water and marine
organisms, terrestrial flora and fauna, oil reserves and mineral
deposits, and risks of flooding and earthquakes are easily recogniz-
able. Increasingly, alas, animals and humans alike have to cope with
polluted air and water, toxic and chemical waste, and deadly viruses.
All of these and similar life-controlling contexts together form the
niche in which a society builds and rebuilds a fitting culture. For
example, it makes perfect sense that Icelanders, Norwegians, and
Japanese value and practice whale fishing, that Californians and
Cypriots grow wines, and that Chinese and South Africans engage
in terrestrial mining.

The reasons for focusing on the climatic and economic characteristics of niches of culture in concert are straightforward. Climatic
demands and money resources are basic living conditions experienced
by nearly every member of every society on earth on a daily basis.
Nonetheless, both contextual conditions vary considerably from one
society to another. As a consequence, they have shaped the history of
every country on all of our inhabited continents. An extra reason to
highlight climate and cash is that they are interdependent factors and
form integrated climato-economic niches. Harsher climates make
money resources more useful; money resources make harsher climates less threatening. Below, the climatic context, the economic
context, and the climato-economic niches are introduced further,
in this order, and are visually related to culture in Figure 1.1.

Climatic Context

My first publication on the consequences of climate for culture
(Van de Vliert & Van Yperen, 1996) turned out to be a finger exercise
for my later work. It made no clear distinctions between weather and
climate; between temperature and precipitation; and between the
cultural consequences of cold, temperate, and hot climates. These

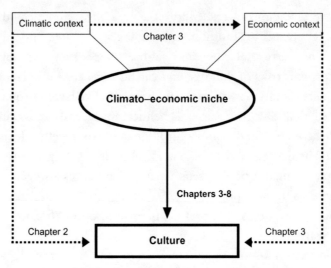

FIGURE 1.1. A model of cultural adaptations to climato-economic niches.

inaccuracies call for clarification because similar dilemmas and errors have plagued scholars ever since Hippocrates (460 B.C.) noted that climate generally shapes physiological needs, psychological well-being, and cultural mores.

Weather versus climate. Whereas weather indicates what is happening to the atmosphere at any given time, climate refers to the generalized weather of an area over at least a 30-year period. Weather changes continuously; climate has been extraordinarily stable for the last 10,000 years. Weather tends to have immediate *physiological* and *psychological* effects at the individual and group levels; climate tends to have *psychological* and *sociological* effects in the longer run and at the societal and global levels of human functioning. Nonetheless, an overview of the extant literature on temperature effects on humans (Parker, 1995), which lists 807 physiological studies, 458 psychological studies and 830 sociological studies, shows no distinction whatsoever between weather and climate. The studies reported here transcend weather by highlighting the psychosocial consequences of climate in the long run and at the societal level of functioning.

Climatic temperature versus climatic precipitation. Climates are made up of temperature, precipitation, wind, humidity, pressure, and so on. To reduce complexity, they are often classified using a combination of the two most important factors: average temperature (frigid, temperate, torrid) and average precipitation (arid, semi-arid, subhumid, humid, wet). In addition, multiple temperature-precipitation combinations within nations are usually averaged to represent the climate of whole nations in a unitary way (the problem of within-nation variation in climate will be addressed in Chapter 2).

For example, in a climate-culture study under the acronym *GLOBE* (House et al., 2004), an international consortium of approximately 170 scholars used the following seven major clusters of climates: *tropical humid* (Colombia, Costa Rica, Ecuador, India, Indonesia, Malaysia, Philippines, Singapore), *savanna* (El Salvador, Guatemala, Nigeria, Thailand, Venezuela, Zambia, Zimbabwe), *desert* (Egypt, Iran, Israel, Kazakhstan, Kuwait, Mexico, Namibia, Qatar, South Africa, Turkey), *subtropical humid* (Argentina, Bolivia, Brazil, Hong Kong, Taiwan), *mediterranean* (Albania, Greece, Italy, Morocco, Portugal, Slovenia, Spain), *maritime* (Britain, Denmark, France, Germany, Ireland, Netherlands, New Zealand, Switzerland), and *continental* (Australia, Austria, Canada, China, Finland, Georgia, Hungary, Japan, Poland, Russia, South Korea, Sweden, United States).

Using such a typological approach to investigate climate-culture links has the advantage that climate is correctly treated as a whole of integrated components. But it also has the disadvantage that the impact of climate cannot be accurately attributed to temperature or precipitation. Take GLOBE's finding that the cultural value of uncertainty avoidance by relying on social norms, rules, and procedures is distinctively stronger in tropical and subtropical climates than in maritime and continental climates (Sully de Luque & Javidan, 2004). Should we explain this finding in terms of climatic temperature or climatic precipitation? Or does a combination of climatic temperature and climatic precipitation account for it? And would we come to the same conclusion if we used the 58 countries listed instead of the 7 clusters of countries as our unit of analysis? To prevent the occurrence of such queries as much as possible, climatic temperature and climatic precipitation are construed here as country-level dimensions with influences on culture that can be separately assessed.

Splitting up climatic temperature and climatic precipitation is defensible also because it makes sense to assume that temperature has an even more important cultural impact than precipitation, for the following reasons. In general, leaving disasters aside, winters and summers seem to be more critical than wet and dry seasons. Whereas bitter winters and scorching summers endanger thermal comfort, crops, and health, very wet and very dry seasons endanger crops in particular. Furthermore, whereas harsh winters and harsh summers are seldom a godsend, much precipitation can be either bad luck resulting from snowfall during already ice-cold winters or good luck resulting from rainfall during otherwise sweltering hot summers. Similarly, clear skies can be either good luck during bitter winters or bad luck during scorching summers.

Last, increasing temperatures tend to increase evaporation, which leads to more precipitation rather than the other way round. According to the Intergovernmental Panel on Climate Change (Houghton et al., 2001), as average global temperatures have risen, average global precipitation, especially land-surface precipitation, has also increased. For all of those reasons, a thermal climate seems to call for more coping and cultural adaptation than a precipitational climate, mostly in and of itself, and partly in conjunction with a precipitational climate. In this work, therefore, I have restricted my investigations to temperature as the predominant dimension of climate and predictor of culture while taking into account the potentially confounding impact of precipitation.

At first blush, climate as the average level of temperature across all seasons is an unambiguous contextual variable. On second thought, it can be viewed in two different ways: through a cold-hot lens, with warmer climates seen as more comfortable, and through a cold-temperate-hot lens, with temperate climates seen as more comfortable than both cold and hot climates. Cold-hot contexts range from cold at latitudes closer to the icecaps to hot at latitudes closer to the equator. Cold-temperate-hot contexts range from comfortable at intermediate latitudes to harsh at latitudes closer to either the icecaps or the equator. Both conceptualizations of climatic contexts have been related to culture elsewhere, and both are discussed and criticized here.

Cold-hot context of culture. The simplest research approach is to search for cold-hot relations between the mean level of climatic temperature and some dimension of culture. As a case in point, Esther Kluwer, Richard Lynn, and I (Van de Vliert, Kluwer, & Lynn, 2000) observed an unmistakable country-level link between increasing temperature and increasing citizen competitiveness. Men and women in warmer countries appear to try harder when they are in competition with other people, finding winning more important in both work and games. We speculated that in former times life was more arduous for families in cold than in hot climates, requiring more cooperation or at least noncompetitiveness to survive. In essence, we hypothesized that remnants of less competitiveness in cooler climates and more competitiveness in hotter climates can be observed in modern-day men and women.

Similarly, Hofstede (2001) showed that decreases in geographic latitude as a global indicator of a country's warmer climate go hand in hand with greater differences in power between individuals or groups. The cold-hot difference in climate is at the beginning of a causal chain, his argument ran, because warmer environments are less problematic and easier to cope with. In the relatively cold climates of, for example, North America and Scandinavia, survival and population growth are more dependent on human intervention in nature, with the complicating effects of more need for technology, more technological momentum for change, more reciprocal teaching, and more questioning of authority. By contrast, in the relatively hot climates of, for example, Central America and South-East Asia, there is less need for human intervention and for technology, leading to a more static society in which teachers are omniscient, teaching is one-way, and authorities are obeyed rather than questioned.

A different illustration of how the cold-hot model has been employed to explain culture relates to predominantly illiterate societies. Fought et al. (2004) compared the languages used by 21 societies in cooler climates and 39 societies in hotter climates (for their research method and for a rival explanation of their findings, see the box "The airco of language"). They proposed that people in cooler climates who have to speak in sheltered and indoor settings can easily make themselves heard even if they use words that contain many consonants (such as b, g, k, p, t), fricatives (such as f, h, s, v, z), and nasal sonorants (such as m and n). By contrast, in hotter climates, where people spend more time outdoors, they need to communicate over longer distances in noisier environments, with the consequence that they need words with more sonorous phonetic segments in the form of vowels (such as a, o, e, u, i) and semivowels (such as w and j). In line with this argument, languages spoken in cooler climates appeared to contain more words with complex combinations of consonants, fricatives, and nasal sonorants (Gdańsk, Saskatchewan, Vladivostok), whereas languages spoken in hotter climates were found to contain more relatively simple words with vowels and semivowels (Dahomey, Kuala Lumpur, Paramaribo).

Cold-temperate-hot context of culture. Like all warm-blooded species, humans have to maintain constant levels of high body temperature. As a rule of thumb, they will be unconscious at internal body temperatures below 30°C and above 40°C, and dead below 20°C and above 45°C. For that reason, humans have a characteristic relation between ambient temperature and physiology, represented

The airco of language

To maintain your internal temperature at around 37°C, heat transfer into your body and heat generation within your body must be balanced by heat outputs from your body. The best controllable tool of thermoregulation through heat output is your mouth. Keeping your mouth shut in cold environments and open in hot environments is both comfortable and functional (do as the dogs do!). Over many generations, this may well have led to cultural adaptations such as northerners being less talkative than southerners. It is equally conceivable that cold-climate humans retain heat better and that hot-climate humans release heat better by using their breath channel as an air conditioner when they talk. This airco view builds a theoretical bridge between climate and language in general and between climate and the articulation of words in particular.

Words consist of vowels and consonants. In the articulation of vowels, the oral part of the breath channel is exposed to the air, with heat release as a result. By contrast, the articulation of consonants is characterized by constriction or closure at one or more points in the breath channel, with heat preservation as a result. Hence, it would serve human thermoregulation if words with many consonants (such as f, p, d, th, ch) evolved in cooler climates whereas words with many vowels (such as a, o, u, ie, ee) evolved in hotter climates. Also, there would be evolutionary advantage in higher frequencies of constricted vowels (such as i, e, ē, ū) in cooler climates and higher frequencies of open vowels (such as a, o, á, ó) in hotter climates. That is exactly what anthropologists have found, although they provide a completely different explanation in terms of required carrying power of speech sounds in indoor settings versus outdoor settings.

Fought and colleagues (2004) investigated approximately 45,000 discrete word sounds in a geographically stratified sample of 60 indigenous societies chosen to represent the 60 macrocultural areas of the world. Each word sound (118 word sounds per language on average) was scored on a carefully constructed 14-point scale of classes of sounds, ranging from voiceless stop consonant to low vowel. The resulting sonority score per society was then related to the degree of climatic cold versus climatic heat. In support of the thermoregulatory explanation, the languages manifested more consonant and less vowel usage in colder areas (tchkash, vrazbrod, etc.), but more vowel and less consonant usage in hotter areas (maraki, tawani, etc.). This finding was robust across the 14 classes of sounds and across six major culture regions (Africa, Circum-Mediterranean, East Eurasia, Insular Pacific, North America, and South America).

The airco of language gives cold words and warm words a new meaning.

in the so-called Scholander curve (Scholander et al., 1950). This curve describes the U-shaped dependence of body heat production or rates of metabolism on ambient temperature. In an intermediate range of ambient temperatures, the thermoneutral zone, the metabolic rate required for the body to maintain a core temperature of approximately 37°C is both minimal and independent of the ambient temperature. Below the thermoneutral zone, metabolism increases to generate enough heat (e.g., by shivering) for the body to survive. Likewise, above the thermoneutral zone, metabolism increases to support active cooling (e.g., by sweating or panting). Thus, the biological costs of keeping body and soul together increase on both sides of the thermoneutral zone. As a consequence, humans thrive in temperate climates and must take protective measures if they are living in colder or hotter regions of the world.

In addition to thermal comfort, temperate climates offer abundant food resources owing to the rich flora and fauna and negligible risks of unhealthy weather conditions. Both colder and hotter climates require more and better protective devices such as clothing, shelter structures, and heating or cooling systems. Work circumstances, work regulations, and work activities have to be adjusted, too. Increasingly colder or hotter climates also require increasing investments of time and effort in the pursuit of food and drink and increasing concern about the climate-dictated composition of nutrients in the diet. Finally, more and more measures have to be taken in increasingly colder and hotter climates to safeguard the health of oneself and one's family, especially in the tropics with its plagues of disease-producing substances, germs, bacteria, and insects. In short, it makes sense to search for U-shaped rather than monotonic relations between mean temperature and culture.

As a case in point, a 53-nation study has provided evidence for more inequality of gender roles in temperate climates than in colder and hotter climates (Van de Vliert, Schwartz, et al., 1999). The interpretation of this finding, a hybrid cross between a speculation and an explanation, ran something like this. In countries with temperate climates, including Japan and Italy, where adaptational investments are less critical, men are supposed to be more assertive, tough, and focused on material success whereas women are supposed to be more modest, tender, and concerned with the quality of life. By contrast, the greater joint investments of males and females in adapting to more extreme climates have led to the development of cultural customs characterized by sacrifice, delay of gratification, and cooperation by both genders. As a consequence, in countries with relatively low temperatures (e.g., Norway and Sweden) or relatively high temperatures (e.g., Indonesia and Thailand), both men and women are supposed to be rather modest, tender, and concerned with the quality of life.

This idea of greater gender equality at the icy poles and the boiling equator fires the imagination. It is also unconvincing. Strikingly contrasting evidence exists that gender role differentiation is rooted in the sexual division of labor, and that the work to be performed in dangerously cold or hot climates drives male and female roles apart. While the men fight the climate outdoors, the women run the household indoors, with the result that there is gender equality rather than inequality in temperate climates and gender inequality rather than equality in harsher climates.

Criticism. The cold-hot and cold-temperate-hot studies discussed above straightforwardly relate average annual levels of climatic temperature in various populated areas to the content of culture in these areas. All such climate-culture studies share two serious weaknesses. First, they overlook the cultural impact of seasonal variations in climatic cold and heat, even though seasonal rhythms in the physiology of man are well documented (Aschoff, 1981). In Chapter 2, a climate index based on winter and summer temperatures is proposed for improving the analysis of the cultural impact of thermal climate. Second, such studies ignore the obvious fact that the cultural impact of the climatic context is dependent on how much money a society has available to cope with a frustratingly cold or hot climate. My view, put forward in Chapters 3 to 8, is that money resources influence the impact of climate on culture.

Economic Context

Like languages and religions, economic systems for creating income and consumption through trade, industry, and provision of services are diversifications of culture. Yet economies perform entirely different functions. In a more straightforward way than languages and religions, property-based operations such as owning, exchanging, earning, saving, cashing, buying, and selling can help prevent and dispel discomfort, hunger, thirst, and illness. There is no mistaking the cultural nature of these property-based operations. At the same time, their relevance to survival itself places them at the root of key causal chains in the further development of cultures. To clarify how the term *cash* is used here, I first pay attention to the origins and functions of money and to the distinction between ready and unready money.

Origins of money. No thing, whether alive or lifeless, is insensitive to extreme temperatures, but warm-blooded animals and humans are sensitive in special ways. In response to cold and heat, they continuously have to satisfy the survival needs of themselves and their offspring. It is in this way that humans have drawn away from all other warm-blooded species by inventing property and money to help them overcome threats to survival.

Early humans lived more or less like animals, as hunters and gatherers. The gradual transition from a nomadic lifestyle to a sedentary lifestyle resulted in the development of media of exchange – first grains and shells, then metals and metallic currencies, and finally cheques, credit card printouts, and electronic acknowledgments of debt. Unlike animals, humans have evolved from hunters and gatherers into traders who now hunt for bargains and save money. Today's bargain hunters demonstrate that hunting has evolved into using money as a means of exchange and as a standard of value reflected in the rate of exchange. And today's savers exemplify that gathering has evolved into using money as a store of value, as an exchangeable resource kept for rainy days. These functions of money as a means of exchange, as a standard of value, and as the basis of capital savings are discussed in more detail below.

Money as a means of exchange. Only a few self-supporting societies in polar and desert regions have not yet developed a full-fledged system of shops and markets and still hunt, gather, and exchange nonfinancial goods to meet their survival needs. Everywhere else, fully developed cash economies are in place to facilitate processes of satisfying basic needs for thermal comfort, nutrition, and health. In these economies, money has a purchasing power that exists independently of the goods it can buy. "Money is either itself an exchangeable commodity (for example, gold coin), or it is a direct symbol of such a commodity (convertible note), or it may be the symbolic representation (*numéraire*) of a commodity standard – cow, barrel of oil, value of a 'basket' of commodities" (Ingham, 2004, p. 6).

Money is an extraordinarily ingenious tool because of the world-wide adherence to the agreement that even worthless pieces of metal or paper and magnetic traces in computer disks can be exchanged for all kinds of valuables. The magic of money is so overwhelming that we don't feel at all ridiculous when we work long hours for an electronic bank transfer or when we trade credit card printouts for valuable goods or services. Anthropologists agree that money has no essence apart from its uses (Furnham & Argyle, 1998). Money enables us to buy clothing, housing, refrigerators, heaters, air conditioners, household energy, meals, drinks, kitchenware, medicines, medical treatment, and even future security. Because such common purchases help directly or indirectly to maintain the human body's constant state, or homeostasis, Parker (2000) calls the items bought *homeostatic goods*. In higher income nations, families appear to spend up to 50% of their household income on a wide variety of such homeostatic goods. This figure rises to 90% in lower income nations, and in the case of abject poverty, many needs for homeostatic goods cannot be met at all by a majority of the population.

Money as a standard of value. That homeostatic goods are for sale indicates that money is a means of exchange. That homeostatic goods have a price indicates that money is a standard against which the importance of the goods is compared and judged. Worldwide, monetary standards are used to coordinate and control negotiable and fixed rates of exchange. Money is not manna; it is not inflexible and will not decay. Money is an extremely flexible and preservable tool, not only because it can so easily be traded for work and for homeostatic goods, but also because its value and exchange rates almost automatically vary in response to current circumstances of supply and demand at individual, national, and global levels. An often consumed homeostatic good elegantly illustrates this adjustment to local circumstances of supply and demand. The price of exactly the same hamburger converted into U.S. dollars differs widely in McDonald's restaurants around the globe. In January 2006, a standard Big Mac cost $1.30 in China, $1.60 in Russia and Egypt, $2.09 in Poland, $2.66 in Mexico, $3.15 in the United States, $4.28 in Sweden, and $4.93 in Switzerland (*The Economist*, January 14, 2006, p. 102).

Ready versus unready money. Ready money is anything accepted and used as a medium of exchange including coin, banknote, token, check, and coupon. Unready money or capital, also traveling under the name of wealth, is the financial value of a stock of accumulated possessions such as financial assets, real estate, consumer durables, and livestock. Although ready money can be converted into frozen or invested money, and the other way round, so that both are highly correlated in practice, the two constructs are quite different in theory. As this book is directed at daily uses of spendable income, it is about the flow of cash a society or household receives or retrieves from capital.

Almost everything we know about the relation between the national economic context and national culture is based on research into the cultural impact of income per head. The most pronounced cash-culture conclusions were drawn on the basis of the World Values Surveys (e.g., Inglehart et al., 1998, 2004; Inglehart & Baker, 2000), a still ongoing series of multiple-nation studies. Drawing on a massive body of evidence covering more than 80 countries, the research team demonstrated that increases in income per head give rise to cultural changes that make individual autonomy, gender equality, and democratic institutions increasingly likely. In parallel, economic progress brings distinctive changes in levels of obedience to authority. Traditional obedience to sacred authorities is followed first by the secularization of authority and then by emancipation from authority (for the impact of economic growth on established world religions, see the box "Belief beyond belief").

Belief beyond belief

The major religions actively seek to convert unbelievers and "false believers" into true believers. Christianity, Islam, and Buddhism attacked rival philosophies of life so successfully that they now have more than 3 billion followers. European crusaders and colonizers as well as Muslim armies brutally killed their rivals. Recently, Buddhist Sinhalese fought Hindu Tamils in Sri Lanka. On a much larger scale, soft attacks took place through conversion by missionaries, traders, and migrants. The greatest champions of the true belief were faithful rulers, including Asoka, the emperor of India, who converted to Buddhism around 261 B.C., and the Roman emperor Constantine, who converted to Christianity in 313.

In a triumphant procession, Christianity spread from today's Israel to North-West Asia and Europe, and later to North America, South America, and Australia. Similarly, Islam overran the Middle East, the Balkan Peninsula, Northern Africa, Indonesia, and the southern Philippines. And Buddhism spread from Nepal to South-East Asia, merging with regional religions in Tibet, China, Korea, and Japan. In times to come, Christians, Muslims, and Buddhists will no doubt continue to try to convert one another. Sooner or later, however, they may have to direct all scattered and opposite forces in pursuit of the unified purpose of beating a common enemy that will otherwise destroy or fatally injure all religions with a monopoly on wisdom.

The odds are that the next worldwide frontier of religious strife will be between institutionalized religions, on the one hand, and economic progress, on the other. In present-day Turkey and Egypt, for example, struggles between Islamic fundamentalists and secular groups are well underway. The reasons are complex, but economic growth certainly plays a part. Ever since 1975, both populations have experienced gradual increases in income per head, life expectancy, and educational attainment. These developments have increased the material, psychosomatic, and cognitive resources of the Turks and

Egyptians, making them financially, medically, and intellectually less and less dependent on the favors of a deity. A similar pattern holds in most religious societies with upward economic development trends. In short, the future enemy of the institutionalized religions is further economic growth.

This is not to say that there will be no religious revivals and radicalizations in prosperous countries, nor that sacral and spiritual beliefs will become extinct. There will always be beliefs in place of the current religious convictions. Humankind will continue to seek answers to such questions as Why do we exist? Where are we going? What will happen to us after death? The World Values Surveys have shown that economic development and rising existential security lead to a fork in our collective path. A decline in the prevalence of established religious institutions is accompanied by a rise of loosely structured systems of personalized religiosity and spirituality (e.g., New Age ideals in the past and the holy well of environmentalism more recently). The long-term shift will be from institutionally fixed forms of dogmatic beliefs to individually flexible forms of spiritual beliefs. For religions, at least, there is life after death.

Many findings of the World Values Surveys are nothing short of exciting. Whoever would have thought that the amount of money in our pockets is indirectly related to our active participation in petitions, strikes, boycotts, and uprisings? And if this had crossed your mind, would you have correctly predicted that richer peoples are more instead of less protest prone than poorer peoples? Inglehart and Welzel (2005) suggest the following explanations for this counterintuitive finding. For a start, higher income levels increase the means to make protests effective. Additionally, higher incomes strengthen self-expression values among the population, thus increasing the size of the pool of potential dissidents and activists as well as the chances that protesters can mobilize large segments of the public for mass campaigns. This broader oppositional platform also gives reformers within the ruling elite a more viable alliance option, strengthening their case against the defenders of the status quo. The reformer camp can convince the defender camp that concessions must be made, as happened during the transitions from dictatorial to democratic regimes in Chile and Spain.

Economic growth has the unmistakable tendency to propel both men and women in the direction of secularization and self-actualization as well as education and economic and political participation. But I couldn't help raising my eyebrows when reading the claim made by some members of the research team of the World Values Surveys that "the only clear predictor of a country's position on the cultural map appears to be its economic development" (Halman et al., 2005, p. 129). What about climatic temperature as a predictor of survival-related values and practices? The studies reported in Chapters 3 to 6, in which the culture measures of the World Values Surveys were used, repeatedly show that the observed cross-national link between cash and culture depends on the country's cold, temperate, or hot climate.

Climato-Economic Niches

The presumption that harsh climates shape the homeostatic utility of a wide variety of purchasable goods echoes earlier work by Montesquieu (1748). His key breakthrough is the insight that people predominantly exchange money for goods and services that satisfy climate-related necessities of life. Cash can indeed protect us against the continuous weather attacks of the climate. Hence, a valid analysis of cultural adaptation to climate should take into account the availability of money resources to cope with cold winters, hot summers, or both. Put another way, a valid analysis of cultural adaptation to income per head should take into account the harshness of climate as a dual indicator of the seriousness of survival problems and the usefulness of money resources. Both formulations highlight the shortcomings of separate analyses of the climatic and economic roots of culture. This is an important point, given broader attention in the form of a mental experiment leading to three hypotheses.

Mental experiment. Consider a fictional sample of people from all over the world who emigrate to Austria. Imagine that we are interested in how well they are adapting to the Austrian context. Do these immigrants choose to hold on to their home cultures and at the same time seek daily interaction with members of the host culture (*integration*), or seek daily interaction with members of the host culture and give up their home culture (*assimilation*), or maybe hold on to their home culture and avoid contact with members of the host culture (*separation*)? One year after arrival in Austria, and again after two years, we ask each of these immigrants to complete a questionnaire to assess the extent to which the person is trying to integrate both cultures.

Imagine further that integration in Austria is least problematic for people from countries with harsh climates and high income levels similar to Austria's (e.g., Canada and the Czech Republic), moderately problematic for people from countries with temperate climates irrespective of their income levels (e.g., South Africa and Uruguay), and most problematic for people from countries with harsh climates similar to Austria's but with much lower income levels than Austria (e.g., Armenia and Kazakhstan). This pattern of immigrant data leads to different conclusions depending on whether they are examined through a climatic lens, an economic lens, or a climato-economic lens.

In a purely climatic analysis, no home-country effect on integration in Austria surfaces because there are no differences for home countries with temperate climates and high-income versus low-income levels, whereas the mutually opposing tendencies for home countries with harsh climates and high-income versus low-income levels balance each other out. In a purely economic analysis, no differences in integration surface for home countries with temperate versus harsh climates, whereas home countries with higher income levels appear to be related to better integration. Only an integrated climato-economic analysis would accurately reveal that climate and income levels in the home country are both relevant because they have an interactive impact on cultural integration in Austria.

This story makes it abundantly clear that Montesquieu had a point when he advanced the thesis that we use money to cope with climate. Following in his footsteps, presuming that climate and cash influence each other's impact, I sought, therefore, to achieve a better understanding of cultural adaptations to climato-economic niches. The research model consisted of a set of three cumulative hypotheses – a context hypothesis, an impact hypothesis, and a niche hypothesis. The ins and outs of this framework are visualized in Figure 1.1 on page 8. The context hypothesis, represented by rectangles connected by dotted lines, focuses on the existence of relations between the climatic context, the economic context, and culture. The impact hypothesis, represented by arrows and a listing of corresponding chapters, specifies the proposed causal directions of the context-culture relations. And the niche hypothesis, represented by the bolder central part of the picture, emphasizes the interactive nature of the joint impact of climate and cash on culture. The three hypotheses are discussed separately below.

Context hypothesis. Each culture is viewed here as a complex adaptation to numerous contexts, including latitude, elevation, water and soil resources, flora and fauna, mineral resources, and the strategic importance of the society's physical location. Being realistic about what can be accomplished at any one time in an inquiry, I restricted my investigations to climate and cash as two bright stars in the night sky of the environmental firmament. The foundation of the research model in Figure 1.1 is the crude assumption that the climatic context and the economic context are related to culture.

Impact hypothesis. Current investigations into human-made levels of atmosphere-warming greenhouse gases such as carbon dioxide and methane serve to remind us that climate is influenced by culture. Analogously, the global competitiveness reports of the World Economic Forum in Geneva remind us that income per head is influenced by cultural customs such as favoritism in decisions of government officials, ethical behavior of firms, hiring and firing practices, and willingness to delegate authority. Recognizing that Figure 1.1 contains a chicken-and-egg problem, I started from the axiom that the contexts come first and are followed by culture. The resulting impact hypothesis posits that climate and cash influence culture.

Niche hypothesis. The title of this book, *Climate, Affluence, and Culture,* is unclear as it leaves open the question of whether climate and cash have independent or interdependent impacts on culture. The mention of animals in this chapter brought clarity to this question. Animals do not live in multiple contexts but in a single conglomerate of contexts known as their habitat. Higher animals like humans are no exception to this rule that one has to adapt to a single niche of interrelated contexts. Self-evidently, our societies may adapt to the climatic context, the economic context, or both in a parallel fashion. But a more accurate understanding of culture may unfold when we consider these contexts to be an integrated climato-economic habitat requiring integrated cultural responses. Hence my emphasis on the hypothesis that the interaction of climatic and economic contexts matters most to culture (see Figure 1.1).

The niche hypothesis in its most stringent interpretation has a number of interesting implications. First, if a society does its utmost to keep the climatic conditions and income positions constant, culture doesn't change much. Perhaps the best-known illustration is the example of the Amish people, who originally lived in Alsace, a small part of France near the German-Swiss border. Thousands of Amish migrated to America between 1815 and 1860, settling in rural areas with climatic and agricultural conditions similar to those prevailing in

Alsace: Indiana, Illinois, Iowa, New York, Ontario, Ohio, and Pennsylvania. Totally opposed to the American dream of large profits and innovation, they explicitly sought a farming life with climato-economic and techno-economic stability. As a consequence, even today, they continue to cling to their traditional values and practices including the use of horsepower and natural fertilizers, growing and rotating a variety of crops, and raising livestock in small numbers.

Second, if a society in a stable climate faces economic collapse, as was the case with the Soviet successor states in 1990–1991, sudden cultural change occurs (Inglehart & Baker, 2000). Conversely, drastic cultural change in opposite directions occurs in cases of rocketing economic growth such as in China at the beginning of this millennium. Third, if a large group of migrants moves to a different climato-economic niche, cultural adaptations are bound to follow. For example, the British settlers in Australia adopted practices of weaker uncertainty avoidance (relying on social norms, rules, and procedures). Additionally, they developed more humane orientations (being fair, altruistic, generous, caring, and kind to others). Finally, they reduced the power distances among all members of society (House et al., 2004).

Fourth, the view of most theorists that cultures are extremely persistent over time may be an artifact of the stability of the climato-economic niches investigated. In the stable Scandinavian niche of a harsh cold climate and high income levels, culture is persistently characterized by caring and sharing rather than fighting as is evident in male-female and leader-follower relationships. But in the 8th to 10th centuries, the ancestors of the Norwegians, Swedes, and Danes – the Vikings – who lived in the same demanding climate but in extreme poverty, were pirates engaging in plundering, raping, kidnapping, and occupying parts of Europe. The lesson to be learned from this reversal in values and practices is that historical explanations of culture make sense only if changes in the climato-economic niches are taken into account as well.

Finally, the research model in Figure 1.1 implies that any cultural adaptation to a climato-economic niche is inextricably connected with a given time period. A particular context-culture link may thus not be generalizable to points in time well beyond its recent past or near future. In consequence, it is important to know that the tests of the model reported in Chapters 2 to 7 cover the period 1980 to 2005. These studies are best viewed as snapshots taken from the never-ending film of how we warm-blooded creatures create life satisfaction, work, cooperation, organization, and a jumble of other components of culture.

PART TWO

CLIMATE, CASH, AND WORK

2

Climate Colors Life Satisfaction

No plant, no animal, no human is indifferent to cold and heat.

Dotted around the globe are many ancient buildings and structures left behind by societies that collapsed or vanished. Not infrequently, these monuments provide stark evidence of the part extremely cold and hot climates can play in human civilizations (Burroughs, 1997; Diamond, 2005). From the Norse who once lived by the shores of iceberg-strewn fjords on Greenland's west coast to the Maya who once lived in the seasonal-desert environment of the Copán Valley in western Honduras, past societies seem to have been overwhelmed by the effects of prolonged adverse weather. Even today, vast areas around the poles are rendered uninhabitable by ice sheets, and huge deserts at lower latitudes are equally effective in limiting human population. Human societies clearly tend to shun overly demanding cold and hot climates.

As elucidated in Chapter 1, humans have a physical and a cultural side. The existence of physically inhospitable areas in harsh climates automatically raises the question, therefore, whether climates also create culturally inhospitable areas – parts of the world where climate has shaped the inhabitants' lifestyle to be so strange and inconsistent that it is extremely difficult for others to make their way there. Or is this a nonissue? No one calls into question that life in the vegetable world and in the animal world has adapted to cold, temperate, and hot climates. Thus, it would be the first wonder of the world if human life were not adapted to climate, because this would mean that human evolution had somehow contrived to wipe out its own climatic underpinnings. There is no need to find out *whether* climates are taken into account when societies create cultures. Rather, the question should be *to what extent* and *in what ways* societies translate climates into values and practices that are passed on and changed from generation to generation in a nongenetic way.

Climate-culture links in man are a touchy subject given their history of untenable single-factor determinism (for an overview, see Sommers & Moos, 1976), even to the point of climate-based racism (e.g., Huntington, 1945). The topic needs to be handled with care, including a clear definition of climate and replications of climate-culture links found. Under the title "Assessing Thermal Climate," I therefore pay ample attention to the choice of a climate index that goes beyond the average level of temperature, incorporating seasonal variations in temperature. Harsh climate is defined, and some testable links between climatic demands, survival needs, and life satisfaction are proposed in the section "Climate, Needs, and Satisfaction." The following section, "Winters, Summers, and Life Satisfaction," contains a report of cross-national associations between greater climatic demands, on the one hand, and less happiness and more suicide as presumed opposite indicators of culturally embedded life satisfaction, on the other hand.

ASSESSING THERMAL CLIMATE

It is common practice in cross-cultural research to use the average level of temperature as an indicator of climate in a given populated area. This leads to observations like "warmer countries have more collectivistic cultures" (Georgas et al., 2004) and "comfortably warm countries have less democratic and more violent cultures than colder and hotter countries" (Van de Vliert, Schwartz, et al., 1999). Such observations are suspect, as the average levels of cold and heat on which they rest neglect seasonal variations in cold and heat. This is a weakness, not only because warm-blooded humans dislike both bitter winters and scorching summers, but also because levels of temperature and variations in temperature are contaminated. In countries closer to the equator, winters and summers are more alike, so that the average temperature is a more meaningful indicator. Conversely, in countries closer to the poles, winters and summers are more different, so that the average temperature is a less meaningful indicator.

Country climates, generally expressed in average monthly degrees Celsius across the country's major cities, are harsher to the extent that winters are colder or summers are hotter, or both. A country's mean temperature level is not a good indicator because country climates, typified by winters and summers, should be treated as two-edged swords. It is a deficiency that the relatively small winter-summer differences of the maritime climate of the Falklands (range from –11°C to +24°C = 35°C) and the relatively large winter-summer differences in temperature of the continental climate of Kazakhstan (range from –33°C to +42°C = 75°C) produce about the same average level of climatic temperature (ca. 5°C). In consequence, it is difficult to construct a valid indicator of thermal climate that ignores winter and summer deviations from a temperate climate. But how warm is a temperate climate in the first place?

There are good reasons for adopting 22°C (ca. 72°F) as a point of reference for temperate climate. Most important, it is the approximate midpoint of the range of comfortable temperatures (Parsons, 1993). In addition, 22°C happens to be the most temperate world temperature in the coldest winter month (on the Marshall Islands) as well as the most temperate world temperature in the hottest summer month (on the Faroe Islands). Average winter and summer deviations from 22°C are indeed fitting indicators of the harshness of climate. In theory, precipitation and humidity can lower or raise the comfortability optimum, but in practice somewhat lower or higher reference points than 22°C appear to have almost identical cultural consequences. Therefore, a winter index can be based on the sum of the absolute deviations from 22°C for the average lowest and highest temperatures in the coldest month, a summer index on the sum of the absolute deviations from 22°C for the average lowest and highest temperatures in the hottest month, and an overall climate index on the sum of all four absolute deviations from temperate climate.[1] On the overall index, climate ranges from most temperate in Burundi and on two islands (Comoros and the Seychelles) to most extreme in Canada and Mongolia. In addition to the overall climate index, the winter and summer indices were also used as predictors of culture in the investigations reported in this book.

It is possible to compute climate indices for the surface areas of cities, villages, provinces, nation-states, and the like. In view of the topic of cultural adaptation, the ideal geographical boundary captures distinct climates as well as distinct cultures. But our inhabited planet is not so neatly organized. Not many national borders are also climatic and cultural boundaries. Nonetheless, it makes a lot of sense to use nation-states as units of measurement in climate-culture analysis. Each country's name, location, and physical geography is taught in school. "Nations are political units with distinctive ecological, historical, political, educational, legal, regulatory, social, and economic characteristics. As such, they constitute systems and have cultures" (Smith et al., 2006, p. 77). And Schwartz (2004) has demonstrated in several ways that nations are meaningful units of cross-cultural analysis. One of his analyses showed that within-country differences in values are smaller than corresponding differences between countries. For all of those reasons, the climate-culture studies reported here were nation-level studies in which nation-level indices of climate and culture were used.

In sum, harsher climates can best be equated with colder winters and hotter summers (for a listing of country scores on the winter index, the summer index, and the total climate index, see Appendix).

Extremely cold winters and extremely hot summers both create unlivable country-level environments that fail to satisfy human needs. Take Africa. Moving inland from the Mediterranean, from the Indian Ocean, and from the Atlantic Ocean toward the burning heart of the continent amounts to moving from more livable and thus more densely populated countries toward less livable and thus more sparsely populated countries (for evidence and discussion, see the box "Desert diets of sand and salt").

Desert diets of sand and salt

For Africans, Asians, Australians, and Americans alike, deserts are not popular areas in which to live. This is taken for granted. It should be food for thought, however, as it tells us much about who we are and why we have preferences for temperate climates. Unlike solar cells, we live on eatables and drinkables instead of rays of sunshine. It is out of the question that we would associate sand and salt with a balanced and healthy diet. Related to this, we are not fireproof; our deep body temperature, heart rate, and sweat rate are not known for being able to cope with torturing degrees of environmental heat stress. As a consequence, on a worldwide scale, we are one another's fair or unfair competitors for habitable areas away from hot deserts. A simple mental experiment can illustrate what I mean.

Imagine the African continent had to be reallocated to the Africans; how would that be done? Give each inhabitant an equally large patch of ground? That would be unfair as some pieces of land are more equal than others. Climate has a lot to do with that. Burundi, for example, mostly a high plateau along the eastern edge of the Great Rift Valley, has a gentle and stable climate with temperatures ranging from 17°C in the coldest month to 31°C in the hottest month. No less than 92% of the land is suitable for farming throughout the year or for grazing animals. Now consider Niger and Lesotho as distinct contrasts. Niger, with the Sahara desert and

Djado Plateau in the north and the Sahel in the south, has a tropical climate with temperatures ranging from 8°C in the coldest month to 48°C in the hottest month. About 88% of Niger's territory consists of infertile wasteland. But Lesotho, a mountainous country in the southern tip of Africa, has a temperate subtropical climate with temperatures ranging from –9°C in the coldest month to 38°C in the hottest month. Meadows and pastures cover 66% of the land and another 11% is used for crop growing rather than animal rearing.

What then is a fair piece of land with a view to providing for oneself and one's family? Perhaps no principle of distributive justice comes closer to perfect fairness than does the hidden criterion of the harshness of climate. If this decision rule were applied, Africans living in increasingly harsh climates would need and get increasingly more land to live on. Nigerians could lay claim to 2.6 times as much ground as Burundians, and the Basotho, the inhabitants of Lesotho, could lay claim to 2.9 times as much ground as Burundians. Indeed, the Burundians, joined only by the people living on the Comoros islands and on the Seychelles, would be fobbed off with the smallest pieces of African soil.[2] If our bodies were designed for extremely hot climates and desert diets, fair allocation would fob off the Sudanese with the smallest pieces of African soil, with hardly larger pieces for the inhabitants of Burkina Faso, Niger, Mali, and Chad.[3]

All this raises the question of whether competition for land, including tribal wars of conquest among the 900 million inhabitants of Africa's 53 nations, is unwittingly based on climatic fairness. My research shows that to a great extent it is. The harsher the climate, the larger the country's surface area and the lower its population density in terms of the number of people per square kilometer.[4] This conclusion still holds if the islands (Cape Verde, Comoros, Madagascar, Mauritius, São Tomé and Príncipe, and the Seychelles) are left out of consideration. Apparently, with ups and downs over many centuries, the peoples in Africa have allocated more land, and indeed more land per head, to societies that have to eke out a living in hotter and more demanding climates. Viewed in this way, it is certainly a sign of fairness that vast deserts are left to nomads who are few and far between. Although deserts are predominantly products of nature, deserted deserts are definitely products of culture.

CLIMATE, NEEDS, AND SATISFACTION

A need is like a needle in the flesh. It is pointed, it hurts, and you want to get rid of it. Officially, a need is a deprivation that energizes a drive to eliminate or reduce the deprivation. There are needs for thermal comfort and appropriate nutrition, needs for health, needs for sex and sexual reproduction, needs for power and affiliation, needs for self-esteem and self-actualization, and so forth. Directly, indirectly, or in certain circumstances, deficiencies in those needs may be related to the harshness and demands of climate. At any rate, as discussed next, the gratification of survival needs for thermal comfort, nutrition, and health is increasingly difficult in colder and hotter areas.

Climatic Demands and Survival Needs

Temperate climates around 22°C are kind to flora, fauna, and humans alike. It was no coincidence that after African genesis, human populations achieved flourishing expansion and evolution once they settled in the temperate zone of the earth. In the fertile crescent of the Middle East and in several other comfortable and relatively healthy areas, humans changed their primary modes of subsistence from hunting animals to herding them and from gathering plants to cultivating them. The subsequent migration patterns of early humans are also in line with the biological theory of the thermoneutral zone and its corollary that humans thrive in temperate climates. The domestication of plants from wheat (8500 B.C., Syria) to potato (400 B.C., Bolivia), and the diffusion of plant cultivation, starting in temperate climates, took a long time to arrive in harsher climates. Likewise, the domestication of animals from the dog (12,000 B.C., Iran) to the reindeer (1000 B.C., Siberia), and the diffusion of livestock breeding, also show evidence of tellingly slow movement from temperate climates into harsher climates (Nolan & Lenski, 1999).

Harsher cold and hot climates have in common that they are more demanding, albeit in qualitatively different ways. Whereas harsher climates are recorded using thermometers, more demanding climates are in the eyes of the beholders. That said, I hasten to add that objective harshness of climate is the best measure I can think of for assessing the subjective demands of climate. In areas with harsher climates, inhabitants inevitably experience more excessive cold or heat, hunger or thirst, and more uncertainty about future temperatures and nutrition. At the same time, they are confronted with less access to good water sources, less amenable vegetation, fewer permanent crops, a less diverse animal realm making hunting and fishing increasingly difficult, more problematic animal husbandry, and less freedom of action and relocation, implying less means to control future events.

In areas with colder winters, hotter summers, or both, therefore, the greater climatic demands are not compensated for by more climatic resources. A striking mismatch exists between climate-based problems and climate-based resources to solve the problems. Fewer resources make harsher climates even more demanding than they already are. Furthermore, cold climates lead to frostbite, pneumonia, asthma, rheumatism, gout, influenza, and common colds, with sickness and absence from work as a consequence. And in the tropics, there are "major vector-borne diseases (malaria, yellow fever, schistosomiasis, trypanosomiasis, ochocerciasis, Chagas' disease, filariasis, among others), in which animals that flourish in the warm climate, such as flies, mosquitoes, and mollusks, play the critical role of intermediate hosts" (Sachs, 2000, p. 32).

For all of those reasons, despite acclimatization – marginal long-term adjustment in anatomy and physiology – excessive cold and heat evoke strong needs for thermal comfort, nutrition, and health. The primary needs for thermal comfort come with secondary needs for special clothing, housing, heating or cooling devices, household energy, and the like. The primary needs for nutrition, including a higher caloric intake in cold climates and more intake of water and salt in hot climates, come with secondary needs for the production, transportation, trade, and storage of food. And the primary needs for health come with secondary needs for medication, care and cure facilities, specific employer-employee arrangements, and other supplies and accommodations.

Climatic Demands and Life Satisfaction

The temperate or demanding climatic context helps or hinders the process of gratifying survival needs for thermal comfort, nutrition, and health. Successful management of demands and needs produces satisfaction; unsuccessful management of demands and needs leads to frustration. Satisfaction as the opposite of frustration thus refers to the internal state of a person who succeeds rather than fails to obtain what was sought. Satisfaction is synonymous with getting and fulfilling, and the opposite of lacking and yearning. As a rule, temperate climates satisfy survival needs whereas demandingly cold or hot climates frustrate them. Because a climate acts on us through the weather, day in day out, year in year out, its demands bombard us with millions of minuscule and overwhelming experiences and expectations of satisfaction versus frustration regarding thermal comfort, nutrition, and health. Even in today's air-conditioned world, it is almost inconceivable that this bombardment of climatic demands would leave unaffected an evaluation of our lives in the areas where we reside. Indeed, on closer consideration, it would not come as a surprise if climatic demands were to lessen life satisfaction.

Following Veenhoven (2000), life satisfaction, or happiness, is the degree to which a person evaluates positively the overall quality of his or her present life as a whole. How much one likes one's life is dependent on an assortment of odd bedfellows ranging from gender, age, income, educational attainment, and life expectancy to feelings of control and freedom, social isolation and conflict, voluntary work and employment, and environmental pollution (Diener & Suh, 2000). Perhaps above all, an evaluation of one's present life is also dependent on the salient cultural values of the society in which one lives (Oishi, 2000). Mapping and explaining links between thermal climate and culturally embedded life satisfaction is an interesting endeavor for a number of reasons.

First, climates influence entire societies rather than certain individuals or groups within these societies. All inhabitants of a given area are exposed to the same climate, undergo the same impact of climate, and are unhappier or happier as a result.

Second, among societies, there are large and stable cultural differences in life satisfaction that vary only moderately in response to current events (Diener et al., 1995; Van de Vliert, 2008b; Veenhoven, 2000). For instance, the inhabitants of Australia, Canada, and Sweden are among the happiest people in the world, and the inhabitants of Cameroon, China, and Panama are among the unhappiest. Moreover, a country's characteristic level of happiness seems to be generalizable across private and work realms of life (Inkeles, 1997; Van de Vliert & Janssen, 2002). The remarkably stable and general cross-national differences in happiness suggest that relatively static rather than dynamic factors in the national context determine the inhabitants' subjective well-being. Static cold and heat, therefore, stand out as possible roots of culturally embedded life satisfaction.

Third, knowledge about climate-satisfaction links may help prevent cultural differences in life satisfaction from being attributed solely to conditions other than the climatic context. As a case in point, cross-national differences in happiness have been viewed as consequences of differences in cultural individualism (Diener et al., 1995), socioeconomic development (Inglehart & Klingemann, 2000), and political freedom in high-income countries and economic freedom in low-income countries (Veenhoven, 2000). However, hidden climatic demands could function as modifiers of the impact of survival needs and drives on degrees of happiness.

Last, climate does not cause bias in the satisfaction response. Unlike feelings of freedom and other self-reported factors, seasonal variations in temperature are unobtrusive predictors of respondents' evaluations of their lives.

WINTERS, SUMMERS, AND LIFE SATISFACTION

The body of science has malleable parts of theoretical flesh and hard parts of empirical bones. The current section contains the hardest part of this chapter. It reports empirical support for the notion that more demanding climates, also leading to fewer resources, lessen culturally embedded life satisfaction. To make my case, I used two completely different indicators of culturally embedded life satisfaction: happiness ratings and suicide rates. Happiness is subjective, suicide objective. Happiness is a feeling, suicide a behavior. Happiness is positive, suicide negative. On a causal path, we find unhappiness at the beginning and suicide at the end. Finally, the happiness index is an indirect country-level average of individual-level ratings, the suicide index a direct country-level proportion.

Winters, Summers, and Happiness

In a series of analyses I investigated whether winter-summer deviations from 22°C are associated with happiness,[5] whether precipitation has an extra effect,[6] and whether obvious alternative explanations could account for the findings. For 81 nation states, aggregated individual ratings of happiness during the 1990s were available for analysis from Ruut Veenhoven's *World Database of Happiness*.[7] This convenience sample consisted of 37 European countries, 20 Asian countries, 14 North and South American countries, 8 African countries, and Australia and New Zealand. The happiness index was based on the responses of representative national samples of residents to statements with four response categories such as "Taking all things together, I would say I am not at all happy, not very happy, quite happy, very happy."

Climate appeared to account for 27% of the variation in the happiness ratings.[8] The results are visually represented in Figure 2.1, illustrated with about 50 country names.[9] Going from left to right, we see much lower happiness in countries with colder winters. Going from top to bottom, we also see somewhat lower happiness in countries with hotter summers. But the largest differences in happiness occur diagonally. In the upper left-hand corner, countries with more temperate winters tend to have happier populations, almost irrespective of whether the summers are bearable (see Tanzania, Puerto Rico, and Singapore) or extremely hot (see El Salvador, Vietnam, and Nigeria). By contrast, in the lower right-hand corner, we find by far the unhappiest peoples in countries with both cold

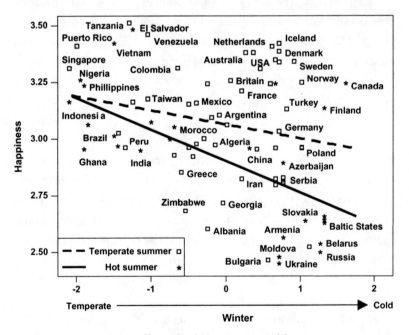

FIGURE 2.1. Joint effect of colder winters and hotter summers on happiness.

winters and hot summers, such as the Baltic States (Estonia, Latvia, and Lithuania), Belarus, Russia, and Ukraine.

Mean-temperature research based on the cold-hot and cold-temperate-hot models discussed in Chapter 1 did not predict these findings.[10] Precipitational climate had a negligible effect, also in combination with thermal climate.[11] Wind, humidity, and pressure did not change the picture in Figure 2.1 either. Apparently, the climate-happiness effect is a temperature effect. All this supports the idea that societies tend to be happier in more temperate climates because colder winters and hotter summers lessen culturally embedded life satisfaction. An intriguing question arises about the observation that Tanzania, with its temperate winters and summers, has the happiest population on earth, at least in this sample of 81 societies. One may wonder whether it is more than a coincidence that the happiest people of today live in the comfortable climate around the Olduvai Gorge in Tanzania where the Homo habilis kicked off human evolution some 2 million years ago.

In the investigations reported in this book, following Kuhn (1977) and McMullin (1983), I accepted as working truths only climatic effects that survived both verification and falsification. After producing many rival explanations of the climate-happiness link that were represented by competitive predictors, I then determined whether the above temperature effect could be broken by adding these competitor variables one by one. Time and again, the joint effect on happiness of colder winters and hotter summers withstood the attack. Four examples may illustrate this robust conclusion.

First, critics have challenged the climate-happiness link, pointing out that several countries span a broad range of latitudes with considerable geographical variation in temperature. I refer here not only to very large countries such as Australia, Brazil, China, and the United States but also to long countries such as Argentina, Chile, India, and Mexico. However, when the 31 largest countries were dropped, the joint impact of winters and summers on the happiness ratings in the remaining 50 countries increased from 27% to 42%. Thus, the larger countries produce an underestimation, not an overestimation, of the actual climate-happiness link. This makes sense if we assume that in extremely large countries, the climate-happiness link applies across the provinces or states within the country but is destroyed in the overarching cross-national picture as a result of averaging out all meaningful differences in local climates and cultures.

Take China, with its extremely cold winters in Manchuria, its cool temperatures even in summer on the Tibetan roof of the world, its desert climate in the Taklimakan and the Gobi, and its subtropical to tropical conditions in the coastal areas of Guangdong and Hainan. Happiness may vary in these climatic areas. The climate-happiness link may well apply to the cultures of the 56 ethnic groups in China's 23 provinces, 5 autonomous regions, and 2 special administrative regions (Hong Kong and Macau). For example, if protest demonstrations, bombings, and assassinations are valid indicators of collective unhappiness, the Uighurs and other Turkic groups living in the landlocked province of Xinjiang, with its harsh continental climate, are really unhappy peoples. All this rich information on variations in local climates and local cultures and the expected relation between them is absent in the single dot for China in Figure 2.1. China is inaccurately listed as having moderately cold winters, temperate summers, and a moderately happy population. Similarly, another dot inaccurately indicates that the United States has moderately cold winters, temperate summers, and a quite happy population. Confirmation of the climate-happiness thesis within these and other large countries would be more than welcome.

Second, the unhappiest peoples all live in Soviet successor states, suggesting that perhaps communist rule in the past rather than thermal climate must be held accountable for the results. Twenty-one out of the 81 countries had an ex-communist heritage. The findings of a supplementary analysis in which this information[12] was used showed that 42% of the cross-national differences in happiness could be associated with greater unhappiness in these ex-communist countries. Over and above climate, a communist past, inextricably bound up with the collapse of communist rule around 1990, accounted for 22% of the variation in happiness but did not break the climate-happiness effect.

Third, income per head, educational attainment, and life expectancy are well-documented determinants of happiness in nations. Since 1990, the United Nations has annually published a cross-national Human Development Index that combines these three clustered indicators into what may be viewed as an objective proxy of the subjective distribution of happiness around the globe. Even so, the Human Development Index, available for 76 out of the 81 countries, was less successful in predicting happiness than were cold winters and hot summers.[13] This objectively established indicator of human development accounted for 13% of the cross-national variation in subjectively experienced happiness; cold winters and hot summers accounted for an additional 39%. These figures strenghten rather than weaken the climate-satisfaction thesis.

Fourth, geographic latitude seems to represent an interesting variable for this kind of ecological research. This variable is not equal to climatic temperature. The thermal impact of such features as altitude, mountains, land masses, and the Gulf Stream, and the discrepancy between geographic equator and thermal equator disqualify latitude as a proper indicator of climatic temperature. Latitude is a much better indicator of variations in sunlight and day-night cycles and may for that reason be positively related to subjective well-being and pleasantness of affect at both the individual and national levels (Basabe et al., 2002). Yet, once again, this rival predictor failed to rebut the observed climate-happiness effect.[14] Colder winters and hotter summers accounted for 21% of the cross-national differences in happiness over and above the 7% accounted for by absolute latitude. Not only is this finding in line with the climate-satisfaction thesis but it also suggests a tentative conclusion of well-nigh cosmic proportions. In and of itself, the tilt of the earth on its axis and its position in relation to the sun has a tiny impact on the happiness of societies.

Winters, Summers, and Suicide

Climate and suicide have long been associated. Implicitly relying on average temperature levels, dozens of authors spread out over dozens of decades have noticed that suicide rates are considerably higher in warmer climates with hotter summers (e.g., Durkheim, 1897; Lynn, 1971). In his 18-nation study, for example, Lynn (1971) found an insignificant relationship between lower temperatures in the coldest month and suicide-based anxiety but a significant relationship between higher temperatures in the hottest month and suicide-based anxiety. Interestingly, he also reported that countries with a larger temperature range between the coldest and the hottest month have higher levels of anxiety and suicide. In retrospect, with his climate-anxiety correlations, Lynn unwittingly skimmed the relevance of the seasonal winter-summer index of climate to explain suicide rates.

To replicate Lynn's winter-summer observation on a larger cross-national scale, I drew data from the first *World Report on Violence and Health* (Krug et al., 2002). In that report, age-standardized suicide rates per 100,000 inhabitants during the 1990s were made available for 75 nation states – 35 European countries, 17 Asian countries, 18 North and South American countries, 3 African countries, and Australia and New Zealand. Assuming that suicide rates are valid indicators of life *dis*satisfaction and that they are cross-nationally comparable, the above climate-satisfaction analyses[5,6] were repeated, with the subjective happiness ratings replaced by the objective suicide rates.

Given the critiques of the reliability of official suicide rates (Taylor, 1982), it came as a surprise that the suicide results unfolded as a kind of mirror image of the happiness results. Climate predicted 43% of the cross-national differences in suicide rates.[15] Going from left to right in Figure 2.2, we see an accelerating increase of suicide in countries with colder winters. Bottom-up, however, we see a steady increase of suicide in countries with hotter summers. As in Figure 2.1, the largest differences occur diagonally.[16] In the lower left-hand corner of Figure 2.2, countries with more temperate winters but hot summers tend to have less suicide-prone populations (see Philippines, Thailand, Panama, Brazil, and Kuwait). By contrast, in the upper right-hand corner, we find by far the most suicide-prone populations in countries with both cold winters and hot summers, including the Baltic States, Russia, Belarus, and Kazakhstan. Again, average temperatures did not predict these findings.[17] Precipitation did not improve[18] the temperature effect on suicide; neither did communist

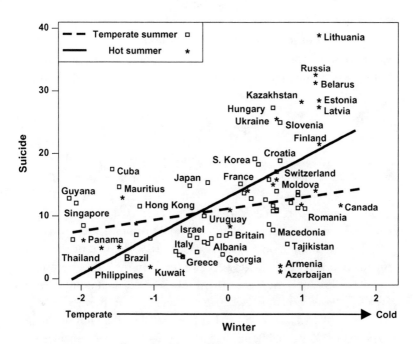

FIGURE 2.2. Joint effect of colder winters and hotter summers on suicide.

rule[19] or geographic latitude[20] break the temperature-suicide effect. This constitutes another series of indications that colder winters and hotter summers lessen culturally embedded life satisfaction.

A striking supplementary result was that, unlike the positive connection found between human development and happiness, there was no connection between human development and suicide.[21] Consequently, the higher suicide rates in countries with colder winters and hotter summers cannot be attributed to lower objective well-being represented by income per head, educational attainment, and life expectancy. Most likely, Durkheim's (1897) four types of suicide – egoistic, altruistic, anomic, and fatalistic suicide – have existential problems as a common denominator that must be traced back to the demands of bitter winters and scorching summers. That climatic cold and heat evoke existential problems is apparent also from their joint association with another major form of lethal violence: homicide (see the box "Yes, violence has climatic links").

For a subset of 58 countries, there were both aggregated individual-level ratings of happiness and country-level rates of suicide. Unfortunately, several countries with continental climates, notably Kazakhstan,

---

Yes, violence has climatic links

If you become so deranged one day that you are ready to take a life, you have a choice. Will it be your own life or someone else's? According to the World Health Organization (Krug et al., 2002), in 2000, leaving war-related deaths aside, an estimated 1,335,000 people worldwide died as a result of suicide (61%) or homicide (39%).

When we zoom in on particular countries, we see that preferences for the two types of lethal violence differ from the above percentages. For instance, there are many more suicides than homicides in Japan (96% vs. 4%), somewhat more suicides than homicides in Moldova (58% vs. 42%), somewhat fewer suicides than homicides in Armenia (40% vs. 60%), and far fewer suicides than homicides in

Colombia (5% vs. 95%). These widely different preferences for suicide versus homicide cry out for explanation in terms of the local circumstances. One of the most important local circumstances is thermal climate. No country is without climate, and no country's inhabitants are immune to it. In the example at issue, climate is less frustrating in Japan and Colombia, and more frustrating in Moldova and Armenia.

After intensive searching and re-searching I discovered two mysterious climatic links between suicide and homicide rates.[22] Countries with less frustrating winters and summers tend to have fixed levels of lethal violence, with widely varying percentage distributions of suicides and homicides. Countries with more frustrating winters and summers, by contrast, tend to have widely varying levels of lethal violence with fixed 50–50 distributions of suicides and homicides. I have not the slightest idea why. And that's good news: no mysteries, no science.

Kyrgyzstan, Tajikistan, Turkmenistan, and Uzbekistan, dropped out. Nevertheless, even in this second-class sample of countries, suicide appeared to be related to unhappiness and, through it, to climate.[23] The overlapping climate-unhappiness and unhappiness-suicide links accounted for 30% of the total climate-suicide link.[24] This climate-unhappiness-suicide path of influence provides extra support for the central notion in this chapter that more demanding winters and summers lessen culturally embedded life satisfaction.

Harsh Seasons and Cultural Solutions

Viewed from the perspective of culture, these connections between climate and life satisfaction are spectacular. The findings are impressive because they deny the generally accepted knowledge that our tropical genesis saddled us with survival problems and necessary cultural adaptations only outside the warmer regions of our planet. In reality, harsh summer seasons are no less problematic than harsh winter seasons. Hotter summers decrease happiness and increase suicide, especially in countries with continental climates where the winters are also problematic. Indeed, our bodies are designed for temperate climates. Although extremely cold and extremely hot climatic contexts are hostile in different ways, both frustrate us and endanger our future. Even after half a million years of cumulative cultural inventions we remain subject to the law of human nature that harsh seasons sap life satisfaction.

By successfully occupying all the major climatic zones of the world, we have created serious problems of unhappiness and suicide in regions with extremely cold winters, extremely hot summers, or both. Are there royal roads to solutions? The Norse colony that once lived in Greenland saw no solution and died out when the already icy climate deteriorated. The animal solution of seasonal migration is infeasible for present-day humans. Wherever possible, the solution of staying in temperate climatic zones or moving there has already been implemented spontaneously (cf. the box "Desert diets of sand and salt" on page 35). What, then, is to be done about the world's climate-related problems of unhappiness, self-inflicted injuries, and suicide? In the year 2000 alone, an estimated 815,000 people died from suicide. Many more lives are profoundly affected emotionally, socially, and economically by the suicidal behavior of family members or friends. All this calls for drastic action.

The World Health Organization (WHO), unaware of the inevitable impact of the harshness of climate, has sounded the alarm. In 1999, the WHO launched a global initiative for the reduction of suicide based on the viewpoint that the complexity of causes of depression, self-directed violence, and suicide necessarily requires a multifaceted approach to prevention (Krug et al., 2002). At the top of the agenda is the strengthening of countries' capabilities to develop and evaluate national policies and plans for suicide prevention. Recommended interventions include changes of the physical environment (e.g., fencing in high bridges), societal approaches (e.g., restricting access to the means of suicide), community-based efforts (e.g., suicide prevention centers), behavioral approaches (e.g., immediate access to helping agencies), and treatment approaches (e.g., pharmacotherapy). After their extensive overview of what can be done to prevent suicide, Krug et al. (2002, p. 206) heaved a sigh: "Cultural factors play a major role in suicidal behavior, producing large differences in the characteristics of this problem around the world. Given these differences, what has a positive effect in preventing suicide in one place may be ineffective or even counterproductive in another cultural setting."

The WHO recommendations for suicide reduction are, of course, most welcome in the countries with the highest rates – Lithuania, Russia, Belarus, Estonia, Kazakhstan, and Latvia. But, as shown in Figure 2.2, all of these countries also have harsh continental climates that may counteract the effectiveness of the recommendations. Large decreases in suicide rates might occur only after the warming of winters, the cooling of summers, or both. A more feasible and more promising direction of planned change, very successfully implemented by Canadians and Scandinavians, is the compensation of harsh seasons by paid work. Money resources can buy all that is required to cope satisfactorily with harsh seasons, and paid work can provide the necessary money resources. These cultural solutions are explored further in the book. Chapter 3 is devoted to the function of cash, and Chapter 4 to the function of work; a climato-economic trichotomy of cultures is developed in Chapter 5 and elaborated in Chapters 6 to 8.

PROPOSITIONS

2.1. Humans are sensitive to climatic deviations from temperateness (22°C; ca. 72°F).

2.2. Colder winters and hotter summers come with greater demands, fewer resources, and stronger needs for thermal comfort, nutrition, and health.

2.3. Colder winters and hotter summers lessen culturally embedded life satisfaction.

RESEARCH NOTES

1. Most studies reported in this book were based on the overall winter-summer index of climate rather than the winter and summer indices (somewhat lower or higher reference points than 22°C yield almost identical results). Note that each degree Celsius has the same weight irrespective of its temperature level. For warm-blooded humans, how-ever, it may be inadequate to describe climate-culture relations using such a linear rule. The objective difference between +20°C and +15°C may produce a smaller subjective difference in environmental difficulty than does the objective difference between −15°C and −20°C. Therefore, equal temperature intervals may be given increasingly heavier weights at increasingly larger deviations from 22°C. Notably, a winter-summer-extremes index could be based on the sum of the squared deviations from 22°C in the coldest and hottest months. However, this alternative index has the disadvantage of departing more from a normal distribu-tion without the advantage of containing additional information. Across 225 countries, city-states, independent islands, and dependent territories (source: Parker, 1997), the winter-summer index and the winter-summer-extremes index are almost identical ($r = .97$, $p < .001$). For that reason, quadratic effects of climate are reported and discussed only when they improve our understanding of culture.

2. The values of the total climate index are 22 for Burundi, Comoros, and the Seychelles, 57 for Niger, and 64 for Lesotho.

3. The values of the summer components of the climate index are 44 for Sudan, 42 for Burkina Faso, 40 for Niger, 39 for Mali, and 38 for Chad.

4. For each country, the size of the surface area and the population density were derived from Parker (1997) (with Congo covering both the Brazzaville part and the Kinshasa part). Harsher climates were associated with larger surface areas [$r(52) = .50$, $p < .001$; $r(46) = .44$, $p < .001$ after exclusion of the islands], and with lower population densities [$r(52) = -.38$, $p < .01$; $r(46) = -.36$, $p < .01$ after exclusion of the islands].

5. I used SPSS regression models in all analyses. Demanding climate was based on average temperatures computed across all major cities in a country, weighted for population (source: Parker, 1997). Demanding winters (W) was the sum of the absolute deviations from 22°C for the average lowest and highest temperatures in the coldest month. Demanding summers (S) was the sum of the absolute deviations from 22°C for the average lowest and highest temperatures in the hottest month. I entered the standardized values of W and S in the first step of the regression analysis, and the interaction term W × S in the second step.

6. Precipitation (P) was a country's midrange monthly rain, snow, sleet, and hail in mm (source: Parker, 1997). After standardizing the predictors, I entered winters (W) and summers (S) in the first step, W × S in the second step, P in the third step, the interaction terms W × P and S × P in the fourth step, and the interaction term W × S × P in the final step.

7. Source of happiness data: www.eur.nl/fsw/research/veenhoven, retrieved August 2, 2005 (scale range from 1 to 4; empirical range from 2.44 to 3.50; $M = 3.01$, $SD = .28$). The test-retest reliability of the happiness ratings was $r(65) = .92$, $p < .001$ over a 10-year period, and $r(23) = .89$, $p < .001$ over a 20-year period, while the validity of the ratings was apparent from their positive relation with self-rated health, $r(74) = .70$, $p < .001$ (same data source) and their negative relation with suicide, $r(60) = -.36$, $p < .01$. Differential response styles such as acquiescence and extremity ratings cannot be held responsible for this relation, as shown in Chapter 3.

8. Joint effect of colder winters and hotter summers on happiness in 81 countries.

Predictors	B	B
Winters (W)	−.10***	−.06*
Summers (S)	−.06*	−.10***
W × S		−.11***
ΔR^2	.18***	.09***
Total R^2	.18***	.27***

$^{\dagger}p < .10.$ $^{*}p < .05.$ $^{**}p < .01.$ $^{***}p < .001.$

There was no multicollinearity (*VIFs* < 1.51), and there were no outliers (Cook's *Ds* < .09).

9. All figures presented in this book are SPSS-generated plots. As they rest on standardizations of colder winters and hotter summers in different samples, a country's position on the temperate-harsh dimensions varies over figures. The cutoff point for the illustration in Figure 2.1 was 67% temperate summers, 33% hot summers. Simple slopes: $r(54) = -.20, p < .10$ for temperate summers; $r(27) = -.61, p < .001$ for hot summers.

10. To correct for the contamination of temperature levels and temperature variations on earth, the average of the lowest and highest temperatures in the coldest and hottest months was regressed on the standard deviation in these four temperature values. The cold-hot model was represented by the standardized residual, the cold-temperate-hot model by the square of this cold-hot predictor. When both predictors were controlled for, ΔR^2 for the joint effect of colder winters and hotter summers on happiness increased from .27 to .28.

11. For thermal and precipitational climate in total, $R^2 = .28$. For the main effect of precipitation, together with the interaction effects of winters-by-precipitation, summers-by-precipitation, and winters-by-summers-by-precipitation, $\Delta R^2 = .01$, n.s.

12. Former communist rule (source: Parker, 1997) was entered first, followed by winters (W) and summers (S) in the second step and W × S in the final step. Total $R^2 = .49$. For former communist rule, $\Delta R^2 = .42, p < .001$; for W and S, $\Delta R^2 = .01$, n.s.; and for W × S, $\Delta R^2 = .06$, $p < .01$.

13. The Human Development Index 1999 (source: United Nations Development Programme, 2001) was used as it covered more countries with happiness ratings than the earlier development indices during the 1990–1999 period under investigation ($N = 76$). Because the ratio of skewness to its standard error was 3.46, the index was log transformed (new ratio .41). The then normally distributed Human Development Index was entered first, followed by winters (W) and summers (S) in the second step and W × S in the final step. Total $R^2 = .52$. For human development, $\Delta R^2 = .13, p < .001$; for W and S, $\Delta R^2 = .34, p < .001$; and for W × S, $\Delta R^2 = .05, p < .01$.

14. The country's absolute latitude – its midrange distance from the geographic equator – was entered first, followed by winters (W) and summers (S) in the second step, and W × S in the final step. Total $R^2 = .28$. For absolute latitude, $\Delta R^2 = .07, p < .05$; for W and S, $\Delta R^2 = .13, p < .01$; and for W × S, $\Delta R^2 = .08, p < .01$.

Climate Colors Life Satisfaction 55

15. Joint effect of colder winters and hotter summers on suicide rates in 75 countries.

Predictors	B	B	B
Winters (W)	3.77***	2.94***	4.66***
Summers (S)	1.48†	2.35**	1.33†
W × S		2.82**	2.16*
W^2			2.34**
S^2			−.07
ΔR^2	.29***	.08**	.06*
Total R^2	.29***	.37***	.43***

Suicide rates ranged from .80 to 38.40 per 100,000 inhabitants (M = 12.04, SD = 7.92).
$^\dagger p < .10$. $^* p < .05$. $^{**} p < .01$. $^{***} p < .001$.

There was no multicollinearity ($VIFs < 1.92$), there were no outliers (Cook's $Ds < .19$), and dropping the 15 countries with the largest geopgraphical variations in temperature produced essentially the same results.

16. The cutoff point for this illustration was 67% temperate summers, 33% hot summers. Simple slopes: $r(49) = .29$, $p < .05$ for temperate summers; $r(26) = .65$, $p < .001$ for hot summers.

17. When the predictors representing the cold-hot model and the cold-temperate-hot model were controlled for, as in research note 10, ΔR^2 for the joint effect of colder winters and hotter summers on suicide rates decreased from .43 to .33.

18. For winters (W), summers (S), and precipitation (P) in total, R^2 = .42. For W and S, $\Delta R^2 = .29$, $p < .001$; for W × S, $\Delta R^2 = .08$, $p < .05$; for P, $\Delta R^2 = .05$, $p < .05$, but final $B_P = 2.29$, n.s.; and for W × P, S × P, and W × S × P, $\Delta R^2 = .00$.

19. For former communist rule, $\Delta R^2 = .17$, $p < .001$; for W and S, $\Delta R^2 = .13$, $p < .001$; and for W × S, $\Delta R^2 = .07$, $p < .01$.

20. For absolute latitude, $\Delta R^2 = .22$, $p < .001$; for W and S, $\Delta R^2 = .07$, $p < .05$; and for W × S, $\Delta R^2 = .09$, $p < .001$.

21. For human development, $\Delta R^2 = .02$, n.s.; for W and S, $\Delta R^2 = .30$, $p < .001$; and for W × S, $\Delta R^2 = .08$, $p < .01$.

22. The cross-national Spearman rank correlation between Krug et al.'s (2002) suicide and homicide rates was insignificant [$r_s(71) = -.11$,

n.s.]. But this changed when the suicide-homicide correlation was computed twice. The correlation became negative for countries with temperate winters, temperate summers, or both [$r_s(46) = -.41, p < .01$], but positive for countries with both cold winters and hot summers [$r_s(25) = .46, p < .02$].

23. For happiness (H), winters (W), and summers (S) in total, $R^2 = .43$. For H, $\Delta R^2 = .13, p < .01$; for W and S, $\Delta R^2 = .23, p < .001$, entry $B_W = 4.56$, $p < .001$, and entry $B_S = 1.55, p < .10$; for W $\times$ S, $\Delta R^2 = .01$, n.s.; and for W^2 and S^2, $\Delta R^2 = .06, p < .05$.

24. For the climate-unhappiness-suicide path to hold true, the following conditions must be met: (a) colder winters and hotter summers must produce higher happiness ratings; (b) colder winters and hotter summers must produce higher suicide rates; (c) higher happiness ratings must produce higher suicide rates; and (d) colder winters and hotter summers must have a significantly reduced effect on the suicide rates when the happiness ratings are controlled for. Condition a is met in research note 8 and is visualized in Figure 2.1. Condition b is met in research note 15 and is visualized in Figure 2.2. Condition c is met because happiness ratings and suicide rates are negatively related: $r(58) = -.36, p < .01$. And condition d is met because the degree of successful suicide prediction decreased from $\Delta R^2 = .42$ to $\Delta R^2 = .30$ when happiness was controlled for. In other words, about 30% of the total climate-suicide link (.13 divided by .42) was accounted for by unhappiness.

3

Cash Compensates for Climate

The worst line ever written is the poverty line of the World Bank.

Poverty is painful, especially in regions where money is needed to cope with extreme cold or heat. Poor Soviet successor states in cold continental climates such as Belarus, Russia, and Ukraine are cases in point. Even more noteworthy, in a hot belt several thousand kilometers in width encircling the earth at the equator, more lower income countries can be found than anywhere else. That belt of painful poverty has come to be known among economists as the equatorial grand canyon (Parker, 2000; Theil & Galvez, 1995; Williamson & Moss, 1993). At the rock bottom of the economic grand canyon, Mali, Niger, Chad, Congo, Sudan, Ethiopia, and Somalia are notorious for their famines, plagues, and ethnic clashes. The triad of cold or heat, poverty, and misery highlights the relevance of the following rhetorical question: Do money resources influence the relation between climatic demands and culturally embedded life satisfaction?

The findings reported in Chapter 2 leave room for two coordinated influences of climate and cash on life satisfaction. The first possibility is that colder winters, hotter summers, or both, produce lower incomes which in turn produce lower happiness ratings and higher suicide rates (see the dotted lines with arrows labeled *Chapter 3* in Figure 1.1 on page 8). In the section "A Climate-Cash-Satisfaction Path?" the degree of temperateness versus harshness of a country's climate is related to the inhabitants' income per head. No clear evidence of a connection between harsh climate and money resources surfaces, ruling out the possibility of a climate-gives-cash-gives-satisfaction path of influence.

The second possibility of a climate-cash impact is that the already lower life satisfaction in countries with harsher climates is even lower in lower-income countries. The basic idea is that we live in climato-economic niches where cash can protect us against colder winters and hotter summers enabling us to buy various things that satisfy climate-based needs. As elaborated in the section "Climato-economic Threats and Challenges," colder and hotter climates alike can be made more livable by richer people who have the resources to meet the climate's demands. To support the explanatory framework, the section "Climato-economic Niches of Life Satisfaction" contains reports of climate-happiness, climate-health, and climate-suicide investigations under the variable condition of a country's income per head. The propositions at the end highlight the finding that a more demanding climate is more painful to the extent that a population is poorer.

A CLIMATE-CASH-SATISFACTION PATH?

The analyses reported in Chapter 2 give no hint that available money is a link between more demanding climates and decreases in life satisfaction. Quite the reverse, the Human Development Index representing collective income, education, and life expectancy failed to account for the links between colder winters and hotter summers, on the one hand, and lower happiness ratings and higher suicide rates, on the other hand. Yet a climate-gives-cash-gives-satisfaction path is still within the bounds of the possible, because the Human Development Index is an inaccurate indicator of income per head. Armenia and Tajikistan, for example, have much worse wage levels than their educational and health systems lead one to expect, whereas

Botswana and South Africa have much better wage levels than their educational and health systems suggest (United Nations Development Programme, 2001). I therefore investigated whether winter-summer deviations from 22°C are associated with income per head[1] and whether winter-summer extremes have an extra effect.[2]

For the 225 countries, city-states, independent islands, and dependent territories for which the gross domestic product has been documented, climate appeared to account for 26% of the variation in income per head.[3] Precipitation had no additional effect.[4] For as yet unknown reasons, countries with colder winters have higher income levels no matter whether the summers are temperate or hot. This result is at odds with the idea that populated areas with harsher climates produce lower incomes and, through them, less life satisfaction. By contrast, countries with hotter summers have lower income levels, perhaps because of the reduction of work output in unbearably hot environments, the intrinsic limit on food productivity (directly or through the diseases and pests afflicting animals and plants), and the burden of continuous attacks on human health (e.g., sleeping sickness, bilharzia, malaria, river blindness, parasitic worms, leprosy, leishmaniasis, yellow fever, and cholera; Kamarck, 1976). This finding confirms the existence of the economic grand canyon alongside the equator. However, colder winters had no effect on the link between hotter summers and lower income levels, neither worldwide nor within the separate continents of Africa, Asia, Europe, and South America. As a consequence, lower income levels cannot account for the finding of especially low happiness ratings and especially high suicide rates in populations having to cope with colder winters on top of hotter summers.

My devil's advocate raised a methodological objection to this analysis. The indicator of income per head used was based on economic activities that are paid for in money, pass through some sort of market, and are taxed by the government. Collective income in the form of gross domestic product per head underestimates the volume of economically significant activities by omitting "the self-consumption of households in agriculture, the unpaid work of housewives, goods and services exchanged informally through barter, and goods and services exchanged in informal transactions not reported to the authorities" (Dogan, 1994, p. 43). The possible impact of the informal "gray" or "underground" economy was ignored. The World Bank recently released an index for the size of a country's informal component of the economy (Schneider, 2002), which allowed a replication of the analysis with a more inclusive indicator of collective income that covers both the formal and the informal economy.

This time, climate predicted 42% of the variation in income per head across 109 nations.[5] Again, the main finding was that countries with colder winters have a higher income per head, whereas countries with hotter summers have a lower income per head. Again, colder winters and hotter summers did not affect each other's link with income per head. Taken together, the conclusion seems clear. Neither countries with colder winters nor countries with both colder winters and hotter summers tend to be lower income countries. Consequently, it is highly unlikely that overall income poverty can help explain the observation that colder winters and hotter summers lessen life satisfaction by functioning as a link between climate and life satisfaction. More scientifically put, no clear evidence of the existence of a climate-cash-satisfaction path of influence was found. Perhaps the climato-economic viewpoint that available money resources influence the impact of climatic demands provides a more viable explanation of culturally embedded life satisfaction.

CLIMATO-ECONOMIC THREATS AND CHALLENGES

A harsh climate is supposed to have a domino effect on warm-blooded humans. An objectively harsher climate produces a subjectively more demanding climate, which elicits and reinforces greater primary needs for thermal comfort, nutrition, and health; these are then translated into greater secondary needs for particular goods and services and in turn increase the usefulness of money to buy those goods and services, and so forth. Among many other things, money can buy clothing, housing, refrigerators, heaters, air-conditioning, household energy, meals, drinks, kitchenware, medicines, medical treatment, and social security.

Self-evidently, in different climates money may be useful for different purchases. Money may be a sine qua non for heating and eating in colder regions and for preventing and recovering from diseases produced by substances, germs, bacteria, and insects in hotter regions. This does not mean that the underlying psychosocial processes of the joint impact of climate and cash are fundamentally different in harsher cold and hot climates. As shown in Chapter 2, temperate versus demanding climates rather than cold winters versus hot summers can best account for variations in our psychosocial functioning. Analogously, in both cold and hot climates but not in temperate climates, societies can use collective income to lessen climatic threats and to seek and meet challenges in extremely cold or hot circumstances.

In short, humans the world over use money resources to make the best of otherwise frustratingly cold winters, frustratingly hot summers, or both. Of course, universal psychosocial processes do not necessarily produce similar cultures. On the contrary, in different climato-economic niches the same train of psychosocial events is bound for different cultural destinations. In Chapter 2 we saw that the same survival needs have gradually produced less culturally embedded life satisfaction in more demanding climates. I argue that the already lower life satisfaction in more demanding climates is even lower in countries with lower income resources. This argument is based on a general and widely known theoretical framework for the joint impact of demands and resources. Translated into climato-economic terms, its core idea is that greater climatic demands function as threats in countries with fewer money resources (hence-forth *poorer countries*) but as potential challenges in countries with more money resources (henceforth *richer countries*).

At least six sociological or psychological theories (brought together by Van de Vliert, Huang, & Levine, 2004) view demands as double-edged swords that can produce either threats and dissat-isfaction or challenges and satisfaction. In different ways, all of these theories successfully predict that demands mismatched by unavail-able or inadequate societal or personal resources to meet them impair psychosocial functioning. Mismatches in demands-resources systems eventually produce dissatisfaction as the actors cannot con-trol the threatening and stressful situation. By contrast, demands matched by adequate societal or personal resources to meet them improve psychosocial functioning. Matches in demands-resources systems eventually produce satisfaction as the actors can control the situation, can turn threats into challenging opportunities, and can experience relief and pleasure instead of disappointment and pain. Application of this demands-resources model to the field of climatic demands and money resources yields the following prediction: Greater climatic demands produce greater threats if they are insuf-ficiently matched by money resources, but greater challenges if they are sufficiently matched by money resources.

Climatic Demands as Threats

In principle, colder winters and hotter summers threaten our lives and lessen our life satisfaction. Cash may compensate, if we have it. But inhabitants of poorer countries are in a worse position than inhabitants of richer countries for buying goods and services to satisfy their survival needs for thermal comfort, nutrition, and health. They collectively suffer more from climatic stress and ill health and are less satisfied as a result. For these deprived people, the lower happiness ratings and higher suicide rates in more demanding climates are, therefore, more pronounced. And in climato-economic niches of bitter winters or scorching summers and abject poverty, people are even in peril of death.

Related to this, the World Bank's definition of poverty implicitly varies as a function of the level of demand of thermal climate. In otherwise equal circumstances, money resources are needed least in temperate climates, much more in hot continental climates, and most in cold continental climates. The poverty line is a dollar a day in African countries with sweltering hot summers, including the Central African Republic, Chad, and Nigeria; it is more than twice as high in East European and Asian countries with ice-cold winters, where more money is needed for heating and clothes (e.g., Belarus, Moldova, Ukraine, Pakistan, Tajikistan, and Uzbekistan). Those poverty-line differences suggest that it is easier to compensate for hot summers than cold winters; in Chapter 8 we see that this impression is an illusion resulting from the earth's present cold bias.

Climatic Demands as Challenges

Inhabitants of richer countries can take physical survival and a decent life for granted and rarely experience weather demands as threats. Colder winters and hotter summers offer societies opportunities for exciting tests of their ability to convert available money resources into life satisfaction for their members. The unemployed, the disabled, the addicts, and the sick are no exception. Richer countries have welfare agencies that take on caretaking responsibilities, making clothing, housing, food, and health services available to almost everyone. "Even in the United States, with a relatively limited welfare state, more than one-quarter of the national product is redistributed through the state for public welfare" (Inglehart & Welzel, 2005, p. 28).

Perhaps a challenging climate is not as simple as it sounds. The golden rule of life, that you can have too little or too much of a good thing, may also be true of climato-economic niches. Especially for richer peoples, thermal climate may perhaps be too easy, just right for challenges, or too difficult. Living in a too-temperate climate may be dull as there are simply too few weather-related goods to spend the money on. Living in a too-demanding climate may lead to helplessness and hopelessness because the many weather-related goods and services represent just a drop in the ocean of survival needs. The existence of such a society-level mechanism of "neither too little nor too much" climatic challenge would be in perfect agreement with much evidence for the commonly accepted individual-level postulate that understimulation and overstimulation, as well as role underload and role overload, produce dissatisfaction and strain (e.g., Fisher, 1986; Gardner & Cummings, 1988; Janssen, 2001; Van de Vliert, 1996). If so, this would also amend the above demands-resources model and its application to the field of climatic demands and money resources. Both undermatching and overmatching as distinct types of mismatches between climatic demands and money resources would produce dissatisfaction and strain.

Thinking further along these admittedly shaky lines leads to some provocative expectations for peoples living in richer countries. Having the cash to compensate for harsh climates, they may find their weather *too easy* if both winters and summers are temperate and undemanding, but *too difficult* if both winters and summers are demanding. By contrast, their weather is *challenging* if only one season is really demanding. As a consequence, the inhabitants of richer countries were expected to evaluate the overall quality of their life most positively if they were living in a challenging climate with either temperate winters and demanding summers, or demanding winters and temperate summers. Tests of this speculative prediction are reported in the next section; again, happiness ratings and suicide rates were used as opposite indicators of culturally embedded life satisfaction.

CLIMATO-ECONOMIC NICHES OF LIFE SATISFACTION

In addition to happiness and suicide, perceptions of one's own health were added as a clearly distinct criterion for life satisfaction. Unlike happiness, health is a survival need. Unlike suicide, health is a sign of successful survival. And more so than happiness and suicide, health is related to purchasable goods and services.

Climato-economic Niches of Happiness

My first introduction to the economic roots of climatic variations in happiness was a kind of scholarly joke that yielded a telling result (see the box "Price tags of happiness"). Overall income differences appeared to be less critical for happiness in the undemanding contexts of temperate winters and temperate summers than in the more demanding contexts of bitter winters, scorching summers, or both. Intrigued by this finding, my research team at the time designed two happiness studies: a preliminary cold-temperate-hot study followed by a main winter-summer study.

Price tags of happiness

What would it take to make all communities on earth equally happy? If we put on blinkers and suppose that climatic demands and money resources are the only determinants of happiness, demands-resources theories give away the secret. To reach the same standard of happiness throughout the world, one has to provide a country's residents with money resources to the extent that the climate they live in deviates from continuous mild temperatures around 22°C. Phil Parker, Xu Huang, and I took delight in testing this seemingly crazy hypothesis. Phil sampled 143 economic development professionals from 34 countries from all corners of the world. They took part in training courses for the World Bank, jointly conducted by

Harvard University, Stanford University, and the European Institute of Business Administration (INSEAD). The trainees, each of whom had traveled extensively in low-income and high-income countries, were asked the following question.

Assume that the average income of a German today is indexed at 100. Based on your knowledge, how much would the average person from your country of origin need to earn to be just as happy as the average German? Please base your answer on the index of 100. If your country of origin is Germany, your answer must be 100. If the average person would be as happy as the average German by earning less, the answer must be between 0 and 100. If the average person would be as happy as the average German by earning more, the answer must be above 100.

The resulting estimates of the income required to generate equal utility to Germany varied from 0 to 130. The figures were lowest for Somalia (0), Mozambique (0), El Salvador (20), Georgia (20), Sudan (25), Egypt (30), Pakistan (30), and Iran (30). The zero scores for Somalia and Mozambique caused a healthy debate among participants, with some accusing those who awarded zero of not understanding the question. The representatives of these countries, however, stood by their estimates. The figures were highest for Denmark (84), Britain (95), Switzerland (97), United States (98), Germany (100), Japan (105), France (105), and Norway (130). Further discussion revealed that the participants rejected the notion that incomes need to equalize for countries to reach equal levels of happiness.

These differences in the price tags of happiness did not occur overnight. It may have taken at least 25 years to develop them. We therefore examined to what extent the price tags of happiness were determined by income levels in the 1970s, and to what extent cold and hot climates had an additional impact. Our hypothesis was not so crazy after all. Through their estimates, the respondents indicated that folks back home needed more money to lead a happy life if they lived in a more demanding climate. Not surprisingly, 32% of the higher money needs could be accounted for by higher collective income. More interestingly, another 42% of the higher money needs could be accounted for by more demanding climates in general (32%) and more demanding climates in countries with specific income levels in particular (10%). Income appeared to serve a less critical function in more temperate climates. However, poorer societies having to cope with hotter summers and richer societies having to cope with colder winters do need more income to be as happy as our German friends.

Cold-temperate-hot study. We compared the happiness of citizens of poorer and richer countries living in more temperate or harsher climatic zones of the earth. To do so, we borrowed a country-level index of happiness from Diener et al. (1995). This index covered 55 nations, was based on four surveys among representative national samples of adults and convenience samples of students, and appeared to be a valid instrument (for details, see Van de Vliert, Huang, & Parker, 2004). We expected that poorer peoples would be unhappier in more demanding climates but that richer peoples would be happier in the same sort of more demanding climates. This expectation was confirmed.

Poorer societies in colder-than-temperate or hotter-than-temperate climates had lower levels of subjective well-being coupled with a somewhat stronger motivation to improve the happiness of others. Mirrorwise, richer societies living in colder-than-temperate or hotter-than-temperate climates had higher levels of subjective well-being coupled with a somewhat weaker motivation to improve the happiness of others. In other words, cultural adaptations to climato-economic niches are stronger for feeling good than for doing good. One should keep in mind, however, that these results

linking climato-economic niches to culturally embedded life satisfaction are tentative because seasonal variations in temperature were
left out of consideration.

Winter-summer study. A more accurate test of the climato-
economic demands-resources explanation of life satisfaction is possible when the average winter and summer deviations from 22°C are
used. This boils down to a replication of the climate-happiness
investigation reported in Chapter 2, under the variable condition
of lower versus higher income per head.

Happiness ratings from the *World Database of Happiness* as well
as purchasing-power indicators of income per head[6] were available
for 77 independent nation-states. In total, colder winters, hotter summers, and income per head accounted for 63% of the variation in the
happiness ratings.[7] Colder winters and hotter summers accounted for
28% of the happiness, income per head for 18%, and colder winters
and income per head in interaction for an additional 17%. These
percentages are broken down in Figure 3.1 into separate pictures
for the 38 relatively poor and the 39 relatively rich countries.

The picture in the poorer countries shows downward slopes of
decreasing happiness in countries with colder winters irrespective of
whether the summers are temperate (dotted line) or hot (solid line).
In a similar vein, the picture in the richer countries shows a downward slope of decreasing happiness in countries with colder winters
and hotter summers (solid line).[8] Thus, in support of the demands-
resources model of climato-economic threats and challenges, colder
winters appear to seriously undermine happiness in poorer countries including several Soviet successor states and in richer countries
with hotter summers including several other Soviet successor states.

Summers also tend to have some impact, albeit in the richer
countries only. The upward dotted bar of the Saint Andrew's cross
indicates that temperate summers tend to increase happiness to the
extent that winters are colder. Conversely, the downward solid bar of
the Saint Andrew's cross indicates that hot summers tend to decrease

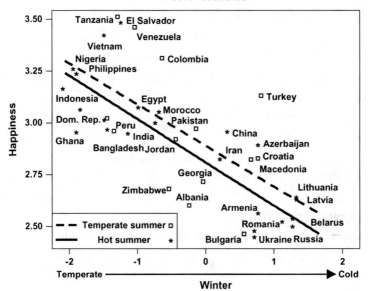

Poorer countries

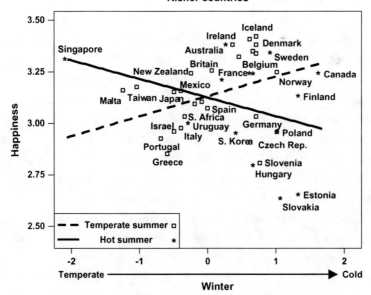

Richer countries

FIGURE 3.1. Joint effect of colder winters and hotter summers on happiness, broken down for poorer and richer countries.

happiness to the extent that winters are colder. These tendencies seem to support the notion of climatic challenges by sketching out the following trichotomy of populations. In countries with an undemanding climate of both temperate winters and temperate summers (see Greece and Portugal in the lower left-hand corner), richer peoples cannot derive extra life satisfaction from spending money resources on climate-related goods and services. By contrast, countries with either demanding summers (Singapore in the upper left-hand corner) or demanding winters (Iceland and Denmark in the upper right-hand corner) challenge richer peoples to use their money resources to cope with the demanding season in satisfactory ways. Finally, in countries with both demanding winters and demanding summers (see Estonia and Slovakia in the lower right-hand corner), even richer peoples are overwhelmed by continuously having to overcome the threats of adverse weather using their money resources.

In line with my theoretical argument, happiness in richer countries might be compromised if the climatic challenges are too easy or too difficult. Too-easy climates may be frustrating as they produce boredom and apathy. Too-difficult climates may be frustrating as they produce helplessness and hopelessness. The weakness that this interpretation of the results is based on findings for a small number of countries comes with the strength that it is the offspring of a family of demands-resources theories in the social sciences. Nonetheless, the only claim made is that poorer societies having to survive more demanding winters are unhappier than all other societies. This claim also rests on a series of unsuccessful attempts to break the strikingly strong joint effect of demanding climate and affluence leading to many resources on the cross-cultural differences in happiness.[9]

One rival explanation brought forward by some skeptical colleagues suggests that the climato-economic effects may in fact be produced by a covariate of income per head – the equal versus unequal distribution of income across regions of the country, by levels of society, or in other ways. These colleagues may have a point.

In many African and South American countries mapped in Figure 3.1 (e.g., Nigeria, Zimbabwe, South Africa, Brazil, and Colombia), a powerful and rich elite controls the economic surplus and the flow of money, creating and maintaining a small minority of "haves" and a huge majority of "have-nots." It is interesting to see what happens when the above test of the demands-resources explanation is repeated with income inequality instead of income per head as the economic predictor. When this was done, the percentages of successful happiness prediction showed that income inequality (2%) was convincingly beaten by income per head (35%).[10]

The conclusion that collective income rather than income equality drives the joint impact of climatic demands and money resources on societal happiness also has practical relevance. Ever since Plato (www.classicallibrary.org/plato/dialogues/laws/book5.htm) warned that "there should exist among the citizens neither extreme poverty nor again excessive wealth," many governments have committed themselves to targets for reducing income inequality. The credos of the French revolution and of the communist movement were also based in part on a presumed link between income equality and happiness (Veenhoven, 2000). The findings of my analysis show that some income inequality as an inevitable consequence of any functioning market economy does not have to be a political nightmare. Especially politicians in the richer countries with challenging winters or summers do not have to fear income inequality as long as their dream of overall economic growth is realized.

It is no news that income level matters to happiness. Much evidence already exists that the inhabitants of poorer countries are less satisfied with the quality of their life as a whole (for overviews, see Diener & Oishi, 2000; Frank, 2005). The new element here is that poorer peoples are especially worse off in colder climates. Perhaps even this conclusion is old wine in new bottles. If Montesquieu (1748) were among us today, he would not be surprised by this finding and would perhaps react with something to the effect of the following: "It is self-evident that awfully poor people are not amused when they have to survive bitter winters. What surprises me is that the publics of richer countries tailor their feelings of happiness to the typical composite of winters and summers. Apparently, it is regarded as a blessing to have no less and no more than one really challenging season, and, apparently, it doesn't matter whether that challenge is extreme cold or extreme heat. The results seem to show that rich people thrive in temperate climates but love occasional peaks of really cold or hot weather."

Montesquieu may not be alone. For policy makers taking for granted that people can be made happier by providing them with a higher income, it may come as a shock that such an economic-development strategy can backfire. The findings suggest that especially citizens of countries with a rather temperate climate throughout the year (Tanzania, Venezuela, etc.) may become unhappier if their country grows richer with insufficient climatic targets on which to spend that money. Economic progress, by contrast, seems especially beneficial for societies facing challenging winters alternated with relieving summers (Albania, Bulgaria, etc.). It might be said that this supporting role of climate confirms that riches alone can make no one happy.

Climato-economic Niches of Health

Even more than happiness and suicide, self-reported health is seen as a manifestation of culturally embedded life satisfaction that depends on climatic demands and money resources. Climates create inhospitable areas by impairing people's experience of health. Thermal comfort and nutrition are necessary conditions of good subjective health. Money can buy immense quantities of goods and services that guarantee and restore objective and subjective health. And both physical and mental health are connected with happiness, on the one hand, and suicide, on the other (Helliwell & Putnam, 2005; Triandis, 2000). It is a truism that better health moves people from suicide toward happiness. Yet, feeling healthy and being happy are different faces of culturally embedded life satisfaction. Several countries scattered around the globe have inhabitants who feel relatively healthy but are nonetheless relatively unhappy (e.g., Albania, Indonesia, Iran, Jordan, Macedonia, South Korea, Spain, Uruguay, and Zimbabwe; Inglehart et al., 1998, 2004). All those considerations made it crucially important to find out whether links between climate and self-reported health exist that resemble the climato-economic contextualization of happiness in Figure 3.1.

For this analysis, I used data from three waves of the World Values Surveys carried out in the 1990s (www.worldvaluessurvey.org; Inglehart et al., 1998, 2004). In each wave, nationally representative samples of on average about 1,500 adult interviewees were asked, "All in all, how would you describe your state of health these days? Would you say it is very poor, poor, fair, good, or very good" (Inglehart et al., 1998, V 83). Data on climate, wealth, and health were available for 71 nations, representing over 80% of the world population. The perceived-health scores were first aggregated within nations and then averaged over repeated measurements, if any. The final scores were based on three measurement waves for 14 countries, on two measurement waves for 24 countries, and on a single measurement wave for 33 countries.[11]

In and of themselves, harsher climates appeared to account for 23%, and income per head for 7%, of the cross-national differences in self-reported health. In mutual interaction, climate and wealth predicted another 14%.[12] The visualization of the results in Figure 3.2 shows, first, further support for the conclusions reported in Chapter 2. Going from left to right, we see that colder winters lessen life satisfaction, here in the shape of poorer health perceptions. Again, however, this held true for the poorer countries only, and a Saint Andrew's cross appeared against the cloud of richer countries.[13] The lower part of the cross seems to weakly suggest that too little stress in climates with temperate winters and summers (see Portugal and

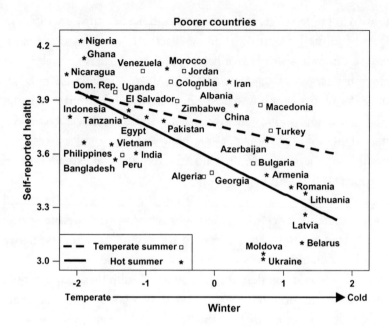

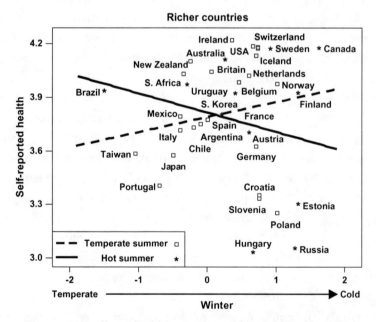

FIGURE 3.2. Joint effect of colder winters and hotter summers on self-reported health, broken down for poorer and richer countries.

Taiwan on the left) and too much stress in climates with cold winters and hot summers (see Hungary and Russia on the right) undermine perceived health. This is in line with the notion that both undermatching and overmatching in demands-resources systems are threatening. By contrast, the upper part of the cross seems to suggest weakly that challenging levels of moderate stress in climates with either hot summers (see Brazil on the left) or cold winters (see Switzerland on the right) strengthen rather than weaken perceived health.

It proved impossible to trivialize these climato-economic niches of culturally embedded feelings of health. My potentially most destructive afterthought was that Figure 3.2 did not amount to anything because it was a clone of Figure 3.1. Self-reported health can be such a strong determinant of happiness (cf. Helliwell & Putnam, 2005; Triandis, 2000) that the two in fact amount to the same thing. Alternatively, the subjective ratings of health and happiness may both be systematically distorted by international differences in response bias (cf. Cheung & Rensvold, 2000; Smith, 2004), with the consequence that we see the same fata morgana twice. When this clone problem was investigated, it vanished into thin air. The climato-economic roots of self-reported health differed from the climato-economic roots of happiness by more than 20%.[14] Moreover, whereas happiness has both winter-economic and summer-economic roots,[8] self-reported health seems to have only winter-economic roots.[13] Thus, to some extent Figures 3.1 and 3.2 provide independent support for the validity of the demands-resources model of climato-economic threats and challenges.

Subjective health and happiness smuggle minor differences into the climato-economic niches of life satisfaction. To further scrutinize these differences, I examined the relation between perceived health and happiness under different conditions of climatic demands and income levels. My presumption was that perceived health is more important for happiness in contexts where life is more in danger. This is exactly what was found, with the marginal note that income levels did not contribute to the differences in the health-happiness relations. In poorer and richer countries with temperate and safe climates, self-reported health and happiness were loosely coupled, like strangers. In poorer and richer countries with demanding and dangerous climates, self-reported health and happiness had strongly positive links, like close relatives.[15] Clearly, self-reported health and happiness stand out as binovular rather than identical twins of life satisfaction.

All in all, climato-economic niches of perceived health play a pivotal part in our lives for four reasons. First, good health is central to life and death because health complaints and illnesses endanger our very existence. Second, day in day out, atmospheric cold and heat make direct and indirect attacks on our health and health perceptions. Third, day in day out, we have to defend our health against weather attacks by spending money. Fourth, our poor, fair, or good health infuses our culture through our comings, doings, and goings.

Climato-economic Niches of Suicide

Poorer people commit suicide more than do their richer compatriots (Krug et al., 2002). It would not be a great discovery, then, if suicide rates were found to peak in poorer countries with more demanding climates. But even this discovery was not forthcoming. Colder winters, hotter summers, and income levels predicted 49% of the variation in the suicide rates[16] in the *World Report on Violence and Health* introduced in Chapter 2. But in no way did the country's income level alter the destructive impact of colder winters and hotter summers on the country's suicide record. In other words, if the world's winter-summer map of suicides in Figure 2.2 is split into separate maps for poorer and richer countries, twin pictures emerge. This means that the climatic niches of suicide are not at all complicated by the economic component of collective income.

Economic misery does not result from poverty alone but from a mosaic of income-related factors, including inflation, unemployment, income inequality, and economic recession. Some of these factors, notably income inequality and economic recession, go hand in hand with higher suicide rates (Krug et al., 2002). But not a clue can be found of an economic condition that influences the relation between climatic demands and the societal inclination to take one's own life. At first blush, money resources can keep the vast majority of a population from feeling unhappy and unhealthy in a demanding climate but cannot keep a small and undoubtedly desperate minority from committing suicide under the same climatic conditions. On second consideration, however, we cannot exclude the possibility that different psychosocial processes in poorer and richer climato-economic niches produce about the same suicide rates (this explanation is discussed further in Chapter 8).

It is a moot question why the higher suicide rates in countries with colder winters and hotter summers are found in both unfavorable and favorable economic circumstances. Gender does not play a part.[17] Age does, but was, therefore, standardized. Furthermore, there is no reason to assume that the higher proportion of suicides is the result of a shared personality structure in populated areas with harsher cold or hot climates. A more likely, yet speculative, explanation is that most populations have roughly the same proportion of suicide-prone members but that stressful winters and stressful summers tend to provoke the deed irrespective of whether the person is short of cash or has plenty of it.

In sum, whereas the climate-happiness and climate-health links are income-dependent, the climate-suicide links are income-free. Thus, the cultural adaptations to climato-economic niches reveal that suicide is not the straightforward opposite of happiness nor an extreme form of bad health. Money resources make the difference between the climate-happiness, climate-health, and climate-suicide links. Cash cannot compensate for all consequences of cold or hot climates that undermine life satisfaction; unhappiness and unhealthiness, yes; suicide, no.

PROPOSITIONS

3.1. Societal income resources can compensate for climatic demands by satisfying needs for thermal comfort, nutrition, and health.

3.2. In poorer societies, colder winters lessen culturally embedded life satisfaction irrespective of whether the summers are temperate or hot.

3.3. In richer societies, colder winters with temperate summers as well as hotter summers with temperate winters increase culturally embedded life satisfaction.

RESEARCH NOTES

1. Gross Domestic Product (GDP) per head in U.S. dollars was derived from Parker (1997) with a view to the number of countries, city-states, independent islands, and dependent territories covered ($N = 225$). Because the ratio of skewness to its standard error was 13.68, this income index was log transformed (new ratio –.58).

2. As in the SPSS regression analyses reported in Chapter 2, I entered the standardized values of demanding winters (W) and demanding summers (S) in the first step, the interaction term W × S in the second step, and W^2 and S^2 in the final step.

3. Joint effect of colder winters and hotter summers on GDP per head in 225 societies.

Predictors	B	B	B
Winters (W)	.41***	.41***	.35***
Summers (S)	–.17**	–.17**	–.15**
W × S		.00	–.07
W^2			.12[†]
S^2			–.12***
ΔR^2	.20***	.00	.06***
Total R^2	.20***	.20***	.26***

[†]$p < .10.$ *$p < .05.$ **$p < .01.$ ***$p < .001.$

There was no multicollinearity (*VIFs* < 1.82), and there were no outliers (Cook's *Ds* < .63).

4. As in the analyses reported in Chapter 2, after standardizing the predictors, I entered winters (W) and summers (S) in the first step, W × S in the second step, Precipitation (P) in the third step, the interaction terms W × P and S × P in the fourth step, and the interaction term W × S × P in the final step. For thermal and precipitational climate in total, $R^2 = .24$; for the four main and interaction effects of precipitation, $\Delta R^2 = .03$, n.s.

5. Joint effect of colder winters and hotter summers on formal plus informal GDP per head in 109 countries.

Predictors	B	B	B
Winters (W)	.85***	.94***	.76***
Summers (S)	−.16	−.11	−.15
W × S		−.19	−.22
W²			.17
S²			−.16**
ΔR^2	.35***	.01	.06**
Total R^2	.35***	.36***	.42*

$^{\dagger}p < .10.$ $^{*}p < .05.$ $^{**}p < .01.$ $^{***}p < .001.$

There was no multicollinearity (*VIFs* < 3.12), and there were no outliers (Cook's *Ds* < .91).

6. As described in Chapter 2, happiness ratings ranged from 1 to 4. In all studies reported, income per head was operationalized in terms of the purchasing power of a country's currency, i.e., the number of units of that currency required to buy a highly similar basket of representative goods and services in U.S. dollars. In this particular study, income per head in 1999 (purchasing power parity; source: United Nations Development Programme, 2001) was used as it covered more countries with happiness ratings ($N = 77$) than the earlier income indices during the 1990–1999 period under investigation. Because the ratio of skewness to its standard error was 3.06, the index was log transformed before it was standardized (new ratio 1.57).

7. Joint effect of colder winters, hotter summers, and income per head on happiness in 77 countries.

Predictors	B	B	B	B	B
Winters (W)	−.09**	−.04	−.11***	−.11***	−.12***
Summers (S)	−.06*	−.11***	−.06*	−.05*	−.04
W × S		−.13***	−.11**	−.04	−.04
Income (I)			.14***	.18***	.18***
W × I				.13***	.14***
S × I				−.03	−.04
W × S × I					−.04
ΔR^2	.16***	.12***	.18***	.16***	.01
Total R^2	.16***	.28***	.46***	.62***	.63***

$^{\dagger}p < .10.$ $^*p < .05.$ $^{**}p < .01.$ $^{***}p < .001.$

There was no multicollinearity (*VIFs* < 2.69), there were no outliers (Cook's *Ds* < .38), and dropping the countries with the largest geographical variations in temperature produced essentially the same results.

8. The correlations between colder winters and happiness were $r(38) =$ −.73, $p < .001$ for the poorer countries, and $r(39) = −.05$, n.s. for the richer countries. On the face of it, this joint influence of colder winters and lower incomes is completely independent of the influence of hotter summers (see the insignificant coefficients for W × S and for W × S × I in the last column of the last table). On further consideration, however, the three-way interaction W × S × I reaches significance ($\Delta R^2 =$ .02, $p < .05$) if only the insignificant main effect of S is left out of the equation. A subsequent supplementary analysis on the 39 richer countries showed that colder winters ($B = .02$, n.s.) and hotter summers ($B = −.07$, n.s.) had a significant interaction effect in the form of a Saint Andrew's cross ($B = −.15, p < .02$), accounting for a considerable proportion of the variation in the happiness ratings (for W and S, ΔR^2 = .11, n.s; for W × S, $\Delta R^2 = .14, p < .02$). From an explanatory rather than descriptive viewpoint, it is important also to note that the addition of I and W × I as predictors did not destroy this Saint Andrew's cross effect of winters and summers in richer countries.

9. For example, precipitation once again had a negligible contribution. In addition to the analyses reported in Chapter 2, the present analysis was repeated with precipitation and the interaction of income per head and precipitation as additional predictors. Owing to the main and interaction effects of precipitation, R^2 increased from .63 to .64; $\Delta R^2 = .01$, n.s.

10. Income inequality was the well-known Gini index (source: United Nations Development Programme, 2001), used to measure the extent to which the distribution of income among individuals or households within a country deviates from a perfectly equal distribution. Lower incomes per head were associated with higher income inequality, $r(74) = -.33$, $p < .01$. On top of winters and summers ($\Delta R^2 = .26$), income inequality ($\Delta R^2 = .00$), and its two-way and three-way interactions with winters and summers ($\Delta R^2 = .02$, n.s.), did not predict extra happiness.

11. The final scores ranged from 3.02 in Hungary and Ukraine to 4.22 in Nigeria (scale range from 1 to 5; $M = 3.74$; $SD= .32$). The test-retest reliabilities were $r(23) = .94$, $p < .001$ for the 1990–1994 period, $r(28) = .90$, $p < .001$ for the 1995–1999 period, and $r(15) = .81$, $p < .001$ for the 1990–1999 period. The validity of the health ratings was apparent from their negative relation with the suicide rates, $r(55) = -.50$, $p < .001$.

12. Joint effect of colder winters, hotter summers, and income per head on self-reported health in 71 countries.

Predictors	B	B	B	B	B
Winters (W)	$-.09^{**}$	$-.05$	$-.12^{***}$	$-.07^{\dagger}$	$-.07^{\dagger}$
Summers (S)	$-.07^{*}$	$-.12^{**}$	$-.08^{*}$	$-.08^{*}$	$-.07^{\dagger}$
W $\times$ S		$-.13^{**}$	$-.09^{*}$	$-.08^{\dagger}$	$-.08^{\dagger}$
Income (I)			$.12^{**}$	$.13^{***}$	$.13^{***}$
W $\times$ I				$.13^{***}$	$.14^{***}$
S $\times$ I				$.03$	$.02$
W $\times$ S $\times$ I					$-.04$
ΔR^2	$.14^{**}$	$.09^{**}$	$.07^{**}$	$.13^{**}$	$.01$
Total R^2	$.14^{**}$	$.23^{***}$	$.30^{***}$	$.43^{***}$	$.44^{***}$

$^{\dagger}p < .10$. $^{*}p < .05$. $^{**}p < .01$. $^{***}p < .001$.

Income (I) was the logged purchasing-power income per head in 1999 (source: United Nations Development Programme, 2001). There was no multicollinearity (*VIFs* < 2.82), there were no outliers (Cook's *Ds* < .16), and dropping the countries with the largest geographical variations in temperature produced essentially the same results.

13. The correlations between colder winters and self-reported health were $r(36) = -.62$, $p < .001$ for poorer countries and $r(35) = -.05$, n.s. for

richer countries. This time, the three-way interaction W × S × I (see the last column of the last table) reached marginal significance when the marginally significant main effect of S was left out of the equation ($\Delta R^2 = .02$, $p < .07$). A more refined analysis of the picture for the 35 richer countries showed that colder winters ($B = .04$, n.s.) and hotter summers ($B = -.07$, n.s.) had a significant interaction effect in the form of a Saint Andrew's cross ($B = -.21$, $p < .05$) accounting for 17% of the variation in the health perceptions. When I and W × I were added as predictors, however, this Saint Andrew's cross effect of winters and summers disappeared, indicating that colder winters in conjunction with lower incomes must be held responsible for all findings in Figure 3.2.

14. Joint effect of colder winters, hotter summers, and income per head on happiness in 70 countries (self-reported health was controlled for; cf. research note 7).

Predictors	B	B	B	B	B
Health	.61***	.51***	.41***	.30***	.29***
Winters (W)		−.02	−.09**	−.08**	−.09**
Summers (S)		−.05*	−.02	−.02	−.02
W × S		−.07*	−.05†	−.01	−.01
Income (I)			.12***	.14***	.14***
W × I				.10***	.11***
S × I				−.04	−.04
W × S × I					−.02
ΔR^2	.49***	.05*	.09***	.07***	.00
Total R^2	.49***	.54***	.63***	.70***	.70***

†$p < .10$. *$p < .05$. **$p < .01$. ***$p < .001$.

15. The complexity of this analysis required the addition of the climatic demands in winter to the climatic demands in summer. The Spearman rank correlations between health and happiness were $r_s(22)= .15$, n.s. for poorer countries with temperate climates, $r_s(13)= .75$, $p < .01$ for poorer countries with demanding climates, $r_s(12)= .39$, n.s. for richer countries with temperate climates, and $r_s(23)= .87$, $p < .001$ for richer countries with demanding climates.

16. Joint effect of colder winters, hotter summers, and income per head on suicide rates in 72 countries.

Predictors	B	B	B	B	B
Winters (W)	4.18***	3.26***	4.88***	4.54***	4.71***
Summers (S)	1.42†	2.27**	1.30	1.69*	1.41
W × S		2.73**	2.13*	2.48**	2.45*
W²			2.35**	2.40**	2.61**
Income (I)				1.45†	2.42*
W × I					−1.36
S × I					−.61
W × S × I					.22
W² × I					−.92
ΔR^2		.31***	.07**	.06**	.03†	.02
Total R^2	.31***	.38***	.44***	.47***	.49***

†$p < .10$. *$p < .05$. **$p < .01$. ***$p < .001$.

Income (I) was the logged purchasing-power income per head in 1999 (source: United Nations Development Programme, 2001). There was no multicollinearity (*VIFs* < 2.91), there were no outliers (Cook's *Ds* < .49), and dropping the countries with the largest geographical variations in temperature produced essentially the same results.

17. Cross-nationally, the total suicide rates were virtually identical with the male suicide rates [$r(75) = .98$, $p < .001$] and the female suicide rates [$r(70) = .81$, $p < .001$].

4

Work Copes with Context

If you won't work, you shan't eat.

Everyone, everyday, everywhere has to produce goods and services that satisfy survival needs. These production activities are, quite simply, work. Work is done in a given climato-economic context that shapes the survival needs, the work, and the satisfaction derived from it. Many climate-related goods and services are produced through household work and other unpaid domestic tasks in straightforward ways. Much satisfaction is indirectly brought about also by working for money to buy a variety of basic goods and services. Indeed, it is a Sisyphean task to strip any work of its direct or indirect connections with the gratification of survival needs. For paid and unpaid production activities alike the bottom line is, "If you won't work, you shan't eat," or, "If you won't work, you shan't survive."

In psychology, it has become customary to divide the reasons for working into context-related or extrinsic motives such as social status and earnings, and content-related or intrinsic motives such as engaging in challenging tasks, use of skills, and freedom of action (for details, see Kasser & Ryan, 2001; Maslow, 1954; Thierry, 1998). Climate-dependent work highlights the production of goods and services for extrinsic reasons of meeting basic necessities of life rather than intrinsic reasons of using and testing one's abilities. The section "Contextualization of Work Motives" provides sketches of the cultural consequences of climatic demands and money resources for the occurrence and salience of extrinsic versus intrinsic work motives.

The proposed joint effect of demanding climate and collective income on embracing extrinsic rather than intrinsic work motives was tested using child labor and working for money as criteria. Labor by children under 15 years of age, reflecting a daily struggle for life, occurs in countries with low to medium levels of development, especially countries with extremely cold winters (e.g., Mongolia), extremely hot summers (e.g., Central African Republic), or both (e.g., Tajikistan). Child labor and working for money are increasingly less important in richer countries. Working for fun by adults who find it more important that a job gives feelings of accomplishment than that it provides a good income occurs in countries like Canada, Norway, and Switzerland, with high levels of development and harsh winters. In consequence, the sections on the climato-economic niches of child labor and of working for money complement each other by covering different countries. They also rest on different research methods and emphasize psychological differences between extrinsically motivated behavior (child labor) and extrinsic behavioral motives (working for money).

CONTEXTUALIZATION OF WORK MOTIVES

Depending on their personal and family situations, people work to keep the household, to earn prestige and money, to achieve something, to meet people, to learn things, to make themselves useful, and the like. People also tailor their reasons for working to the broader array of characteristics of the place where they live. For example, whereas work is regarded as a duty toward society by more than 90% of the citizens of Malta, Tanzania, and Vietnam, this obligation is experienced by less than 50% of the citizens of Bosnia and Herzegovina, Great Britain, and Greece (Inglehart et al., 2004).

Also, the extent to which a job is respected by people in general is seen as very important in Bangladesh, Morocco, and Turkey but is unimportant in Denmark, Lithuania, and Slovakia (Inglehart et al., 2004). No province, no industrial sector, no family is immune to such predominant work values. Work values and motives, indicating why members of a society do paid or unpaid work, are intelligent responses to a complex context.

Whereas workers in Austria, Hungary, and Japan especially value extrinsic motives of earnings (Hofstede, 2001), workers in Brazil, Greece, and Transkei especially value intrinsic motives of achievement (Lynn, 1991). A 42-nation study revealed that the inhabitants of many Arab countries are high in extrinsic motives of outperforming competitors whereas the inhabitants of many South American countries are high in intrinsic motives of performance improvement (see the box "The right expat for the right state"). Thus, telling cross-national variations in work motives exist, and these can be used to gauge cultural differences and to relate them to their climato-economic niches.

The right expat for the right state

It is becoming increasingly important for human resource managers to be competent in arranging international assignments for expatriate workers and finding person-country matches. A matter of special importance is a proper match of the work motives. Some employees want to perform better than others irrespective of how well they are doing in an absolute sense. They are competitors, driven by extrinsic work motives that cause them to seek satisfaction in winning rather than working. Other employees want to perform better than they did before or are doing right now, irrespective of how well comparable others are doing. They are improvers, driven by intrinsic work motives that cause them to seek satisfaction in working rather than winning. Previous research has shown that the extreme cases are rare. Most employees are partly competitor and partly improver.

In a study of great relevance to expat assignments, Onne Janssen and I have investigated whether and to what extent workers in different nation-states are competitors, improvers, or both (Van de Vliert & Janssen, 2002). Across 42 nations, some workforces, including those of Germany and Switzerland, are low in both types of work motives. Other workforces are one-sidedly high in extrinsic work motives of competing, as in Bangladesh and Iraq, or one-sidedly high in intrinsic work motives of improving, as in Argentina and Venezuela. Workers in Egypt and Mexico are high in both. Culture-specific extrinsic versus intrinsic work motives exist and should be reckoned with.

We also investigated what this means for the resulting satisfaction. Satisfaction was represented by country-level indices of job satisfaction, company satisfaction, subjective well-being, life satisfaction, and a reliable combination of all of these. The results were impressive and dramatic. On all five indicators, the extrinsic work motives of competing were associated with dissatisfaction rather than satisfaction. By seeking satisfaction in winning rather than working, especially Arab workers in the Middle East and domestic workers in Bangladesh and India find themselves in a state of relative dissatisfaction. In contrast, the intrinsic work motives of improving were found to go hand in hand with job satisfaction, company satisfaction, subjective well-being, and life satisfaction. By seeking satisfaction in working rather than winning, especially inhabitants of Scandinavia and of the Atlantic-coast countries of South America find themselves in a state of relative satisfaction.

Here's one thing every international human resource manager should realize. The world of work has states of extrinsic motivation and dissatisfaction as well as states of intrinsic motivation and satisfaction. In this regard, no expat is a tabula rasa, and no host country a desert island. Competitors will be less dissatisfied in a competitive-oriented country. Improvers will be even more satisfied in an improvement-oriented country. Hence the challenge: find the proper match of expat state and nation-state.

A cluster of predominantly extrinsic work motives seems to safe-guard survival through successful coping with the climatic context. Climate enhances employment. People work because they want to maintain a comfortable temperature, need food, fear illness, and so forth. These, and similar work motives of wanting, needing, and fearing, differ in the degrees of specificity and directness of the survival activity pursued. The most specific and direct forms of survival activity include dressing and eating. Somewhat less specific and direct survival activities have to do with cooling or heating, cooking, taking care of the body, and the like. Good illustrations of more general and indirect forms of survival activity are shopping, kitchen gardening, and seeing a doctor. Among the most general and indirect survival activities are doing paid work and managing one's financial matters.

All of these survival activities are so inextricably bound up with climate that it seems very possible to relate them to the demands-resources contexts outlined in Chapter 3. My point of departure was Maslow's (1943, 1954) thesis that extrinsic motives satisfying lower order survival needs must be achieved before intrinsic motives sat-isfying higher order growth needs can gain momentum. Maslow's theory of the hierarchy of human needs is more complex than this two-layer model, but the other parts of the theory are not applicable across societies owing to variations in values (Hofstede, 2001). In any case, there is no denying the priority of survival needs over other needs. As a consequence, ecological niches that satisfy needs for ther-mal comfort, nutrition, and health constitute a necessary albeit insuf-ficient condition for intrinsic work motives to sprout and to develop roots and shoots. This insight led me to formulate three types of cultural adaptation of work motives to climato-economic niches.

First, earnings and similar extrinsic work motives were expected to be much more important in poor countries with harsh cold or hot climates than in richer countries and in countries with less demand-ing climates, where work is less critical for survival. This also holds for extrinsically motivated child labor. Second, intrinsic work motives were expected to dwarf extrinsic work motives in rich cold or hot regions, where economic development has gradually transferred the acquired relation between harsh climate and hard work from controlling climatic threats to meeting climatic challenges. Third, in poor and rich countries with undemanding climates, work was expected to be characterized by a mixture of moderately strong extrinsic and intrinsic work motives. Child labor and working for money are appropriate criteria for testing these climato-economic predictions.

CLIMATO-ECONOMIC NICHES OF CHILD LABOR

Although both children and adults have survival needs, most work nowadays is done by adults in most parts of the world. In all modernized nations, dying children and working children have become overlapping shadows of the past. Elsewhere, infant mortality and child labor continue to be gigantic problems for which all earthlings are to blame. Paradoxically, this black cloud may have a silver lining for scientists. Reprehensible old-fashioned practices of child labor may shed more light on the essence of work as a survival strategy than does labor in modern families and organizations. Children can do many things that help satisfy the stronger survival needs for thermal comfort, nutrition, and health in harsher cold or hot climates. They can do a wide variety of household chores and domestic activities, enabling other family members to earn money, or they can even earn money themselves.

This is not to say that children never enjoy their work contributions nor that they never reap nonfinancial benefits. Child labor can involve a good deal of intrinsically motivated and useful learning by doing. The point is that we should look at child-labor motives of parents instead of child-labor motives of children. For fathers and mothers, work contributions of their children cannot have intrinsic payoffs. Parents make choices between immediate benefits for the family and long-delayed costs for their children of sending them to work now, and do so for extrinsic reasons. Child labor on the basis of survival considerations is an outstanding example of extrinsically motivated behavior.

Discussion of child labor is restricted here to general and indirect forms of survival activity. In all countries, children have to take part in specific daily activities of clothing and feeding, and washing hands or dishes. But huge international differences exist in the extent to which children are also engaged in economic and domestic activities that secure survival of their nuclear family in the longer run. These investments of children in meeting survival needs are generally known and monitored as child labor. The United Nations Children's Fund (UNICEF) considers youngsters "to be involved in child labour activities under the following classification: (a) children 5 to 11 years of age that during the week preceding the survey did at least one hour of economic activity or at least 28 hours of domestic work, and (b) children 12 to 14 years of age that during the week preceding the survey did at least 14 hours of economic activity or at least 42 hours of economic activity and domestic work combined" (Mocca et al., 2005, p. 131).

Zooming In on the Problem

The juvenile workforce is not active in all corners of the world. Affluent countries have banned child labor. In 72 countries for which UNICEF has documented child labor during the 1999–2004 period, the percentage of children involved ranged from 2% in Jamaica to 66% in Niger. A breakdown for regions yielded the following figures: 9% in the Middle East and North Africa, 10% in East Asia and the Pacific, 11% in Latin America and the Caribbean, 14% in South Asia, 32% in Eastern and Southern Africa, and 41% in Western and Central Africa. Child labor in these regions is a tremendous problem because it denies the next generation a full course of education and, as a result, the opportunity to generate a decent income in the future.

On closer consideration, however, labor may be a children's friend compared with the worst enemy of children in these regions, the Grim Reaper. Like child labor, infant mortality is not randomly spread out over the surface of the earth. On the contrary, and unfortunately, child labor and infant mortality are often found in the same places, as if the one was a parasite of the other. Across the 72 nations mentioned in the UNICEF documentation, there is a 40% overlap of child labor and infant mortality,[1] much too much to be a coincidence. Do working children have higher mortality rates? Or are working children making all-out and vain attempts to prevent the deaths of younger siblings?

At this point, my own theoretical reading of the 40% labor-mortality overlap is that child labor and infant mortality tend to co-occur in miserable climato-economic circumstances. Child labor seems a sensible response to the misfortune of cold or heat and destitution, an intelligent cultural strategy to survive as a family at the expense of primary education.[2] A gender breakdown of the data shows that both boys and girls are recruited for paid and unpaid work, which emphasizes the all-embracing nature of the survival problem. My practical reading of the 40% labor-mortality overlap is that we can solve the problem of child labor only if we solve the problem of infant mortality as well. As a researcher interested in measurement issues, I view the variable of child labor as a proxy for survival behavior. And as a work and organizational scholar interested in the consequences of climate, I believe that the over-representation of dying and working children in Africa and in parts of Asia and South America urgently requires a systematic explora-tion of its climato-economic roots.

Connections between climate, cash, and culturally embedded child labor deserve research attention for at least three reasons. First, as one of the world's biggest problems, child labor cries out for university professors to walk into this extremely relevant field, mapping the complexities and consolidating them in simpler overall understandings. Second, as a footprint of real behavior, child labor can be of great worth in our quest for solid cross-cultural knowledge about the value and function of work in different climato-economic niches. Last, child labor may reveal itself as the undeniable flip side of undeniable climato-economic niches of infant mortality. Produce or perish may be the existential dilemma for the boys and girls working in a harsh climate and living in dire poverty.

The primary purpose of the analysis to be reported was to relate child labor, presumably driven by extrinsic survival motives, to its climato-economic niches. I argued as follows. Whereas learning children and playing children cost money, working children generate money, or at least non-money resources that substitute for money resources to satisfy survival needs. Consequently, learning and playing children make it more difficult for their parents, whereas working children make it less difficult, to successfully cope with a cold or hot climate. This simple fact of life may not be important or noticeable in rich societies. In poor societies, however, and especially in poor societies in harsh cold or hot climates, working children may be as common or even more common than learning and playing children. Indeed, in miserable climato-economic niches where it is hard to gratify the family's survival needs, fathers and mothers may find it difficult to encourage learning and playing in their children, thus resisting the pressures of forgone income and undone jobs in and about the home.

Putting Child Labor in Context

UNICEF's national percentages of working children under 15 years of age allowed a check of the above line of reasoning. In 50 out of the 72 countries, the child-labor figures were both based on the above-quoted standard definition and representative of the entire country.

This sample of countries is unique in that it is biased toward Africa, toward hot summers, and toward poverty. Take the poverty bias. At the time of the research, the United Nations classified 36 countries in the world as extremely poor and characterized by low development, 86 countries as rather poor and characterized by medium development, and 55 countries as relatively rich and characterized by high development. The biased convenience sample consisted of 21 of the 36 extremely poor countries (58%), 27 of the 86 poorer countries (31%), and only 2 of the 55 richer countries (Bahrain and Trinidad & Tobago; 4%).

Indicators of colder winters and hotter summers and of collective wealth in the form of income per head were calculated in the same way as in the studies reported in the preceding chapters.[3] Notwithstanding the absence of really cold and really rich countries, climatic demands (14%), collective income (27%), and climate and wealth in interaction (17%) accounted for 58% of the cross-national differences in child labor.[4] Figure 4.1 provides the details, broken down for the 21 poorest and the 29 moderately poor countries (with the "richer" countries of Bahrain and Trinidad & Tobago labeled *moderately poor*).[5]

The poorest countries in the first part of Figure 4.1 are all from the African continent (in the center of the picture, just above Mali, there was no space to include the labels of Rwanda and Tanzania). The display of the 21 countries forms a downward slope of decreasing child labor in countries with colder winters, with the lowest percentages of working children reported for countries with colder winters and temperate summers (see Malawi, Lesotho, and Zambia in the lower right-hand corner). For a proper understanding of this graph, note that the midrange temperature in the coldest winter month varies from +20°C in Sierra Leone and +18°C in Burundi to +6°C in Malawi and –1°C in Lesotho. As a consequence, for inhabitants of these extremely hot countries, a temperate winter is a mixed blessing, whereas a cold winter is a godsend. That is, hot

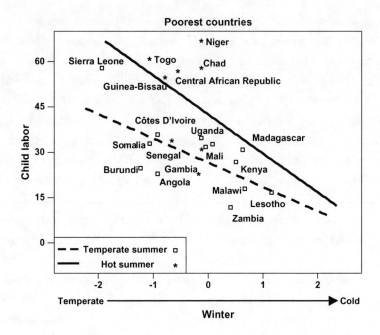

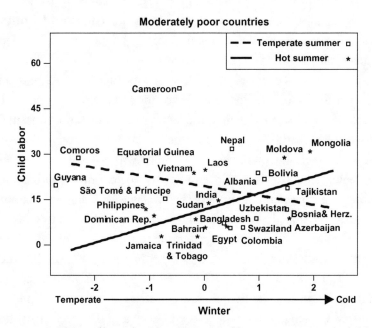

FIGURE 4.1. Joint effect of colder winters and hotter summers on child labor, broken down for the poorest and moderately poor countries.

summers alternated with temperate winters are more demanding than hot summers relieved with cold winters. Viewed in this way, Figure 4.1 shows clear support for the hypothesis that child labor peaks in the poorest countries with the harshest climates. As can be seen, the percentage of working children is maximal in countries with hot summers and temperate winters (e.g., Togo), intermediate in countries with temperate summers and temperate winters (e.g., Somalia), and minimal in countries with temperate summers and cold winters (e.g., Zambia).

The second part of Figure 4.1 contains the results for the moderately poor countries (in the center of the picture, just above Egypt, there was no space to include the labels of Lebanon and Venezuela). In general, the percentages of working children are lower than in the poorest countries. But the most striking feature is that the broken downward bar for temperate summers and the solid upward bar for hot summers again form a Saint Andrew's cross (cf. Figures 3.1 and 3.2). Undemanding climates with temperate winters and temperate summers, and with too little stress, increase child labor in moderately poor countries such as Comoros and Guyana. Moderately demanding climates with optimal stress from either cold winters or hot summers decrease child labor in moderately poor countries, including Jamaica and Bosnia & Herzegovina. Demanding climates with cold winters and hot summers, and with too much stress, increase child labor in moderately poor countries such as Moldova and Mongolia. The resemblances between the Saint Andrew's crosses in Figures 3.1, 3.2, and 4.1 make sense if we accept that child labor reflects a strategy for producing badly needed satisfaction of survival needs for the nuclear family. The same characteristics of climato-economic niches that lead to less life satisfaction lead to more child labor.

These interpretations of the research results in the two parts of Figure 4.1 support not only the viewpoint that child labor is more common in the poorest countries but also the crucially important qualification that child labor is most common in the poorest countries with the harshest climates. The adjectives *crucial* and *important* are added by way of an attempt to break away from the triviality of the common assumption that child labor is caused by poverty. Sure, poverty accounts for 27% of the cross-national differences in child labor. But only in conjunction with harshness of climate does poverty account for 58% of child labor. In and of themselves, climate and cash each paints an inaccurate and misleading picture of the culture of child labor. Scholars, world leaders, and intervenors alike would be wise to start paying attention to the more valid climatoeconomics of child labor.

We should scrutinize in particular the intriguing finding that the percentages of working children in Sierra Leone (one of the poorest countries) and in Cameroon (one of the moderately poor countries) are much higher than in comparable countries with temperate winters and summers, such as Burundi and Comoros, respectively (see Figure 4.1). Differences in birth, death, and fertility rates between Sierra Leone and Burundi, and between Cameroon and Comoros, cannot explain the differences in child labor. Nor do differences in political rights and civil liberties seem to play a major part. Whereas individual citizens enjoy somewhat more democracy and freedom in Sierra Leone than in Burundi, they have somewhat less freedom in Cameroon than in Comoros. What about climatic precipitation as an explanation?

In the predominantly hot and poor countries investigated, rain stands out as a possible alternative or supplementary explanation of child labor. Indeed, rain makes a world of difference between desert and steppe climate, wet and dry savanna climate, and monsoon climate. Sierra Leone gets much more rain than Burundi (452 mm vs. 65 mm per month), whereas Cameroon gets less rain than Comoros (159 mm vs. 228 mm per month). What, if any, impact does this have? The rather small number of 50 countries precluded the possibility of analyzing the joint impact of precipitation, winters, summers, and collective income on the percentages of working children. Instead, the supplementary study had to be split up into several analyses.[6] Controlling for the degree of precipitation made no odds. Likewise, there was no joint impact of degree of precipitation and other climato-economic factors on child labor. So, there is no indication whatsoever that falling back on child labor is related to rainfall.

Another rival explanation of the percentages of working children may be hidden in income inequality as a complication of collective poverty. Indeed, the higher and steeper a country's income pyramid, the more children are working at its foot.[7] In Guinea-Bissau, for example, where the richest 10% of the population earns more than 80 times as much as the poorest 10% of the population, 54% of the children work. When income inequality was controlled for, however, the picture in Figure 4.1 did not change at all. In addition, the impact of climate and wealth on child labor was in no way dependent on the degree of income inequality. In conclusion, neither precipitation nor income inequality appears to have the power to compromise the overall conclusion that more working children can be found in lower income countries with harsher climates.

Infant Mortality

With climate-culture links for child labor in relatively poor countries established, the part played by infant mortality was given further attention. The point of departure was that child labor refers to children 5 to 14 years of age, whereas infant mortality is the probability of dying between birth and 5 years of age. Thus, the working children cannot be the same ones as the dying children. This leaves two explanations of the 40% labor-mortality overlap. It is possible that miserable climato-economic niches produce infant mortality, which in turn produces child labor to help prevent death in the

family. Alternatively, miserable climato-economic niches may produce child labor, which in turn produces infant mortality because
of the inadequacy and insufficiency of the children's contribution
to family survival. Infant mortality can play each part only if it
occurs in roughly the same climato-economic niches as child labor.
This appeared to be the case;[8] a duplicate of Figure 4.1 resulted.
The findings of supplementary analyses show that the climato-
economic niches have unique effects on infant mortality (20%
out of 64%) and child labor (16% out of 60%), over and above a
massive effect on the joint occurrence of infant mortality and child
labor (44%). Thus, climato-economic niches have an unmistakable
impact on the coalition forces of infant mortality and child labor,
with no evidence predominantly pointing in the direction of either
a climate-mortality-labor path or a climate-labor-mortality path of
interpretation.

Emergency measures to end child misery are in order. As the
world entered the 21st century, heads of state and government adopted a number of quantified and monitorable Millennium Development Goals (United Nations Development Programme, 2001). Two
of these goals are to reduce the world's infant mortality rates by two-
thirds and to achieve universal completion of primary schooling as
an antipole of child labor. The deadline is 2015. Both goals are based
on the common understanding that economic development ban-
ishes many evils of human suffering, including infant mortality
and child labor. These are great initiatives, although room for
improvement remains. There seems to be little awareness yet of
the complicating impact of climate. The present discoveries imply
that projects providing financial aid and economic stimulation are
especially effective in reducing child misery in extremely poor countries with extremely hot summers and insufficiently cold winters.
Figure 4.1 nominates the Central African Republic, Chad, Guinea-
Bissau, Niger, and Togo for targeted projects addressing the needs of
children at risk of mistreatment and mortality.

CLIMATO-ECONOMIC NICHES OF WORKING FOR MONEY

Measuring Work Motives Worldwide

As stated earlier, different peoples have different reasons for working. "In some cultures work is a virtue, and work success is a divine sign of worthiness; in other cultures work is a necessary evil" (Triandis, 1973, p. 30). In the terminology used here, in some societies work is a nuisance driven by extrinsic work motives; in other societies it is a pleasure driven by intrinsic work motives. In the 1970s, Hofstede (2001) observed that opportunities for high earnings were of little importance in Sweden and Taiwan but of great importance in Germany and Jamaica, and that the use of skills and abilities on the job was of little importance in Jamaica and Nigeria but of great importance in Japan and South Korea.

From the 1970s onward, in all waves of the World Values Surveys, interviewers showed a card listing at least 11 work motives, asked which the respondents found important in a job, and noted the motives mentioned. There was no obligation to choose, with the consequence that some respondents (22%) mentioned at most 3 motives whereas others (21%) mentioned at least 10. Across 75 countries and 2 related territories (Northern Ireland and Puerto Rico), the four motives mentioned most frequently as reasons for working were good pay (82%), good job security (71%), pleasant people to work with (71%), and an interesting job that meets one's abilities (64%; Inglehart et al., 2004). Owing to the large variations in the number of motives mentioned, these figures for the importance of work motives have built-in usability problems. For a certain work motive, they cannot be compared across countries. For a certain country, they cannot be compared across motives. To address this problem, the following alternative question was included during the fourth wave of the World Values Surveys from 1999 to 2002.

In a subset of 41 countries, the interviewers doing the World Values Surveys were instructed to say, "Now I would like to ask you something about the things which would seem to you, personally, most important if you were looking for a job. Here are some of the things many people take into account in relation to their work. Regardless of whether you're actually looking for a job, which one would you, personally, place first if you were looking for a job?" They then presented the respondent with a card showing the following options:

1. A good income so that you do not have any worries about money.
2. A safe job with no risk of closing down or unemployment.
3. Working with people you like.
4. Doing an important job which gives you a feeling of accomplishment.

The design of this question has several strengths. The options are the ones most frequently mentioned as reasons for doing paid work. The obligation to choose is based on the theoretically relevant contrast between predominantly extrinsic work motives (options 1–2) and predominantly intrinsic work motives (options 3–4). And the bottom-up structure of a good income (option 1) peaking in a feeling of accomplishment (option 4) does justice to Maslow's (1954) axiom that the gratification of lower order survival needs is a necessary but insufficient condition for the gratification of higher order growth needs.

To complement the study of extrinsically motivated child labor, I concentrated on the extrinsic motive of working for money at the expense of the intrinsic motive of working for achievement. I used the national percentage of income responses (option 1) minus the national percentage of accomplishment responses (option 4) as a cross-national indicator of the extrinsic motivation to work for money. In a prepublication (Van de Vliert, Van Yperen, & Thierry, 2008), it was made certain that this measure has the same meaning in countries with different climates, different degrees of wealth, or both.[9] Additionally, it was made certain that this measure represents the importance of the extrinsic work motives clustered around high earnings[10] and does so for employers, managers, professional workers, office workers, and skilled and unskilled manual workers alike.[11]

Putting Working for Money in Context

Demanding climate (10%), collective income (36%), and the interaction of colder winters and collective income (16%) accounted for 62% of the cross-national differences in the extrinsic motives of working for money.[12] Hotter summers had a negligible effect, even in conjunction with colder winters, greater wealth, or both. The joint effect of colder winters and greater wealth is visualized in Figure 4.2 as a crossing wedge-shaped pair of lines, a broken upward line for poorer countries and a solid downward line for richer countries. In full support of the model of cultural adaptations, the strongest extrinsic work motives were found in the poorest countries with the coldest climates in the upper right-hand corner (Azerbaijan, Moldova, Georgia, Armenia, and Macedonia); the weakest extrinsic work motives were found in the richest countries with the coldest climates in the lower right-hand corner (Norway, Australia, Canada, Switzerland, and the United States). Moderately strong extrinsic work motives were found in countries with undemanding climates on the left-hand side irrespective of whether these countries were relatively poor (Dominican Republic and Tanzania) or relatively rich (Singapore and Brazil).[13]

Like the greater acceptance and utilization of child labor in lower income countries with harsher climates, the greater endorsement of working for money in those countries is not influenced by climatic precipitation nor by income inequality.[14] Similarly, the country's inflation rate, the size of the informal gray economy, and the use of performance-related pay in the country's organizations failed to nullify the impact of more climatic demands in conjunction with less money resources. Even latitude, longitude, and their geographic

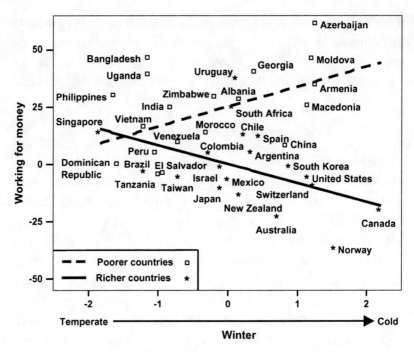

FIGURE 4.2. Effect of colder winters on working for money, broken down for poorer and richer countries.

combinations as proxies for regional differences in religious, historical, political, and institutional contexts are unrelated to the perceived importance of wages (Van de Vliert, Van Yperen, & Thierry, 2008). The country's typical level of life satisfaction discussed earlier was the only covariate of the more or less extrinsic motives clustered around and represented by working for money.[15] Indeed, inhabitants of poorer countries with colder climates are both less satisfied with their life as a whole and more strongly motivated to work for a good income to avoid having any worries about money.

The observed variations in the perceived importance of wages have implications for practitioners' cross-national policies of implementing pay of equal value for work of equal value (Van de Vliert & Van der Vegt, 2004), also known as pay equity (Figart, 2000; Michael et al., 1989) and as comparable worth (England, 1992; Gunderson, 1994). One strategic consideration concerns the part *pay of equal value*. Economists define cross-national pay of equal value in terms of *purchasing power parity* – the money required to buy a highly similar basket of representative goods and services in different countries (for under- and overpayment relative to a country's level of wealth, see Van de Vliert, 2003). Analogously, international human resource managers could define cross-national pay of equal value in terms of *motivating power parity* – the money required to drive a highly similar set of survival-need satisfactions in different countries. The motivating power parity could be used to pay otherwise comparable employees more to the extent that they have to live in harsher climatic environments or less to the extent that they have to live in poorer economic environments.

Another strategic consideration concerns the part *work of equal value*. In otherwise identical circumstances, the same productivity improvement is expected to have more added value in poorer countries with harsher climates (like Belarus and Ukraine) than in richer countries with harsher climates (like Finland and South Korea) and in countries with more temperate climates irrespective of whether they are relatively poor (like Nigeria) or relatively rich (like Taiwan). Consequently, the principle of equal pay for work of equal value dictates that employees in poorer countries with harsher climates are paid more than employees in other countries who do similar work. Note that international human resource managers who adopt such a work-of-equal-value policy of payment have to quit the widespread policy of reducing labor costs by exporting jobs to countries in the developing world.

General Conclusions

Working for money in colder countries and child labor in hotter countries have three things in common. Both are context-related, both go up in more demanding climates to the extent that the income per head goes down, and both go down in more demanding climates to the extent that the income per head goes up. These observations lead to firm conclusions about the worldwide prevalences of context-related and content-related work tendencies because they demonstrate generalizability from cold to hot regions, from adults to children, and from motives to behaviors. In combination with the observations about the existence of climato-economic niches of life satisfaction in Chapter 3, the present findings support the following conclusions.

In countries with harsh climates, overall poverty fails to satisfy survival needs and produces unhappiness as well as strong tendencies to work for survival rather than for achievement. In these climates, overall societal wealth satisfies survival needs and produces happiness as well as weak tendencies to work for survival rather than for achievement. By contrast, climates with temperate winters produce happiness irrespective of the degree of societal wealth. In those less demanding climates, working for survival is less of a necessity, with the consequence that moderate tendencies of working for money and child labor predominate. The wording of these conclusions leaves open whether climato-economic niches produce context-related work through life satisfaction, life satisfaction through context-related work, or context-related work and life satisfaction in parallel. This formulation is chosen to emphasize my primary interest in unidirectional arrows of causality from climato-economic niches to cultural consequences, but bidirectional arrows of simultaneity between distinct components of culture.

As for the arrows of causality, it continues to catch the eye that hot summers rather than cold winters tend to drive child labor, whereas cold winters rather than hot summers tend to drive working for money. With hindsight, it is clear that these seemingly contradictory findings are an artifact of the research procedure of convenient sampling of countries, which led to a complete absence of really rich countries with cold winters in the case of child labor and a complete absence of really poor countries with hot summers in the case of working for money. None of the world's 20 richest and coldest countries is included in the child-labor Figure 4.1, whereas none of the world's 20 poorest and hottest countries is included in the working-for-money Figure 4.2. The limited results of both studies contain a serious warning against quick-and-dirty sampling of societies when investigating the roots of culture. At the same time, the complementary results nicely illustrate how subsequent studies can make up for each other's weaknesses. Taken together, the findings reported in this chapter suggest that humans react like chameleons by changing their work orientations in response to the climato-economic environments in which they have to satisfy survival needs.

PROPOSITIONS

4.1. To produce satisfaction of needs for thermal comfort, nutrition, and health, culturally embedded work is fine-tuned to climatic demands and societal wealth.

4.2. Child labor and working for money increase in more demanding climates to the extent that a society is poorer.

4.3. Working for achievement increases in more demanding climates to the extent that a society is richer.

RESEARCH NOTES

1. The percentage of children involved in labor activities and the under-five infant mortality rate (source: Mocca et al., 2005) were strongly positively related, $r(72) = .63$, $p < .001$.

2. Cross-nationally, the internal consistency of the measure of child labor for boys and girls was .98, $p < .001$. The validity of this measure was apparent from its negative relation $[r(71) = -.63, p < .001]$ with the net primary school enrollment rate and attendance ratio (source: Mocca et al., 2005).

3. For the harshness of winters, the ratio of skewness to its standard error was 4.25, with the consequence that this predictor had to be log transformed before it was standardized (new ratio −1.17). Income per head in 2002 (purchasing power parity; source: United Nations Development Programme, 2004) was used as the most appropriate index of wealth for the 1999–2004 period under investigation. Because the ratio of skewness to its standard error was 12.54, this index too had to be log transformed before it was standardized (new ratio 2.48).

4. Joint effect of colder winters, hotter summers, and income per head on the percentage of working children in 50 countries.

Predictors	B	B	B	B	B
Winters (W)	−4.92*	−5.15*	−4.72*	−3.61	1.64
Summers (S)	3.36	3.90	3.03	−4.54	−6.63*
W × S		−1.52	−1.38	.36	10.59*
Income (I)			−11.35***	−12.68***	−12.34***
W × I				1.30	6.81*
S × I				−8.09**	−8.82***
W × S × I					11.39**
ΔR²		.13*	.01	.27***	.10**	.07**
Total R²		.13*	.14*	.41***	.51***	.58***

¹p < .10. *p < .05. **p < .01. ***p < .001.

There was no multicollinearity (*VIFs* < 5.82), and there were no outliers (Cook's *Ds* < .92).

5. The correlations between colder winters and child labor were $r(21) = −.50$, $p < .05$ for the poorest countries and $r(29) = .08$, n.s. for the moderately poor countries. A supplementary analysis of the 29 moderately poor countries showed that colder winters ($B = −.92$, n.s.) and hotter summers ($B = −1.36$, n.s.) had a significant interaction effect ($B = 2.71$, $p < .05$, one-sided), accounting for 11% of the variation in child labor.

6. Precipitation (P) was the square root of a country's midrange monthly precipitation in mm (source: Parker, 1997). The ratio of skewness to its standard error was 4.88 for P and .50 for the square root of P. First, P was entered in the first step, winters (W) and summers (S) in the second step, W × S in the third step, income (I) in the fourth step, W × I and S × I in the fifth step, and W × S × I in the final step.

Second, S was entered in the first step, W and P in the second step, W × P in the third step, I in the fourth step, W × I and P × I in the fifth step, and W × P × I in the final step. Third, the second analysis was repeated after winters and summers changed places. Finally, income (I) was entered in the first step, W and S in the second step, W × S in the third step, P in the fourth step, W × P and S × P in the fifth step, and W × S × P in the final step.

7. Again, income inequality was the well-known Gini index (source: United Nations Development Programme, 2001). In the subsample of countries for which these data were available, income inequality was unrelated to income per head [r (40) = −.17, n.s.], but was associated with more child labor [r (40) = .32, p < .05].

8. Joint effect of colder winters, hotter summers, and income per head on the under-5 mortality rate in 50 countries.

Predictors	B	B	B	B	B
Winters (W)	−26.33**	−26.61**	−24.51**	−23.62†	9.96
Summers (S)	2.59	3.24	−1.05	−28.86†	−42.21**
W × S		−1.86	−1.19	4.82	70.19***
Income (I)			−55.97***	−61.88***	−59.74***
W × I				.66	35.95**
S × I				−29.77*	−34.39**
W × S × I					72.86***
ΔR²	.12*	.00	.32***	.06†	.13***
Total R²	.12*	.12*	.44***	.50***	.63***

†p < .10. *p < .05. **p < .01. ***p < .001.

There was no multicollinearity (*VIFs* < 5.82), and there were no outliers (Cook's *Ds* < 2.01).

9. Bosnia and Herzegovina, Montenegro, and Serbia had to be removed because these countries were at war during the 1990s, so that no income data were available. The national scores for financial work motivation ranged from −37.70 in Norway to 60.50 in Azerbaijan (*M* = 10.41; *SD* = 21.70). The reliability of the measure of working for money was demonstrated by comparing and combining separate scores for blue-collar workers, white-collar workers, and managers within each country (Cronbach's α = .94). As expected, the national percentage of income responses and the national percentage of

Climate, Cash, and Work

accomplishment responses as opposite poles of the overall dimension of extrinsic versus intrinsic work motives tended to exclude each other, $r(38) = -.64$, $p < .001$. With a view to the cross-national equivalence of this index, my research group has scrutinized the broader nomological network of financial attitudes mapped out by the World Values Surveys (Inglehart et al., 2004).

We (Van de Vliert, Van Yperen, & Thierry, 2008) used median splits to divide the countries in pairs of clusters: countries with relatively temperate versus relatively demanding climates; relatively poor versus relatively rich countries; and countries with symmetrical low-low or high-high scores on demanding climate and national wealth versus countries with asymmetrical low-high or high-low scores on demanding climate and national wealth. Next, we computed six intercorrelation matrices, one for each of these six clusters of countries. Each matrix contained 21 correlations between the country-level percentages of inhabitants who said the following: working for money is the most important thing; accepting a bribe in the course of one's duties may be justifiable; receiving money without working for it is okay; claiming government benefits to which one has no right may be justifiable; cheating on taxes may be justifiable; avoiding a fare on public transport may be justifiable; and giving part of one's income for use in preventing environmental pollution is unacceptable. The 15 metacorrelations between the six sets of 21 intercorrelations ranged from .54 ($p < .01$) to .97 ($p < .001$), with an average of .75 ($p < .001$), indicating that the inhabitants of countries in widely different climato-economic contexts conceptualize working for money equivalently in terms of a broader nomological network of financial attitudes.

10. If the working-for-money measure is valid, stronger financial work motives should be related to more painful financial situations. And that is precisely what we found. The lower the logged purchasing-power income per head in 2000 (source: United Nations Development Programme, 2002), the higher the extrinsic motivation of working for money, $r(38) = -.66$, $p < .001$. In the same vein, the higher the World Bank index for the size of the informal *gray* or *underground* economy (source: Schneider, 2002), the higher the extrinsic motivation of working for money, $r(35) = .57$, $p < .001$.

11. Cross-nationally, the degree of satisfaction with the financial situation of one's household (ranging from $1 = $ *dissatisfied* to $10 = $ *satisfied*; source: Inglehart et al., 2004, p. 419) was negatively related to the motivational strength of a good income, $r(38) = -.55$, $p < .001$. Across 38 nations, this held true for employers/managers of establishments

with 10 or more employees and supervisors of office workers ($r = -.50$, $p < .01$), employers/managers of establishments with fewer than 10 employees and supervisors of workers other than office workers ($r = -.45$, $p < .01$), professional workers such as lawyers, accountants, and teachers ($r = -.58$, $p < .001$), office personnel and other non-manual workers ($r = -.57$, $p < .001$), skilled manual workers ($r = -.56$, $p < .001$), and semi-skilled and unskilled manual workers ($r = -.52$, $p < .001$).

12. Joint effect of colder winters and income per head on working for money in 38 countries.

Predictors	B	B	B	B	B
Winters (W)	−2.45	−5.78	2.94	3.78	5.18
Summers (S)	4.28	6.21	1.26	1.98	1.30
W × S		8.59			−3.02
Income (I)			−15.13***	−15.16***	−15.73***
W × I				−8.36***	−8.82**
S × I				2.02	3.10
W × S × I					.33
ΔR^2		.05	.05	.36***	.16**	.00
Total R^2	.05	.10	.46***	.62***	.62***

$^{\dagger}p < .10.$ $^{*}p < .05.$ $^{**}p < .01.$ $^{***}p < .001.$

Income (I) was the logged purchasing-power income per head in 2000 (source: United Nations Development Programme, 2002). There was no multicollinearity (*VIFs* < 5.82), there were no outliers (Cook's *Ds* < .92), and dropping the countries with the largest geographic variations in temperature produced essentially the same results.

Replacement of income per head in 2000 with income per head in earlier years showed a gradual decrease in the interactive impact of colder winters, hotter summers, and income per head on working for money ($\Delta R^2 = .16$ for 2000, .09 for 1995, .06 for 1990, .05 for 1985, .03 for 1980, and .01 for 1975). Apparently, unlike the long-term adaptation of child labor to climato-economic niches reported in research note 3, the adaptation of extrinsic work motives to climato-economic niches is a short-term process.

13. The simple-slope correlations between colder winters and working for money were $r(19) = .48$, $p < .05$ for the poorer countries and $r(19) = -.45$, $p < .05$ for the richer countries.

14. Separate controls for precipitation ($\Delta R^2 = .01$, n.s.), income inequality ($\Delta R^2 = .00$), inflation rate (source: United Nations Development Programme report, 2000; $\Delta R^2 = .01$, n.s.), gray economy (source: Schneider, 2002; $\Delta R^2 = .01$, n.s.), and performance-related pay (source: World Economic Forum, 1999–2002; $\Delta R^2 = .01$, n.s.) did not change the results. With a view to the sample size (only 38 countries), joint effects of these control variables in interaction with colder winters, hotter summers, and income per head were left out of consideration.

15. Joint effect of colder winters and income per head on working for money; life satisfaction from Chapter 3 (happiness in 38 countries and subjective health in 36 countries) was controlled for.

Predictors	B	B	B	B	B
Happiness	-43.94^{**}		-27.15^*		-30.71^*
Health	$-22.47^{\dagger}$			-7.65	$-.80$
Winters (W)		3.78	.36	4.11	1.01
Summers (S)		1.98	1.64	1.64	
Income (I)		-15.16^{***}	-11.73^{***}	-14.82^{***}	-12.39^{***}
W × I		-8.36^{***}	$-4.90^{\dagger}$	-7.21^*	-3.35
S × I		2.02	.31	2.22	
ΔR^2			$.05^*$	.00	$.05^*$
Total R^2	$.46^{***}$	$.62^{***}$	$.67^{***}$	$.62^{***}$	$.67^{***}$

$^{\dagger}p < .10.$ $^*p < .05.$ $^{**}p < .01.$ $^{***}p < .001.$

There was no multicollinearity ($VIFs < 2.64$), and there were no outliers (Cook's $Ds < .75$).

PART THREE

SURVIVAL, COOPERATION,
AND ORGANIZATION

5

Survival, Self-Expression, and Easygoingness

Climate and cash are the Adam and Eve of all cultures.

All world citizens have to learn to cope with climatic cold and heat using money. This holds true for people from individualistic cultures in Western Europe to collectivistic cultures in East Asia, from masculine cultures in Southern Africa to feminine cultures in Northern Europe, and from democratic cultures in North and South America to autocratic cultures in Central America. Climate-related values and practices are learned with the greatest of ease, without awareness of their age-long evolution and of survival as their ultimate objective. As a consequence, hidden cultural remnants of our climato-economic past are waiting to be discovered as companions of our climato-economic present. The joint effects of colder winters, hotter summers, and income per head on life satisfaction and work, reported in the preceding chapters, are cases in point.

It would be overly precise, if not downright naïve, to propose that the impact of a country's climato-economic firmament could be pinpointed at a single component of culture. Rather, a societal culture is a syndrome of values and practices passed on from generation to generation and gradually fine-tuned to its particular climato-economic niche with an accuracy that is often underestimated. In this vein, in the section "Picturing a Triangle of Cultures," three broad tapestries of culture are first laid out: *survival culture, self-expression culture*, and *easygoing culture*. These cultural syndromes are next conceptually related to their alleged contexts of climatic demands and money resources.

In the section "Climato-economic Niches of the Triangle of Cultures," I report further cross-sectional evidence of the crude ecology of culture unfolded in Chapter 1 through Chapter 4. A longitudinal investigation of the covariation of climato-economic change and culture change supported the results. One finds survival cultures in economically deprived societies in demanding climates, self-expression cultures in economically prosperous societies in demanding climates, and easygoing cultures in societies in temperate climates irrespective of their economic situation.

PICTURING A TRIANGLE OF CULTURES

So far, winter and summer deviations from temperateness have been treated as separate predictors of culture, leading to unnecessarily complex and feature-rich pictures. If they are combined into a single indicator of the harshness of climate, all pictures in Chapter 2 through Chapter 4 become similar triangles pointing to less happiness, less subjective health, more child labor, and more working for money in poorer countries with more demanding climates. These triangles are thought to reflect and represent broader survival-related cultures.

Survival-Related Cultures

People living in more temperate climates and richer people living in colder or hotter climates experience less survival stress and are, therefore, more satisfied and happier with their life, health, and work than are poorer people living in harsher climates. Survival-related satisfaction is not a lonely piper but part of an orchestra. A lot of evidence (for overviews, see Fredrickson, 2005; ; Lyubomirsky et al., 2005) shows that happier people are also more knowledgeable, creative, active, flexible, effective, resilient, and economically productive. In addition, happier individuals are more socially integrated, sociable, tolerant, generous, and altruistic. The entire orchestra is a metaphor for a cultural syndrome. Freely rendered from Triandis (1995, p. 43), a cultural syndrome is a pattern of shared values, norms, roles, beliefs, attitudes, and practices that is organized around a theme and that can be found in certain geographic regions during a particular historic period.

In the current book, the theme is the production of survival-related satisfaction, the geographic regions are climato-economic areas, and the historic period (1980–2005) peaks at the turn of the millennium. As discussed below, the production of survival-related satisfaction can be viewed from the unipolar perspective of survival culture, the bipolar perspective of survival versus self-expression cultures, and the tripolar perspective of survival, self-expression, and easygoing cultures.

Unipolar survival cultures. Unipolar measures of culture such as those that tap power distance and uncertainty avoidance range in only one direction: from minimum to maximum. Survival values and practices are minimal where life is safe and maximal where life is in danger. In this vein, the longitudinal World Values Surveys (Inglehart & Baker, 2000; Inglehart et al., 2004; Inglehart & Welzel, 2005) repeatedly showed that a population with a stronger survival-culture syndrome gives higher priority to physical and economic security, is unhappier, is more reluctant to sign petitions, views homosexuality as less justifiable, and tends to be more careful about placing trust in people.

Bipolar survival versus self-expression cultures. Bipolar measures of culture such as those that tap individualism-collectivism and masculinity-femininity range in two directions, from the midpoint to each of the two poles. Time and again, the World Values Surveys group has empirically shown that the antipole of survival culture is self-expression culture. Thus, self-expression values and practices increase at the expense of survival values and practices. As the opposite of survival culture, the syndrome of self-expression culture emphasizes that a population is happy, gives priority to self-realization and quality of life over physical and economic security, signs petitions, views homosexuality as justifiable, and does not believe it is necessary to be very careful about placing trust in people. In the sample of nations investigated, survival values and practices are maximal in Moldova, Ukraine, and Russia, whereas self-expression values and practices are maximal in Australia, Sweden, and the Netherlands.

Easygoingness as midpoint between extreme cultures. Viewed from a unipolar perspective, the bipolar survival versus self-expression measure is made up of two unipolar measures linked together at the midpoint where survival and self-expression are both minimal (see Figure 5.1). As a consequence, there are three rather than two salient points of culture – the two poles and the midpoint. In addition to the two antipoles, the center can stand out as a third marker point of culture, definable in terms of what it is *not* (neither survival nor self-expression). In my view, middle-of-the-road cultures between antipoles deserve a more decent treatment than that.

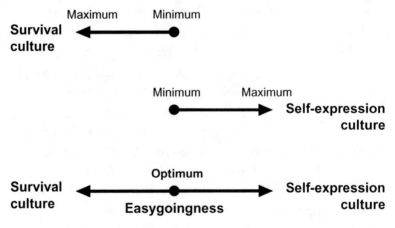

FIGURE 5.1. Unipolar and bipolar measures of survival and self-expression cultures.

Seen through a unipolar lens, the midpoints of survival culture and self-expression culture are not salient (just a dot), ambiguous (half empty? half full?), and suboptimal (half-hearted values and practices). Seen through a bipolar lens, however, the midpoint of survival versus self-expression cultures is the outstanding optimum between two opposites (see Figure 5.1). Halfway between the extremes, decreases in survival culture turn into increases in self-expression culture, and the other way round. There is the free-standing medium, free from the onerous task of achieving survival, free also from the onerous task of achieving self-expression. Indeed, around the center spot are cultures with members who are in an excellent position to overcome a good deal of constraints, concerns, plans, and rules originating from either survival or self-expression and to lead a relatively relaxed and easy life instead.

Easygoingness as a third pole of culture. If we force ourselves to see the midpoint of easygoingness as a third pole of culture, we erect a triangle by pushing easygoing culture out of the line of survival versus self-expression cultures (see Figure 5.2). This is an innovative operation. The above unipolar, bipolar, and midpoint perspectives do not go beyond a single dimension. This tripolar perspective, by contrast, creates three distinct dimensions, the syndromes of survival, easygoing, and self-expression culture represented by the three corners of the triangle. Although the easygoing culture remains a survival-related syndrome, it goes beyond the survival versus self-expression

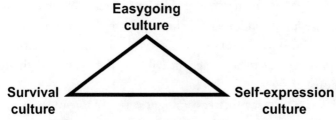

FIGURE 5.2. The triangle of survival-related cultures.

syndromes of culture as a result of the removal of many components of stress and strain.

Compared with survival culture and self-expression culture, easygoing cultures are characterized less by constraint – the situational condition of being checked, restricted, or compelled to avoid or perform some action.[1] Similarly, easygoing cultures are less uncertainty avoidant: they rely less on social norms, rules, and procedures.[2] Finally, whereas members of both survival and self-expression cultures emphasize secular-rational values and practices over religious-traditional values and practices, members of easygoing cultures emphasize religious-traditional values and practices over secular-rational values and practices.[3] This pattern of findings for components of easygoing cultures makes a great deal of sense considering that religious-traditional values and practices tend to protect societies against a variety of rational constraints, ambiguities, and uncertainties. The results strongly support the idea of easygoing culture as a distinct third type of survival-related culture.

An excellent example of a region where easygoing cultures prevail is the Caribbean. The Caribbean lifestyle on Jamaica, Haiti, Puerto Rico, Guadeloupe, Martinique, Barbados, and numerous smaller islands is relatively relaxed. The location of the Dominican Republic in Figure 4.2 exemplifies that these islanders tend to shun both working for money and working for achievement. Instead, they share a passion for singing and dancing in a natural, easy rhythm. As some travel brochures and Web sites say, "Dancing everywhere in the Caribbean is an energetic melding of lower carriage movement, shuffle-stepping, and swaying hips" (http://caribbean-guide.info/past.and.present/culture). Neither survival pressures nor self-expression pressures seem to weigh heavily on the islanders' thoughts, emotions, and actions.

This is not to say that easygoingness is a synonym for peacefulness. Both harmony and hostilities may result from easygoingness because lenient and liberal regulations and sanctions may either de-escalate or escalate conflict (Van de Vliert, 1997, 1998). Lenient and liberal regulations and sanctions are two-edged swords that may help explain why domestic violence is nowadays uncommon in Jamaica and Barbados but common in Haiti and in the Dominican Republic. The Caribbean illustration raises the further question of whether easygoing cultures can be conceptualized as adaptations to the climatic context, the economic context, or both.

Contextualizing the Triangle of Cultures

Climatic context? Close scrutiny of the culture maps resulting from the World Values Surveys reveals that the triangle of survival culture, self-expression culture, and easygoing culture is clearly present, that survival and self-expression cultures tend to be secular-rational cultures in more demanding climates, and that easygoing cultures tend to be religious-traditional cultures in more temperate climates.[3] The special role of easygoingness in the triangle of cultures draws attention to its links with religious traditions and temperate climates. Easygoing cultures may be long-term adaptations to religion ("Don't worry, trust in God") or long-term adaptations to temperate climate ("Don't worry, survival is easy").

An analysis to solve this part of the cultural-adaptation puzzle uncovered that religious traditions and harshness of climate account for 0% and 28% of the cultural differences in easygoingness, respectively.[4] Presumably, societies in temperate climates have evolved easygoingness in response to the climate whereas societies in more demanding climates have evolved tighter cultures in response to the incessant burden of climatic survival (and self-expression as a sublimation of it). This finding seems consistent with Robbins et al.'s (1972) observation that temperate climates tend toward loose cultures in which behavioral prescriptions are neither clearly defined nor reliably enforced. They pitted these loose cultural systems against tight cultural systems found in climates with extreme temperatures where behavioral prescriptions are both clearly defined and reliably enforced (for a recent review of cultural tightness-looseness, see Gelfand et al., 2006).

Economic context? The World Values Surveys group attributes survival and self-expression cultures almost entirely to the economic context of the collective level of wealth (Inglehart & Baker, 2000; Inglehart et al., 2004; Inglehart & Welzel, 2005). According to Halman et al. (2005, p. 129; see also Bell, 1973; Marx, 1867), "the only clear predictor of a country's position on the cultural map appears to be its economic development." Unmistakably, economic growth tends to propel societies in the direction of higher incomes, healthier lives, better education, and more political and economic participation. The effects go beyond these socioeconomic indicators annually published for the United Nations Development Programme. The World Values Surveys group has additionally found that the rise of industrial society is also linked with coherent culture shifts away from survival values and practices toward subjective well-being, trust, tolerance, and self-expression (Inglehart & Baker, 2000).

Self-evident as this economy-drives-culture contextualization may appear to be, the message is certainly not trivial. Contrast the economy-drives-culture standpoint with what outspoken advocates of the opposite culture-drives-economy camp have to say (e.g., Fukuyama, 1995; Harrison & Huntington, 2000; Landes, 1998; McClelland, 1961; Weber, 1904). Take Hampden-Turner and Trompenaars (1993). In *The Seven Cultures of Capitalism: Value Systems for Creating Wealth*, their point of departure is that a deep structure of values and practices is the invisible hand that regulates economic activity. They propose that wealth is created by overcoming seven universal dilemmas in culturally unique ways. The seven contrasts that have to be managed successfully are internal environment versus external environment, rules versus exceptions, hierarchy versus equality, achieved status versus ascribed status, individual interests versus collective interests, breaking down versus putting together, and rashness versus carefulness. Whether the economy-drives-culture camp or the culture-drives-economy camp is closer to the Holy Grail of truth, one thing seems beyond dispute. Each of the opposite causal arrows defended by the two camps is more likely than the alternative causal arrows from economy to climate, and from culture to climate.

In short, seemingly neverending debates about the links between climate, cash, and culture keep us from getting too lazy in our thinking. One may view these debates as a kind of competition for survival-related explanations of culture, with climatic, economic, and climato-economic contexts as competitors. I trust that the integrated climato-economic context will win out in the end.

Climato-economic niches. We have already shown a connection between environments of poverty in harsh climates and societies that embrace a survival culture with components of life dissatisfaction, working for money, and rule and role orientations. A fit exists also between temperate climatic environments and societies that cultivate easygoingness. Poverty versus wealth does not make much difference in such environments for the members' feelings of life satisfaction or for their work motivation. There is a fit, too, between rich-harsh environments and self-expression values and practices. Like members of societies in temperate climates, members of richer societies in harsher climates also tend to lead a happy and healthy life, but, it seems, for completely different reasons. For them, money makes all the difference to upholding their self-expression culture, including near-obsessive working for themselves, for fun, and for improvement against the continuous counteractions of the demanding climate.

Two types of environment or context, therefore, were expected to move societies beyond the tortuous maze of survival troubles: easygoing cultures thrive in temperate climates irrespective of the societal income per head, and self-expression cultures thrive in demanding climates only if the society is rich.

CLIMATO-ECONOMIC NICHES
OF THE TRIANGLE OF CULTURES

Climato-economic packages of survival versus self-expression values and practices can be unpacked using cross-sectional studies in which all measurements are obtained in a single time period. This approach makes causal interpretation of observed relations problematic. Alternatively, the same climate-cash-culture packages can also be unpacked using longitudinal studies based on two or more time points of measurement. This alternative approach comes with the tricky question of whether culture measures at different points in time tap the same components of culture (Cronbach & Furby, 1970; Golembiewski et al., 1976).

Aiming to have the best of both worlds, I tested the triangle of cultural adaptations to climato-economic niches twice. A cross-sectional *generalization study* extended the previous analyses of culturally embedded life satisfaction and work motivation by demonstrating the generalizability of the findings to survival, self-expression, and easygoing cultures. In a longitudinal *change study* I checked to see whether economic decline versus economic growth resulted in adaptations of survival, self-expression, and easygoing cultures depending on the demandingness of cold, temperate, and hot climates.

The generalization study and the change study of the global villagers' cultures were secondary analyses of the above-discussed data from the World Values Surveys (www.worldvaluessurvey.org; Inglehart et al., 1998, 2004). That construct of survival versus self-expression values and practices represents broad cultural syndromes; it was also constructed using a well-thought-out strategy of measurement (see the box "How to discipline apples, oranges, and bananas"). In addition, as specified below, there is testimony to its cross-national solidity and usableness.

How to discipline apples, oranges, and bananas

Survey researchers face the problem of combining answers to separate questions into meaningful factors. In fact, they face three mutually exclusive problems. The survey responses to be combined can be too heterogeneous, too homogeneous, or too far from the best of both worlds, that is, not sufficiently homogeneous and heterogeneous at the same time. Interestingly, cross-cultural researchers from different scientific disciplines appear to weigh these problems differently. Psychologists, economists, and macrosociologists are distinct prototypes.

Psychologists overemphasize the heterogeneity problem. They preach and teach that one should never add apples and oranges, let alone bananas. Each factor should be internally consistent and independent from other factors. Thus, the validity of a culture measure is built on specificity rather than generality. For example, Triandis and colleagues (Singelis et al., 1995; Triandis & Gelfand, 1998) have developed internally consistent, factorially independent, and cross-culturally applicable scales to tap individuals' endorsement of horizontal individualism, vertical individualism, horizontal collectivism, and vertical collectivism. Shall I take the psychologists' example, and serve apples?

In striking contrast, economists overemphasize the homogeneity problem. They preach and teach that one should always combine as many fruits as possible to get indices that adequately represent inevitably complicated realities. Thus, the validity of a culture measure is built on generality rather than specificity. For example, the World Economic Forum in Geneva annually produces a number of competitiveness indices aimed at highlighting the factors and policies that determine the sharply different growth experiences of over 100 countries. The most recent global competitiveness index (Lopez-Claros et al., 2005) combines 90 variables representing institutions, infrastructure, macroeconomy, health and primary education, higher education and training, market efficiency, technological readiness, business sophistication, and innovation. Shall I take the economists' example and serve fruits?

The World Values Surveys are conducted by macrosociologists who, unlike psychologists and economists, aim to overcome both the heterogeneity problem and the homogeneity problem. They profess that they "deliberately selected items covering a wide range of topics," that they could have obtained "more tightly correlated clusters of items" referring to a specific topic, but that they refused to do so because their "goal was to measure broad dimensions of cross-cultural variation" (Inglehart & Baker, 2000, pp. 24–25). Thus, the validity of the macrosociologists' measures of survival culture and self-expression culture used here is built on both homogeneity and heterogeneity. I am serving their mixed fruit.

Generalization Study

Recall that the total climate index is the sum of the smallest and largest deviations from 22°C in the coldest and hottest months. The measure of national wealth as a well-known antecedent condition of culture also remained as it was.[5] In contrast, in this generalization study, much attention had to be paid to the cross-national reliability,[6] equivalence,[7] and validity[8] of the continuous measure of extreme survival culture, intermediate easygoing culture, and extreme self-expression culture. This was not in vain; survival versus self-expression values and practices consistently stood out as a solid and usable dimension of culture. Notably, the empirical evidence supported the idea that happiness, subjective health, child labor, and working for money versus working for achievement are, so to say, combinable under the umbrella of survival, easygoing, and self-expression cultures as three overall adaptations to climato-economic niches.[9]

Climatic demands (0%), income per head (52%), and climate and wealth in concert (20%) accounted for 72% of the cross-national variation in survival versus self-expression culture.[10] The details of these results are plotted in Figure 5.3, illustrated with 67

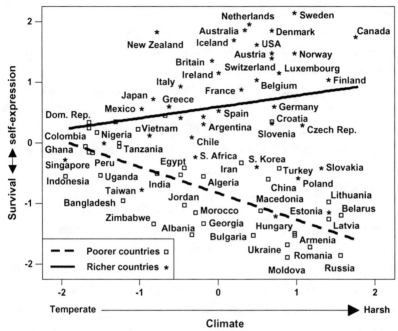

FIGURE 5.3. Effect of more demanding climate on survival versus self-expression culture, broken down for poorer and richer countries.

country names; 10 others were crowded out (Azerbaijan, Brazil, El Salvador, Israel, Malta, Pakistan, Philippines, Portugal, Uruguay, and Venezuela). As exemplified below, the countries at the bottom tend to have survival cultures, the countries at the top tend to have self-expression cultures, and the countries in the middle tend to have easygoing cultures. It is important to realize and remember that the upward slope for the richer countries becomes steeper to the extent that fewer countries are regarded as really rich.[11]

In the lower right-hand corner of Figure 5.3, we see that survival cultures such as those in Moldova and Russia thrive in regions with demanding climates where the inhabitants are poor and short of money resources to cope with climate. In the upper right-hand corner, we see that self-expression cultures such as those in Canada and Sweden thrive in regions with demanding climates where the inhabitants are rich and have plenty of money resources to cope with climate. In the middle left, we see that easygoing cultures thrive in regions with temperate climates irrespective of whether the inhabitants are rather poor (e.g., Ghana) or rather rich (e.g., Singapore). As a consequence, and in full support of the model of cultural adaptations to climato-economic niches, Figure 5.3 shows a triangle of cultures with the easygoing corner in temperate climates and the missing side between survival cultures and self-expression cultures in demanding climates.

The overrepresentation of European countries is a matter of concern. However, when the 9 African, 9 South American, and 19 Asian countries were treated as more equal than the European countries, by giving them a proportionally higher weight, the three climato-economic niches of the three types of culture were not swallowed up by a cross-continental fog. If anything, the culture niches became even clearer. Climatic demands and income per head in concert initially accounted for 20% of the cross-national variation in survival, self-expression, and easygoing cultures; this figure now rose to 28%.[10] Thus, there is not the slightest indication that the biased sampling of societies undermines the cross-continental applicability of the observed adaptations of culture to the climatic and economic circumstances. Quite the reverse, the overrepresentation of European countries increases rather than decreases the worldwide generalizability of my climato-economic theory of culture in the making.

In sum, the climato-economic niches of culture proposed here are generalizable from culturally embedded life satisfaction and work motivation to survival, self-expression, and easygoing cultures, and across the world's inhabited continents. Another indication of the generalizability of the earlier findings is that, once again, no support was found for competing pictures containing rival explanations (for details, see Van de Vliert, 2007a, 2007b).

Change Study

Cross-sectional links between lower incomes and survival orientations suggest that lower incomes lead to survival cultures. Analogous
links between higher incomes and self-expression orientations likewise suggest that higher incomes lead to self-expression cultures.
Strictly speaking, both suggestions are illusions of culture change,
which may well get stronger if they occur for household incomes and
national incomes alike. As a case in point, families living in lower
income countries with more demanding climates appear to endorse
survival culture over self-expression culture to the extent that their
household incomes in these already lower income countries are
lower as well.[12] Such cross-sectional findings strongly suggest that
changes in income lead to changes in cultural values and practices.

Illusions of culture change are conjured up also by the visual-
izations of the research results presented in this book. The culture
differences between poorer and richer countries in harsher climates,
represented as the missing side of a triangle of cultures, also make it
seem likely that changes in income lead to changes in culture. However, evidence to the contrary is at our fingertips. To shatter the
illusion of wealth-based culture change, all we have to do is to
inspect the corner of the triangle of cultures in temperate climates.
There, differences in wealth are not convincingly related to deviations from the easygoing culture in the direction of either survival or
self-expression culture. So, comparing economy-culture links in different climatic conditions is one way to prevent the occurrence of
illusions of economic causes of culture. Another research measure to
prevent victimization by an economy-drives-culture illusion is the
use of changes between different points in time.

The change study had the same purpose as the generalization
study – to test the viability of the model of cultural adaptations to
climato-economic niches. Other than their identical purpose, the
studies were very different. Notably, repeated measures of extreme

survival culture, intermediate easygoing culture, and extreme self-expression culture over 9- to 19-year-periods between 1981 and 2002 were available for only 38 nations.[13] The role of national wealth was also quite different because income per head as a cross-sectional indicator of money resources had to be replaced with economic growth as a longitudinal indicator of money resources.[14]

A systematic analysis of the rates of change revealed that no less than 54% of the changes in culture in the 38 countries covaried with changes in niches of climatic demands and economic growth.[15] Climatic demands contributed at least 37% in and of themselves and at least another 11% together with economic growth. Given the view of most theorists that cultures are extremely stable over time, this degree of covariation of climato-economic change and culture change is impressive for the limited span of time investigated. A map of the locations of 33 countries in this field of context-based changes in culture is provided in Figure 5.4 (there was no room to list Australia, Bangladesh, France, Germany, and the Netherlands). The most striking feature of this picture is that in temperate climates at the left, the lower left quadrant of growing emphasis on survival culture is empty whereas the upper left quadrant of growing emphasis on self-expression culture is full. Apparently, in temperate climates, economic decline versus growth is not important for survival-related cultures.

In more demanding climates, it is more difficult to move from survival culture toward self-expression culture, as is apparent from the downward sloping lines in Figure 5.4, although lower economic growth produces more movement toward survival culture (broken line) than does higher economic growth (solid line).[16] The inhabitants of Russia, Latvia, Lithuania, and Estonia all moved further from self-expression culture toward survival culture after the collapse of communist rule and the subsequent economic decline—an average of minus 5% per year at the end of the 20th century. By contrast, the inhabitants of countries with favorable economic

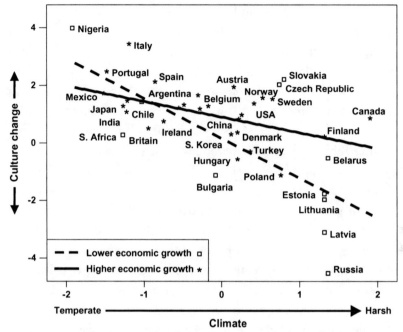

FIGURE 5.4. Effect of more demanding climate on culture change, downward toward survival or upward toward self-expression, broken down for countries with lower and higher economic growth.

growth rates in the same climatic zone, such as the Canadians and the Finns, hardly moved from survival values toward self-expression values. All this sounds plausible and looks real as it rests on longitudinal information that is less sensitive to illusory change. But plausibility and sense of reality do not guarantee authenticity.

On closer consideration, the influence of economic growth was found to be retraceable to the influence of national wealth, with the consequence that Figure 5.4 is a new chip off the old block of previous pictures. This insight surfaced when income per head was controlled for. The joint impact of climatic demands and income per head on culture change appeared to overarch and dwarf the joint impact of climatic demands and economic growth on culture change.[15] This finding has far-reaching implications for each of the three corners of the triangle of cultures. In the survival corner, climatic demands and poverty produce not only survival cultures but also economic decline and a corresponding extra *movement in the direction of survival culture.* The self-reinforcing nature of this process of cultural adaptation may well explain why the climato-economic niches of survival cultures are more pronounced than the climato-economic niches of easygoing and self-expression cultures. In the self-expression corner, climatic demands and wealth produce not only self-expression cultures but also prevention of economic decline and of a corresponding movement in the direction of survival culture. And in the easygoing corner, temperate climates produce not only easygoing cultures but also prevention of movement away from the easygoing culture in times of economic change.

All in all, the above makes several significant contributions to the classification, visualization, and explanation of societal cultures. Prototypically, survival cultures are characterized by many constraints, secular-rational orientations, unhappiness, unhealthiness, much child labor, and working for money. Self-expression cultures are characterized by many constraints, secular-rational orientations, happiness, healthiness, absence of child labor, and working for achievement. In between these two, easygoing cultures are characterized by few constraints, religious-traditional orientations, happiness, health, and moderate degrees of child labor and of working for money and for achievement. The World Values Surveys group has visualized this classification as a descriptive triangle of cultures (see, for instance, Inglehart & Welzel, 2005). In Figure 5.3, the same classification is visualized as an explanatory triangle of cultures, in which survival cultures are seen as adaptations to harsh-poor climato-economic niches, self-expression cultures as adaptations to harsh-rich climato-economic niches, and easygoing cultures as adaptations to temperate climatic niches.

PROPOSITIONS

5.1. Survival cultures thrive in poor societies in demanding climates.

5.2. Self-expression cultures thrive in rich societies in demanding climates.

5.3. Easygoing cultures thrive in societies in temperate climates irrespective of their level of wealth.

RESEARCH NOTES

1. The overall survival versus self-expression syndrome reported by Inglehart and Baker (2000, p. 27) has 31 components with positive and negative loadings on the survival versus self-expression factor. Interestingly, the 31 components also vary in constraint. Constraint was measured on a 4-point scale ranging from 0 (*no constraint*) to 3 (*much constraint*). Little constraint is reflected in 20 factual descriptions of one's own and other people's opinions, intentions, and behaviors. Some to considerable constraint is reflected in six evaluations of interactions with parents, children, and neighbors. And much constraint is reflected in five statements about possible problems in daily life, to wit: being in poor health; feeling that one does not have much free choice or control over one's life; the financial situation of one's household as a cause for worry; the pressure that a good income and safe job are more important than a feeling of accomplishment and working with people one likes (job motivation index); and the rejection of foreigners, homosexuals, and people with AIDS as neighbors (out-group index). The absolute loadings of the 31 components on the survival versus self-expression factor represent easygoingness, ranging from maximal easygoingness, |.42|, to minimal easygoingness, |.86|. As expected, easygoingness was negatively related to constraint, $r(31) = -.46$, $p < .01$.

2. Uncertainty avoidance was the extent to which a society relies on social norms, rules, and procedures to alleviate unpredictability of future events (source: House et al., 2004, pp. 740–741). A multiple regression analysis showed that, across 40 countries, the linear ($\Delta R^2 = .30$; $B = .19$, $p < .001$) and quadratic ($\Delta R^2 = .06$; $B = .09$, $p < .05$) terms of standardized survival versus self-expression culture accounted for 36% of the variation in uncertainty avoidance. The signs of the unstandardized regression coefficients (given between brackets) indicate that

reliance on constraining behavioral prescriptions is lower for intermediate degrees of survival versus self-expression culture.

3. Survival versus self-expression culture was standardized (1st predictor), and then squared to get an operationalization of easygoing culture (2nd predictor). Across 77 countries, survival versus self-
expression culture ($\Delta R^2 = .02$, $B = .08$, n.s.) and their middle reaches
of easygoing culture ($\Delta R^2 = .19$; $B = .43$, $p < .001$) had a U-curved
relation with religious-traditional versus secular-rational culture
(source: www.worldvaluessurvey.org; Inglehart et al., 1998, 2004).
When the demandingness of climate was controlled for ($\Delta R^2 = .45$;
$B = .65$, $p < .001$), this U-curved relation between survival versus self-
expression culture and religious-traditional versus secular-rational
culture disappeared ($\Delta R^2 = .19$; $B = .43$, $p < .001$ changed into $\Delta R^2 =
.01$; $B = .12$, n.s.), demonstrating that temperate climates must be asso-
ciated with easygoingness, religiosity, and traditionality simultaneously.

4. Joint effect of religious-traditional versus secular-rational culture (RT-
SR) and demanding climate on survival versus self-expression culture,
and easygoing culture in 77 countries.

Predictors	Survival versus self-expression			Easygoingness		
	B	B	B	B	B	B
RT-SR	.14	$.31^{\dagger}$	$.30^{\dagger}$	$.49^{***}$	.23	.23
Climate (C)		−.26	−.27		$.39^{**}$	$.39^{**}$
(RT-SR) × C			−.14			−.02
ΔR^2	.02	.03	.01	$.21^{***}$	$.07^{**}$	$.28^{***}$
Total R^2	.02	.05	.06	$.21^{***}$	$.28^{***}$	$.28^{***}$

$^{\dagger}p < .10.$ $^{*}p < .05.$ $^{**}p < .01.$ $^{***}p < .001.$

For this analysis and for other analyses reported in this chapter,
demanding climate (C) was the sum of the absolute deviations from
22°C for the average lowest and highest temperatures in the coldest
winter month and for the average lowest and highest temperatures in
the hottest summer month. Easygoingness was the standardized survival versus self-expression culture squared. There was no multicollinearity (*VIFs* < 1.82), and there were no outliers (Cook's *Ds* < .12).

5. Income per head in 2000 (purchasing power parity; source: United Nations Development Programme, 2002) was used as the most appropriate index of wealth for the 1999–2002 period under investigation. Because the ratio of skewness to its standard error was 3.40, this index had to be log transformed before it was standardized (new ratio –1.62).

6. A country's survival versus self-expression factor score was first based on 14 items (Inglehart, 1997) but was later restricted to 8 items that appeared in the same format in all waves of the World Values Surveys (Inglehart & Baker, 2000). To avoid response bias, the 8 items had varying response scales, including a 4-item subindex tapping whether the respondent gives priority to self-expression and quality of life over physical and economic security (2-point scales), and 4 singular items tapping whether the respondent "has signed a petition" (3-point scale), "thinks that homosexuality is justifiable" (10-point scale), "would say that most people can be trusted" (2-point scale), and "taking all things together" describes himself or herself as "happy" (4-point scale). In subsamples of countries, this 8-item index was almost perfectly correlated with the initial 14-item index [Pearson $r(43) = .96$, $p < .001$; Inglehart & Baker, 2000, p. 25] and had a high test-retest reliability [Spearman $r_s(8) = .98$, $p < .001$, after 1–2 years; $r_s(9) = .83$, $p < .01$, after 2–3 years; own calculations]. The survival versus self-expression index ranged from –1.93 in Moldova (high survival, low self-expression) to +2.17 in Sweden (low survival, high self-expression; $M= 0$; $SD= 1.06$).

7. The measurement equivalence of the construct of survival versus self-expression culture across climato-economic niches was established in four steps (for details, see Van de Vliert, 2007a). First, all subindices and items measuring survival versus self-expression culture and religious-traditional versus secular-rational culture were intercorrelated at the individual level, resulting in a matrix with 45 intercorrelations. Second, 4 sets of 2 countries were selected on the basis of a systematic 2 (demanding climate: extremely temperate vs. extremely harsh) × 2 (national wealth: extremely poor vs. extremely rich) sampling design. The countries sampled were Nigeria and Tanzania (temperate/poor), Belarus and Russia (harsh/poor), New Zealand and Taiwan (temperate/rich), and Canada and Finland (harsh/rich). Third, similar to step 1, for each of the 8 countries, a matrix with 45 intercorrelations was produced. Fourth, all sets of 45 intercorrelations were intercorrelated. The associations between the world set and the country sets of intercorrelations showed cross-national equivalence of the conceptualizations of survival versus self-expression culture in Nigeria ($r = .62$,

$p < .001$), Tanzania ($r = .82, p < .001$), Belarus ($r = .81, p < .001$), Russia ($r = .85, p < .001$), New Zealand ($r = .86, p < .001$), Taiwan ($r = .87, p < .001$), Canada ($r = .96, p < .001$), and Finland ($r = .91, p < .001$).

8. The measurement validity of the construct of survival versus self-expression culture is apparent from its consistent and strong relations with a considerable number of comparable dimensions in the extant literature (Hofstede, 2001; House et al., 2004; Huntington, 1996; Inglehart, 1997; Inglehart & Baker, 2000; Inglehart et al., 1998, 2004; Inglehart & Welzel, 2005; Ronen & Shenkar, 1985; Schwartz, 2004; Smith et al., 2006).

9. As predicted, survival versus self-expression culture was positively related to the indicators of happiness [$r(77) = .78, p < .001$] and subjective health [$r(70) = .64, p < .001$] used in the studies reported in Chapter 3, and was negatively related to the indicators of child labor [$r(68) = -.24, p < .05$] and working for money rather than for achievement [$r(34) = -.68, p < .001$] used in the studies reported in Chapter 4.

10. Joint effect of demanding climate and income per head on survival versus self-expression culture in 77 countries (also weighted for cross-continental generalization to correct for the over-representation of European countries).

Predictors	Unweighted for generalization			Weighted for generalization		
	B	B	B	B	B	B
Climate (C)	$-.04$	$-.34^{***}$	$-.28^{**}$	$-.08$	$-.34^{***}$	$-.21^{**}$
Income (I)		$.82^{***}$	$.95^{***}$		$.55^{***}$	$.85^{***}$
C x I			$.52^{***}$			$.51^{***}$
ΔR^2	.00	$.52^{***}$	$.20^{***}$	.01	$.35^{***}$	$.28^{***}$
Total R^2	.00	$.52^{***}$	$.72^{***}$	.01	$.36^{***}$	$.64^{***}$

$^{\dagger}p < .10$. $^{*}p < .05$. $^{**}p < .01$. $^{***}p < .001$.

In the analysis "Weighted for generalization," each country was weighted for the within-continent underrepresentation of the number of countries over 10,000 square kilometers. The 9 African countries in the study were given a weight of 5.32, the 19 Asian countries a weight of 2.56, the 9 South American countries a weight of 2.44, and the remaining 40 countries a weight of 1. There was no multicollinearity (*VIFs* < 1.72), and there were no outliers (Cook's *Ds* < .32).

Replacement of income per head in 2000 with income per head in earlier years showed gradual decreases in the interactive impact of demanding climate and income per head on survival versus self-expression culture (unweighted: ΔR^2 = .20 for 2000, .14 for 1995, .09 for 1990, .05 for 1985, .07 for 1980, and .06 for 1975; weighted: ΔR^2 = .28 for 2000, .20 for 1995, .11 for 1990, .09 for 1985, .10 for 1980, and .05 for 1975). This suggests that cultural adaptations to climato-economic niches do not necessarily take very long, as is often thought.

11. Simple slopes for a 50–50 split (38 vs. 39), a 60–40 split (46 vs. 31), and a 70–30 split (54 vs. 23) of poorer and richer countries: $r(38)$ = −.68, $p < .001$, $r(46)$ = −.61, $p < .001$ and $r(54)$ = −.53, $p < .001$ for poorer countries; $r(39)$ = .17, n.s., $r(31)$ = .40, $p < .05$ and $r(23)$ = .55, $p < .01$ for richer countries. The simple slopes shown in Figure 5.3 are for the most conservative 50–50 split of poorer and richer countries.

12. Sixty-six within-country correlations between the respondent's household income and the respondent's personal endorsement of survival versus self-expression values and practices ranged from .04 to .45 (M_r = .22; SD_r = .08). As expected, only for inhabitants of lower income countries in more demanding climates did a person's own household income make a difference. Unlike inhabitants of richer countries in more demanding climates (e.g., Finland and USA; simple slope $B = -.01$, n.s.), inhabitants of poorer countries in more demanding climates (e.g., Belarus and Latvia; B = .03, $p < .01$) endorsed survival culture over self-expression culture to the extent that they earned less (for details, see Van de Vliert, 2007a).

13. Based on hundreds of analyses and intellectual speculation, my arbitrary point of departure was that culture is stable during years 1–3, destabilizes during years 4–8, and starts to change only after almost a decade, from 9 years onward. The annual change in survival versus self-expression culture was expressed in two ways: as the difference between the factor scores at the two points in time divided by the number of years between these two points in time, and as the annual percentage of change in the factor score (after addition of an increment of 3 to allow the percentage to be calculated from positive scores above 1). These slightly different operationalizations [$r(38)$ = .97, $p < .001$] produced virtually the same results. Results for the annual percentage of culture change are reported because this percentage is identical in form with its main predictor – the economic growth rate. The annual rate of change in survival versus self-expression

culture ranged from −4.60 in Russia (higher survival, lower self-expression) to +3.89 in Nigeria (lower survival, higher self-expression; $M = .60$; $SD = 1.66$).

14. As usual, economic growth was the percentage of annual decline versus growth in gross domestic product per head (GDP/h; source: World Bank Atlas, 1965–2002). The negative versus positive growth rates were computed over periods ranging from 5 years before the earliest culture survey to the year of the latest culture survey. After the distribution of the 9 negative and 29 positive growth rates was transformed into a 5-point ordinal scale, there were no departures from normality. Standardized economic growth, ranging from −2 in Latvia, Lithuania, and Russia to +2 in Chile, China, and South Korea ($M = 0$; $SD = 1.04$), was insignificantly related to ln GDP/h in 2000 [$r(38) = .31$, n.s.].

15. Joint effect of demanding climate, income per head, and economic growth on change from survival culture to self-expression culture in 38 countries.

Predictors	Uncontrolled for income per head			Controlled for income per head		
	B	B	B	B	B	B
Climate (C)	−1.01***	−.85***	−.69**	−.83***	−.77***	−.71***
Income (I)				.59**	.40*	.47*
C × I				.56**		.40*
Growth (G)		.42†	.34		.22	.18
C × G			.59**		.51**	.31
ΔR²	.37***	.06†	.11**		.05*	.04†
Total R²	.37***	.43***	.54***	.60***	.59***	.63***

†$p < .10$. *$p < .05$. **$p < .01$. ***$p < .001$.

For the annual percentage of change from survival culture to self-expression culture, see research note 13. Income (I) was the logged purchasing-power income per head in 2000 (source: United Nations Development Programme, 2002). Economic growth was measured on the 5-point scale discussed in research note 14. There was no multicollinearity (*VIFs* < 1.55), and there were no outliers (Cook's *Ds* < .34).

16. The simple-slope correlations between more demanding climate and culture change were $r(11) = -.67$, $p < .05$ for the countries with lower economic growth and $r(27) = -.50$, $p < .01$ for the countries with higher economic growth.

6

Cooperation

Cooperation is the master key to genetic survival, and climatic survival is the master key to cooperation.

Cultures the world over are both constant *and* in continuous transition. A major reason for the constancy of cultures may well be that they thrive in stable climato-economic niches that do not yo-yo like the daily weather and the amount of money in our pockets. And a major reason for the never-ceasing transition of cultures may be that we, the carriers of cultures, are born and die. Birth and death have the inevitable consequence that some values and practices are not picked up by children from adults, or transmitted by adults to children, whereas newly developed values and practices are successfully passed on to following generations.

The parent-child relation is the crucial core of the dynamic stability of culture. One of the most rudimentary things parents have to teach their children, by setting good examples and giving instructions and feedback, is cooperativeness. Babies are selfish, and toddlers must learn to have less than maximal concern for their own goals (unselfishness) and more than minimal tolerance and respect for other people's goals (prosociality). This is a difficult process with increasingly more trials and, at best, increasingly fewer errors.

Considerable differences exist around the globe in the degrees to which unselfishness and prosociality play a part in daily life (Bierhoff, 2002; Kabasakal & Bodur, 2004; Schroeder et al., 1995).

For example, parents and other adults tend to encourage children to value and practice unselfishness rather than prosociality in Montenegro and Indonesia, but prosociality rather than unselfishness in Moldova and Spain (Inglehart et al., 2004, variables A35 and A41). This distribution of distinct combinations of unselfishness and prosociality raises the question of whether the climato-economics of culture can be used once more to introduce some sort of order. Do adults in different climato-economic niches evolve different strategies of more or less cooperative enculturation of their children? And do the adults themselves also live up to these more or less cooperative do's and dont's, especially where this is critical, such as in work situations?

This chapter highlights the extent to which societies get their children into cooperative moods and habits and endorse democratic leadership. The section "Cooperating in Pursuit of Survival" relates climatic, climato-genetic, and climato-economic survival perspectives to cooperative values and practices. The final part of this survival section contains a translation of the model presented in Chapter 5 into a triangle of selfish, easygoing, and cooperative adaptations of culture to climatic demands and collective wealth. In the following sections, evidence of the existence of climato-economic niches of cooperation is presented and discussed. It is hard to deny or disparage this further support for the burgeoning climato-economic theory of culture because the results were double-checked using different sources of survey information about cooperation in children and leaders.

COOPERATING IN PURSUIT OF SURVIVAL

Each new world citizen learns to cooperate with others in numerous ways. Perhaps the most basic examples are cohabitation and trade. Whereas cohabitation favors genetic survival over time, trade facilitates climatic survival in a particular place. In the case of cohabitation, procreation and joint pleasure are higher order goals, male and female satisfaction lower order goals. In the case of trade, exchange and joint gain are higher order goals, buyer and seller satisfaction lower order goals. These fundamental perspectives have led to the formulation of several theories of cooperative integration of concern for one's own goals and for other people's goals. One genetic-survival theory, for example, postulates that individuals are most unselfish and prosocial toward their parents, siblings, and children (sharing 50% of their genes), less unselfish and prosocial toward their grandparents, uncles, aunts, nephews, nieces, and grandchildren (sharing 25% of their genes), and least unselfish and prosocial toward nonrelatives ("charity begins at home"; for supporting evidence in animals and humans, see Gaulin & McBurney, 2001).

From my point of view, climatic survival in a particular place is a necessary but insufficient condition of genetic survival over time. Only when the existence needs of the nuclear family are not utterly frustrated by a lack of thermal comfort, nutrition, and health can one maximize the proliferation of one's gene pool. Hence, cooperating in pursuit of climatic survival is more elementary than cooperating in pursuit of genetic survival. Put otherwise, a back-to-basics approach to survival gives scientific priority to climate over genes as a source of societal values and practices. The greater urgency of coping with freezing cold and boiling heat makes it incomprehensible that the genetic roots of culture have received much more attention than its climatic roots.

Climatic survival is the foundation of the theory of climate-culture overload; a combination of climatic and genetic survival underpins the paternal investment theory. But neither of these theories is a proper match for the climato-economic theory of cooperation, which highlights the joint importance of climate and cash. Below, the parts of each of these theories that address the climate-related origins and evolution of cooperative cultures are summarized.

Climatic Survival and Cooperation

The simplest model of climate-culture effects pays no attention to curvilinear relations between climate and culture nor to the impact of seasonal variations in temperature. It guides the search for straightforward roots of culture in mean temperature levels varying from cold at latitudes closer to the icecaps to hot at latitudes closer to the equator. This overly simple cold-hot model was adopted in my first publication on climatic effects (Van de Vliert & Van Yperen, 1996). In that study, we formulated a weather explanation and a climatic explanation of the finding that employees in colder countries experience less role overload in the form of excessive work demands. The weather explanation proposed that less ambient heat produces less negative affect and, through it, less role overload. The climatic explanation proposed connections between survival, positive goal interdependence, cooperative culture, and role overload. As discussed next, this climatic explanation of culture highlighted the increasingly demanding nature of increasingly colder climates.

Societies in cold climates with prolonged winters have evolved situations of positive goal interdependence. In these climates, meeting basic needs for food, safety, and security is much more demanding than it is in warm climates, so a more positive relation exists between the attainment of one's own and other people's goals. As a consequence, over many generations, people have evolved more shared responsibilities and more need for adequate technology as a condition for joint survival in cold climates. On a social level, they have learned to stand or fall together. Survival in cold climates requires large-game hunting by groups that share their skills and kills. Individuals have to unite against the threats of snowstorms and frost, especially in the event of climatic deterioration as happened long ago to the Norse colony in Greenland. Or they may coalesce against other societies, as was once the case with the

Scandinavian Vikings, whose chosen method of survival was plundering and occupying more southerly parts of Europe.

Positive goal interdependence in cold climates produces a culture of cooperative attitudes and behaviors within one's primary groups. Considerable research has shown that group members in circumstances of greater positive goal interdependence manifest more integrative intentions and actions. They are more open-minded regarding others' arguments and desires, more concerned about others' outcomes, and more inclined to search for compromises and solutions, simply because self-interest requires negotiating and problem solving (Deutsch, 1973; Johnson & Johnson, 1989; Tjosvold, 1991). Support for the link between colder climates and more cooperative cultures came from the findings that inhabitants of cooler countries are less competitive and that their cultures are characterized more by egalitarian commitment and harmony.

As the final link of the chain of connections, more cooperative cultures resulting from greater positive goal interdependence in colder climates are characterized by greater willingness to allow another person's actions to replace one's own actions, which encourages division of labor, role specialization, and delegation of work. Other features of more cooperative cultures are more positive attitudes toward others and a greater readiness to extend social support. These sets of behavioral tendencies counteract experiences of role overload. Conversely, societies in warmer climates have to face fewer survival problems, evolve less positive goal interdependence, and create less cooperative or more competitive cultures, with more experiences of role overload as a result.

The observed climate-culture relation withstood 47 statistical attacks by economic indicators, organizational features, and personal characteristics (for details, see Van de Vliert & Van Yperen, 1996). Although those and other simple and straightforward climate-culture links may appeal to the imagination, some courtship with genetic factors may provide a more realistic perspective.

Climato-genetic Survival and Cooperation

In the book *Not by Genes Alone: How Culture Transformed Human Evolution*, Richerson and Boyd (2005) propose that culture is adaptive because it can do things such as social learning that genes cannot do for themselves. Their proposition is based in particular on an extensive discussion of the increased variation in thermal climate during the last part of the Pleistocene (roughly 80,000 to 10,000 years ago). In their words, "Because cumulative cultural evolution gives rise to complex adaptations much more rapidly than natural selection can give rise to genetic adaptations, complex culture was particularly suited to the highly variable Pleistocene environments" (Richerson & Boyd, 2005, p. 146). As cold and hot climates changed places quickly, climatic survival merged with genetic survival. Parental cooperation was invented to overcome climatic crises and keep the nuclear family alive and well.

The intense temperature variations of the last glacial period were followed by the relatively warm and stable Holocene climates of the last 10,000 years or so (Burroughs, 1997; Ditlevsen et al., 1996). Cold, temperate, and hot climates no longer rambled, making joint paternal and maternal investments in child rearing less crucial for survival, especially in temperate climates. One explanation for the origin and evolution of cooperative cultures uses this link between parenting and genetic existence after death. This paternal investment theory (Bjorklund & Kipp, 1996; Hewlett, 1992; Miller, 1994) is derived from the biological construct of differential parental care (Clutton-Brock, 1991; Trivers, 1972). It can best be presented in the form of four cumulative propositions – a genetic-survival proposition, a trade-off proposition, a climatic-survival proposition, and a culture proposition.

- *Genetic-survival proposition.* Women have to invest much more time and effort in the heavy burdens of pregnancy, breast feeding, and procreation-related health problems than men. As a consequence, a woman can best serve her interest of genetic survival by mating with a single man who will provide not only good genes but also resources for herself and for their children. By contrast, a man can best serve his interest of increasing the proliferation of his genes by mating with many females, regardless of their "genetic quality." In further consequence, compared with women, men will be less choosy in mate selection and more competitive with other males for access to females.

- *Trade-off proposition.* Given this evolution of sex differences, men have more leeway to trade off different reproductive strategies. Men have greater choice between investing in providing abundant resources for a single family and investing in multiple partners to increase offspring. Historically, the choices men made are thought to have been partly dependent on the climatic circumstances.

- *Climatic-survival proposition.* It is increasingly difficult for families to meet basic survival needs in increasingly cold or hot climates. In addition to maternal investment, the survival of mothers and offspring in those harsher climates requires much more paternal investment in the family. Although maternal and paternal investment will be complementary in part, some pushing and pulling in the direction of more gender role equality will have evolved as well (Coltrane, 1988). By comparison, in temperate climates, men have more freedom to invest in siring children with multiple mates in the expectation that many of these children will survive. In the long run, the fathers' release from child care, household chores, and other work will have resulted in greater gender-role differences in temperate climates.

- *Culture proposition.* Greater paternal investment in the family in more demanding climates produces more cooperative cultures. In families in colder or hotter climates, both maternal and paternal investments are characterized more by sacrifice, delay of gratification, and the evolution of predominantly cooperative attitudes and behaviors. This cooperative orientation in the nuclear family generalizes to much of societal behavior and infuses it (cf. Bonta, 1997). In the end, compared with societies in temperate climates, societies in more demanding cold or hot climates will have evolved more cooperative, and thus less selfish and competitive, cultures with smaller role differences between mothers and fathers.

In essence, the paternal investment theory predicts that gender role equality will thrive in regions with more demanding cold or hot climates, irrespective of income per head. Tests of this prediction are possible using the United Nations' gender empowerment index, GLOBE's cultural value dimension of gender egalitarianism, and Sullivan's gender gap index.[1] Three times in a row, the analyses failed to confirm the notion that climato-genetically anchored gender role differences are smaller in more demanding climates. On the contrary, gender role equality decreased rather than increased in poorer countries with more demanding climates.[2] Thus, the climatic-survival and culture propositions are less applicable in some niches of greater climatic demands than in others. Consequently, the climato-genetic survival perspective cannot accurately explain cross-national differences in male-female cooperation as a basis of cooperative culture.

Yet another weakness in the climato-genetic explanation of cooperation is the ambiguity of the term *paternal investment*. In the studies on work motives reported in Chapter 4, doing paid work and doing unpaid work were unfolded as different routes to the same goal of satisfying family needs for thermal comfort, nutrition, and health. Fathers who take the paid-work route to proliferate their genes find themselves in a role-reinforcing process of providing enough cash to enable their nuclear families to cope with a threatening climate. They maintain or even widen the gender gap. By contrast, fathers who take the unpaid-work route to proliferate their genes find themselves in a transitional process from the role of provider to the role of caregiver. By and large, they narrow the gender gap. The findings of the above analyses suggest that fathers in poorer countries with harsher climates favor cooperation through paid work and widening gender gaps over cooperation through unpaid work and narrowing gender gaps.

Climato-economic Survival and Cooperation

Climato-economic niches of cooperation have been discussed in earlier chapters. The findings of the study on trading work activities for money, reported in Chapter 4, made it clear that the base level of cooperative trading is most salient and relevant in poorer societies in more demanding climates and least salient and relevant in richer societies in more demanding climates. For nonfinancial cooperation, however, different or even opposite rules of thumb seem to apply. The findings reported in Chapter 5 highlighted that inhabitants of countries in more demanding climates have a cultural connection with social discrimination. If people are poor, they tend to distrust one another and to reject foreigners, homosexuals, and people with AIDS as neighbors. If they are rich, they tend to trust one another and to accept the groups mentioned as neighbors. Because interpersonal trust and interpersonal acceptance are foundations of cooperation, it follows that nonfinancial cooperation is expected to occur least in poorer societies in more demanding climates and most in richer societies in more demanding climates.

These expectations about the endorsement and occurrence of nonfinancial cooperation can be more fully understood in terms of the demands-resources theories introduced in Chapter 3. Societies faced with climatic demands mismatched by scarcity of money resources will evolve selfish ways of interaction, reflecting desperate attempts to control threatening and stressful situations. The members' selfish orientations will be part of an overall survival culture passed on to children and valued and practiced by leaders as cultural representatives of their communities. By contrast, societies faced with climatic demands matched by abundant money resources will evolve less selfish and more prosocial ways of interaction, reflecting successful attempts to turn threats into opportunities and stress into relief. Their children and leaders will radiate a cooperative orientation as the cornerstone of their overall self-expression culture. In between these extremes, societies faced with a less demanding temperate climate, where money resources are less important, will evolve an easygoing culture, free from the onerous tasks of either enforcing selfish decisions or creating cooperative solutions.

Tentative support for this model of selfish, easygoing, and cooperative adaptations of culture to climato-economic niches comes from a cross-national study of voluntary workers' motives for helping others for no monetary pay (see the box "Habit and habitat of the good samaritan"). The generalizability of the triangle of cultural adaptations from unpaid volunteers to the entire societal population is clearly questionable. For that reason, in the studies reported below, children and leaders were chosen as highly relevant and broad layers of society that were expected to be subject to the same joint impact of climatic demands and money resources on cooperative culture.

Habit and habitat of the good samaritan

Why do you help someone knocking at your metaphorical door? The wellspring of hospitality and generosity is clear: The one in need could be a god. Gods have the amazing gift of being able to transform helping needy people into helping yourself. Relatedly, a common theme running through all major religions is that you should concern yourself with the well-being of other people, especially when they need your help.

Many folktales and parables with religion-tinted story lines and with barely hidden hints about admirable helping behavior are also doing the rounds. When societies find it necessary to praise helping to the skies and to evolve roles and rules to ensure helping, one can reasonably surmise that people have a natural tendency to be too selfish. Indeed, being ready to help the distressed is not a natural habit. Helping, when it occurs, is seldom motivated by pure altruism, sometimes by pure egoism, but most often by a cooperative combination of both.

Given that most good samaritans on our planet mix altruism and egoism, Xu Huang, Bob Levine, and I became interested in the balance between altruistic and egoistic reasons for helping. No, not financial helping or helping for financial reasons, but the reasons for doing unpaid voluntary work. Altruistic volunteer motives include religious beliefs, a feeling of solidarity with the poor and disadvantaged, and the desire to give people who are suffering hope and dignity. Egoistic volunteer motives include the need for something worthwhile to do, wanting to meet people, and the desire to gain new skills and useful experience. A 33-nation analysis of this tableau of motives for helping others revealed, for example, that the Chinese tend to be higher in altruistic motives, Germans higher in egoistic motives, Italians low in both, and Brazilians high in both. What really excited us was a set of links between the helpers' helping habits and the helpers' country habitats.

In lower income countries with demandingly cold climates such as the Baltic States, voluntary workers had either predominantly altruistic or predominantly egoistic motives. In countries with temperate climates, including those in Southern Europe, altruistic and egoistic reasons for engaging in unpaid volunteer work were unrelated. And in higher income countries with demandingly cold climates such as Norway and Sweden, voluntary workers mingled altruistic and egoistic motives. All of these tendencies held true for both men and women. My advice? Place ads for good samaritans (m/f) in the Scandinavian media.

CLIMATO-ECONOMIC NICHES OF COOPERATIVE CHILDREN

Like animals, humans have the built-in capacity for fight or flight. Humans escaped from this forced-choice cage by inventing and refining financial and nonfinancial cooperation. With exceptions, even cohabitation gradually moved from the battlefield of fighting or flighting to the playing field of cooperating. The clever thing about cooperation is that the animal win-lose code was cracked, was then supplemented with win-win codes, and was finally incorporated into processes of child enculturation. Win-win outcomes, varying from meager compromises to fantastic solutions, result from interactions characterized by less than maximal concern for one's own goals, more than minimal concern for other people's goals, and the like. These compromises and solutions can be reached only if the parties have learned, and are able and willing, to behave unselfishly, prosocially, or both (for details, see Van de Vliert, 1997).

To complicate matters, there are also cooperative variants of fighting and flighting. In fair fighting, for instance, the combatants follow mutually agreed-upon rules of right and wrong behavior to defeat the other. Bach and Wyden (1969) consider openness, honesty, equality, and reciprocity relevant criteria for fair fighting between spouses. The ultimate goal should be to pursue a better mutual relationship with the opponent through fair struggles, not to go for the all-out win through knockout. An illustration of flighting with a cooperative touch is the walk-away negotiation. Buyers, sellers, recruiters, applicants, and others frequently feign the existence of other potential negotiation partners. Even if a person goes so far as to literally walk away, that flight reaction may still represent a manipulative move in a serious game of coming to terms. Compromise in particular often wears the stole and hat of give-and-take bargaining in combination with the mantle of walk-away negotiation.

Adults in different societies value, practice, demonstrate, and teach compromise, problem solving, fair fighting, and walk-away negotiation to a different extent. Their children observe, listen, imitate, and test this whole gamut of modes of conflict handling. Children do not have to reinvent the wheel because, as part of their selfish versus cooperative enculturation, they use social learning tactics like "copy and obey Mom and Dad," "copy and obey the successful," and "go with the majority." These social learning tactics allow them to shortcut costly individual trial-and-error learning and leapfrog directly to adaptive values and practices (Boyd & Richerson, 2005). One may even say that children keep more or less cooperative cultures alive by acquiring negotiating and fair-fighting skills and abilities in a nongenetic way. This application of social learning tactics need not be a subconscious process.

Some scholars postulate that culture is culture only when the owners are not aware of its existence. But culture can also be learned, adapted, and transmitted in conscious ways, as is the case with many do's and dont's. The most fundamental and efficient way to check whether the cultural transmission process indeed occurs is to investigate to what extent the stance of acting unselfishly or prosocially is passed on from old-timers to newcomers and from adults to children. Do adults in more demanding climates find it more important that children learn to be selfish to the extent that their community is poorer? Conversely, are grown-ups coping with harsher climates more strongly in favor of fostering cooperativeness among children to the extent that their community is richer?

To answer this question, the perceived importance of selfish and cooperative enculturation was derived from the 1999–2002 World Values Surveys (source: www.-worldvaluessurvey.org; Inglehart et al., 2004). In interviews, 106,343 adults from 74 nations were asked, "Here is a list of qualities that children can be encouraged to learn at home. Which, if any, do you consider to be especially important?" Among the qualities listed were unselfishness, and tolerance and respect for other people.[3] Each respondent was categorized as endorsing selfish enculturation (considered neither unselfishness nor tolerance and respect for other people important) or cooperative enculturation (considered unselfishness or tolerance and respect for other people important).[4] The percentage of adults who endorsed cooperative enculturation then served as an estimate of each country's degree of cooperative enculturation.[5] The resulting enculturation index ranged from most selfish and least cooperative in Algeria (61%), Romania (62%), and Georgia (64%), via intermediate levels in Belarus (77%), Portugal (77%), and Singapore (78%), to least selfish and most cooperative in the Netherlands (93%), Sweden (94%), and Denmark (95%).

Using the same predictors of demanding climate and national wealth as used in the generalization study reported in Chapter 5, Gerben Van der Vegt, Onne Janssen, and I sought to replicate the by-now familiar triangle of cultural adaptations to climato-economic niches. This was not in vain. Not only did we find a picture of selfish, easygoing, and cooperative enculturation of the world's children (illustrated in Figure 6.1), but we were also able to present this additional triangle as yet another rib of the umbrella of survival, easygoing, and self-expression cultures put up in Chapter 5. Survival versus self-expression values and practices accounted for 42% of the variation in selfish versus cooperative enculturation, including the 31% accounted for by thermal climate and national wealth.[6] It felt like coming home after a trip abroad. Supplementary analyses with respect to the cross-continental generalizability of the results and the exclusion of rival explanations of precipitation and income inequality further strengthened the experience of a homecoming event, with only one exception.

When climate was broken down for winters and summers, colder winters did not receive any complicating help from hotter summers in producing the findings.[7] To get the simple picture in Figure 6.1 right, one needs to read it as follows.[8] In poorer countries in colder climates, notably the Soviet successor states in the lower right corner, adults in the child's environment embrace survival culture; they

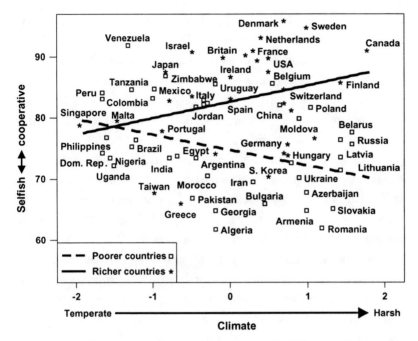

FIGURE 6.1. Effect of more demanding climate on selfish versus cooperative enculturation of children, broken down for poorer and richer countries.

serve as models of selfishness and give lectures about looking after one's own interests first. In poorer and richer countries in temperate climates, such as the Philippines and Singapore in the middle left, easygoing parents and other adults leave few trodden paths of either selfish or cooperative values and practices for the younger generation. Finally, in North America in the upper right corner and in other richer countries in colder climates, adults in the child's environment radiate self-expression culture by setting examples and providing instructions about acting unselfishly or prosocially. And the children? Children are creative copiers, with their originality limited by the originals they copy.

The above results support and exemplify Bronfenbrenner's (1979) ecological perspective, which has influenced the psychology of parenting and child development worldwide. Bronfenbrenner situates the

education and enculturation of children within layers of more prox-
imal and more distal contexts. The child is in interaction with micro-
level environments in the family, in the classroom, during leisure time,
and so forth. These micro-level interactions are embedded within
meso-level environments of the place of residence, the school, the
wider community, and so on. The meso-level interactions in turn
are further embedded within macro-level environments of culture,
politics, economy, and the like. More advantageous contexts are
thought to have a more constructive influence on child development.
In line with this ecological perspective, more advantageous matches of
climatic demands and money resources produce less selfish and more
cooperative enculturation of the next generation of world citizens.

The umbrella function of survival, easygoing, and self-expression
cultures refines our understanding of the differing processes of encul-
turative trade-offs between selfishness and cooperativeness. Driven by
dissatisfaction with life, financial problems, working for survival, and
social distrust, adults in poorer countries with colder-than-temperate
climates overemphasize selfishness, also in front of the children. By
contrast, grown-up inhabitants of richer countries in colder-than-
temperate climates yield and spread more cooperativeness from their
psychosocial seedbeds of physiological and financial rosiness, enjoyment of task achievements, and acceptance of dissimilar others. Apparently, this is how societies throughout the world use adult-child
enculturation to preserve values and practices that transform climatic
and economic contexts into livable ecological niches.

Ample room remains for further research into adult-child relay
of culture conservation. For example, the World Values Surveys also
document the respondent's sex, marital status, and number of children. It would be interesting to see a comparison of mothers' and
fathers' strategies of selfish versus cooperative enculturation of their
children as adaptations to the climato-economic niches in which
their nuclear families have to survive. The change study reported
in Chapter 5 could be repeated for mothers' and fathers' movements

away from selfish toward cooperative enculturation, or the other way round. In addition, other qualities in the list of things that children can be encouraged to learn at home such as saving money, hard work, and obedience also deserve future attention.

For now, we have to make do with the observed enculturation tendencies. It goes almost without saying that climato-economic niches of selfishness and cooperativeness help explain why societies differ so greatly. The daily news reports continue to record huge cross-cultural differences in the amount of conflict that exists and in what people do when conflict occurs (for scientific overviews, see Gelfand & Brett, 2004; Rahim & Blum, 1994; Ross, 1993; Ting-Toomey & Oetzel, 2001; Van de Vliert, Schwartz, et al., 1999). Related to this, outside the focus of the media, societies vary greatly in the degrees to which intimate partners, students, employees, customers, and clients are treated and managed with empathy and helpfulness. These differences in selfishness versus selflessness and competitiveness versus cooperativeness have many roots. One of the least obvious roots, uncovered here, is the functional adaptation of child enculturation to the given context of climatic demands and money resources.

CLIMATO-ECONOMIC NICHES OF DEMOCRATIC LEADERS

According to Yukl (2002), leadership connotes images of powerful, dynamic individuals who shape the course of nations, command victorious armies, or direct corporate empires from atop gleaming skyscrapers. In the same vein, exploits of brave and clever leaders and leader-like heroes, alive or dead, real or imaginary, are the essence of many legends and myths. A people attributes things to its leaders that appear most essential to its existence and culture, such as setting visionary goals, spotting great dangers, overcoming major obstacles, and coming up with important inventions. These processes of creating legends and attributing heroic deeds and feats to leaders suggest that leaders are products of culture rather than producers of culture. This may not be far from the truth. In the long run, leaders may survive only if they help carry their followers' culture forward. In short, if you search for high concentrations of cultural materials, you find leaders.

My search for high concentrations of selfish, easygoing, and cooperative cultures exposed me to the Global Leadership and Organizational Behavior Effectiveness Research Program (GLOBE; Dorfman et al., 2004). Based on the responses of about 17,000 managers from over 900 organizations in countries throughout the world, the GLOBE group described how distinct societies score on perceptions of ineffective and effective leaders. The managers rated how important each of about 100 characteristics and behaviors is for a leader to be "exceptionally skilled at motivating, influencing, or enabling you, others, or groups to contribute to the success of the organization or task." The rating scale ranged from 1 ("greatly inhibits a person from being an outstanding leader") to 7 ("contributes greatly to a person being an outstanding leader"). Country-level indices of leadership ideals were produced for autocratic,[9] self-protective, autonomous, humane-oriented, team-oriented, and charismatic leadership.[10] On theoretical and empirical grounds, for the research reported here, autocratic, self-protective, team-oriented, and charismatic leadership ideals were transformed into a single overarching index ranging from selfish autocratic leadership, via intermediate leadership, to cooperative democratic leadership.[11]

As in the preceding study of child enculturation, two analyses were done: one to test the model of cultural adaptation, and the other to explore whether the results could be subsumed under the umbrella of survival, easygoing, and self-expression cultures. Again, the expectations proved to be correct. Across 60 societies, climatic demands (4%), income per head (13%), and climate and wealth in concert (14%) accounted for 31% of the variation in autocratic versus democratic leadership culture.[12] And, once more, all of these climato-economic differences in autocratic versus democratic leadership culture could be retraced to climato-economic differences in survival versus self-expression culture and their middle ranges of easygoing culture. It will be an eye-opener for many a criticaster that the climato-economics of survival culture and selfish orientation, and of self-expression culture and cooperative orientation, could be corroborated with autocratic and democratic leadership as criteria.

In a two-dimensional space, Figure 6.2 gives the positions of 56 countries on the three dimensions of temperate versus harsh climate, low versus high income per head, and autocratic versus democratic leadership culture (crowding out four others). A quick comparative glance reveals that Figure 6.1 and Figure 6.2 look alike. Both pictures show a downward sloping line for the poorer communities, an upward sloping line for the richer communities, negligible differences between poorer and richer communities in temperate climates, and

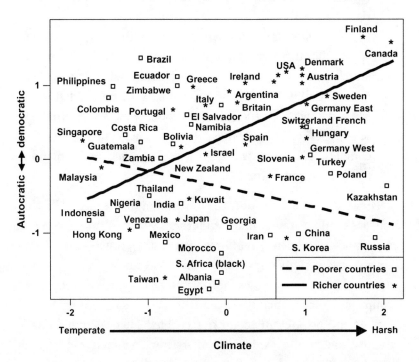

FIGURE 6.2. Effect of more demanding climate on autocratic versus democratic leadership, broken down for poorer and richer countries.

significant differences between poorer and richer communities in harsher climates.[13] In addition, both pictures have been carved out much more by colder winters than by hotter summers or an alliance of colder winters and hotter summers.[14] Taken together, the two triangles reflect consistency, parsimony, and accuracy, and inspire confidence in the following conclusions about leadership cultures.

Although each leader and each leadership culture is unique, there is no denying that a common denominator exists. The leadership ideals and analyses on which Figure 6.2 rests suggest three common denominators.

- More autocratic and relatively selfish leaders thrive in survival cultures that evolve in poorer countries in colder climates, as represented by China, Kazakhstan, and Russia in the lower right corner.
- Leaders who embrace neither autocratic nor democratic approaches thrive in easygoing cultures that evolve in temperate climates irrespective of the collective level of wealth, as represented by Malaysia and Zambia in the middle left.
- More democractic and relatively cooperative leaders thrive in self-expression cultures that evolve in richer countries in colder climates, as represented by Austria, Denmark, and Finland in the upper right corner.

These conclusions support the impression that leaders, like children, are products rather than producers of their culture. Of course, leaders may subsequently reinforce their culture, notably by subconsciously or consciously spreading selfish, easygoing, or cooperative values and practices among subordinates. Data gathered by the Hay-Group among more than 150,000 members of organizational groups in 53 of the 60 GLOBE countries enabled Hein Wendt, Martin Euwema, and me to explore whether team members model their cooperative teamwork[15] on the attitudes of their more or less democratic leaders. In line with the framework of cultural adaptation, we found less cooperative teamwork in poorer countries in more demanding climates but more cooperative teamwork in richer countries in the same climates. We also found that greater endorsement of democratic ideals by their leaders accounts for 60% of team members' greater mutual cooperativeness.[16] This may indicate that followers imitate their leaders or that both more democratic leaders and better teamworkers bring into practice their more cooperative upbringing in harsher and richer climato-economic environments.

If this leader-follower theory survives replication studies, it will help "to describe how, to map where, and to explain why superiors rely on their subordinates as sources of information and as targets of delegation" (Van de Vliert & Smith, 2004, p. 400). All this would provide a set of new insights with important implications. Scholars are challenged to investigate whether changes in national wealth under constant climatic conditions produce changes in leadership construals and to contextualize group-level theories of leadership. Research into expatriates and migratory workers experiencing culture shock after carrying their own leader-follower values and practices into a host country may also be accomplished along lines suggested by the theory. For example, how long does it take migratory workers from cold and poor East European countries and from hot and poor African countries to integrate into cold and rich West European countries?

On a more general note, my observation that leaders are takers rather than makers of their culture may serve as a source of modesty and caution to change agents. Practitioners in nonprofit and profit domains alike must wake up to the reality that climate and cash shape not only hardware amenities such as infrastructures and demographics but also software amenities such as upbringing and leadership. Human resource trainers and consultants can no longer take it for granted that leadership approaches are equally malleable in any direction anywhere. They have to come to grips with robust climato-economic niches of autocratic, easygoing, and democratic leadership culture around the globe.

The current state of the science in the climate-leadership field, most clearly articulated by the GLOBE group (House et al., 2004), is a two-step model of climatic influence on societal culture and, through it, on organizational leadership culture (for empirical evidence, see also Hofstede, 2001; Van de Vliert, 2006b; Van de Vliert & Smith, 2004). A questionable implication of this two-step model is that leadership culture is not part and parcel of societal culture. It may be more fruitful to think of leadership culture not as an indivisible whole but rather as a multilayered phenomenon. In the lower layers, each club, nonprofit organization, and firm separately adapts its leader-follower values and practices to a mosaic of individual-level and group-level factors. Intranational variations in leadership culture are substantial and need to be explained in ways that are not climate related.[17]

In the upper layer of whole societies, all clubs, nonprofit organizations, and firms in a society adapt their leader-follower values and practices to the same overarching conditions outside their own grouping, including climate and wealth in concert. Hence, they share autocratic, democratic, and other leadership components of their national culture. And they may share more. Leadership is a peninsula of the organizational mainland rather than an isolated island. It makes sense, therefore, to propose that the climato-economic theory of culture is generalizable from the occurrence and effectiveness of leadership to the occurrence and effectiveness of other characteristics of organizations. This viewpoint is the starting point of the discussion in the next chapter, which progresses beyond the selfish, easygoing, and cooperative functioning of leaders and followers in a country's organizations.

PROPOSITIONS

6.1. Selfish child enculturation and autocratic leadership cultures thrive in poor societies in demanding climates.

6.2. Easygoing child enculturation and easygoing leadership cultures thrive in societies in temperate climates irrespective of their level of wealth.

6.3. Cooperative child enculturation and democratic leadership cultures thrive in rich societies in demanding climates.

RESEARCH NOTES

1. Again, demanding climate was the sum of the absolute deviations from 22°C for the average lowest and highest temperatures in the coldest winter month and in the hottest summer month. Logged income per head in 1990 was used to predict gender empowerment in 2000 (source: United Nations Development Programme, 2000). Gender empowerment is a composite index of gender equality in three basic dimensions of empowerment – economic participation and decision making, political participation and decision making, and power over economic resources (for a cross-national study of the circumstances in which gender empowerment backfires, see Van de Vliert & Van der Vegt, 2004). Logged income per head in 1985 was used to predict cultural values of gender egalitarianism assessed by the GLOBE group around 1995 (source: House et al., 2004), and logged income per head in 1980 was used to predict Sullivan's (1991) gender gaps in health, marriage, education, employment, and social equality within nations.

2. Joint effect of demanding climate and income per head on gender empowerment in 71 countries, cultural gender egalitarianism in 52 countries, and gender gap in 84 countries.

Predictors	Gender empowerment		Gender egalitarianism		Gender gap	
	B	B	B	B	B	B
Climate (C)	.00	$-.03^{*}$	$.12^{\dagger}$	.11	$-.73$	$-.27$
Income (I)	$.15^{**}$	$.12^{***}$	$.13^{*}$	$.14^{*}$	-2.32^{***}	-1.99^{***}
C × I		$.05^{***}$		$.13^{*}$		-1.36^{***}
ΔR^2	$.69^{***}$	$.06^{***}$	$.22^{***}$	$.06^{*}$	$.38^{***}$	$.05^{***}$
Total R^2	$.69^{***}$	$.75^{***}$	$.22^{**}$	$.28^{***}$	$.38^{***}$	$.43^{***}$

$^{\dagger}p < .10.$ $^{*}p < .05.$ $^{**}p < .01.$ $^{***}p < .001.$

There was no multicollinearity ($VIFs < 2.09$), and there were no outliers (Cook's $Ds < .25$).

3. The interviewees were asked to choose up to 5 especially important qualities out of the following list of 10 qualities that children can be encouraged to learn at home: unselfishness, tolerance and respect for other people, independence, hard work, feeling of responsibility, imagination, thrift, determination, religious faith, and obedience ($0 = not\ important$; $1 = important$). The interviewer gave each quality that was mentioned a code of 1. For the present investigation, interviewees with more than five codes of 1 were removed.

4. A majority of 78% of the respondents endorsed cooperative enculturation, finding unselfishness or tolerance and respect for other people, or both, important.

5. One-way analysis of variance and intraclass correlation coefficients supported the aggregation of individual responses to create the country-level variable for cooperative enculturation. This index was in validatory ways related to indices of altruism and competitiveness (for details, see Van de Vliert, Van der Vegt, & Janssen, in press).

6. Joint effect of demanding climate and income per head on selfish versus cooperative enculturation of children in 74 countries (survival versus self-expression culture was also controlled for).

Predictors	Survival versus self-expression culture uncontrolled for			Survival versus self-expression culture controlled for		
	B	B	B	B	B	B
Culture				5.09^{***}	5.04^{***}	4.82^{***}
Climate (C)	−.42	$−1.77^{\dagger}$	$−1.57^{\dagger}$		−.03	−.09
Income (I)		4.18^{***}	4.89^{***}		.08	.33
C × I			2.83^{**}			.27
ΔR^2	.00	$.22^{***}$	$.09^{**}$	$.42^{***}$	.00	.00
Total R^2	.00	$.22^{***}$	$.31^{**}$	$.42^{***}$	$.42^{***}$	$.42^{***}$

$^{\dagger}p < .10$. $^{*}p < .05$. $^{**}p < .01$. $^{***}p < .001$.

The data refer to 73 countries because Indonesia was an outlier. After removal of Indonesia, there was no multicollinearity ($VIFs < 1.19$), and there were no other outliers (Cook's $Ds < .16$).

7. Joint effect of colder winters and income per head on selfish versus cooperative enculturation of children in 73 countries.

Predictors	B	B	B	B	B
Winters (W)	.59	1.27	−.41	−.51	−.90
Summers (S)	−3.11***	−3.76***	−2.54*	−2.32*	−1.79
W × S		−1.69	−1.04	.57	.62
Income (I)			3.25**	4.14***	4.30***
W × I				3.11***	3.60***
S × I				−.59	−1.04
W × S × I					−1.39
ΔR^2	.14**	.02	.10**	.11**	.01
Total R^2	.14**	.16**	.26***	.37***	.38***

$^{\dagger}p < .10.$ $^{*}p < .05.$ $^{**}p < .01.$ $^{***}p < .001.$

There was no multicollinearity ($VIFs < 2.62$), and there were no outliers (Cook's $Ds < .17$).

8. The simple slopes in Figure 6.1 are both significant: $r(42) = -.36, p < .01$ for poorer countries; $r(31) = .28, p < .06$ for richer countries.

9. As discussed elsewhere (Van de Vliert, 2006a), for unknown and questionable reasons, the characteristics and behaviors of autocratic leadership (elitist, ruler, autocratic, dictatorial, domineering, bossy, nonegalitarian, nondelegator, micro-manager, individually oriented) were reverse coded and labeled *participative leadership*.

10. The aggregatability (average $r_{wg(J)} = .78$; average $ICC_1 = .18$), internal consistency (average Cronbach's $\alpha = .84$), and interrater reliability (average $ICC_2 = .95$) of each of the six leadership ideals were good (for details, see Hanges & Dickson, 2004, pp. 132–137, 147–148). In addition, ample evidence shows measurement equivalence and construct validity of the information in the profile of leadership ideals across the 61 societies from 58 countries (Van de Vliert & Einarsen, 2008).

11. To eliminate response bias in scale use, GLOBE's six leadership ideals were centered around their mean score within each of the 61 societies from 58 countries. Factor analysis produced a bipolar factor that predicted 77% of the variance in autocratic, self-protective, team-oriented, and charismatic leadership ideals. Autocratic (−.87) and

self–protective (–.83) leadership ideals loaded on the autocratic and
selfish pole; team-oriented (.85) and charismatic (.96) leadership
ideals loaded on the opposite democratic and cooperative pole of
this dimension. After removal of an outlier (Qatar = –3.20), the final
autocratic versus democratic leadership index ranged from –.1.80 in
Egypt (high selfishness, low cooperativeness) to +1.61 in Finland (low
selfishness, high cooperativeness).

12. Joint effect of demanding climate and income per head on autocratic
versus democratic leadership ideals in 60 societies from 57 countries
(survival versus self-expression culture in 49 countries was also controlled for).

Predictors	Survival versus self-expression culture uncontrolled for			Survival versus self-expression culture controlled for		
	B	B	B	B	B	B
Culture				.59***	.51**	.39*
Climate (C)	.18	.09	.10		.07	.07
Income (I)		.34**	.29**		.09	.14
C × I			.37***			.20
ΔR^2	.04	.13**	.14***	.38***	.01	.02
Total R^2	.04	.17**	.31***	.38***	.39***	.41***

$^{\dagger}p < .10.$ $^{*}p < .05.$ $^{**}p < .01.$ $^{***}p < .001.$

Income (I) was the logged purchasing-power income per head
in 1995 (source: United Nations Development Programme, 1998).
There was no multicollinearity (*VIFs* < 2.88), there were no outliers
(Cook's *Ds* < .15), and the results survived attacks by the rival predictors of precipitation and income inequality.

The analyses were repeated six times; income per head in 1995
was replaced with income per head in 1990, 1985, 1980, 1975,
1970, and 1965. This showed that it takes 10 years for the interactive impact of climatic demands and income per head to reach
its maximum effect on autocratic versus democratic leadership
culture (an increase from $\Delta R^2 = .14$ in 1995 to $\Delta R^2 = .16$ in
1985; $n = 52$). Nevertheless, the more conservative 1995 estimates

are reported because they cover 60 societies from 57 instead of 52 countries.

13. As expected, the simple slopes in Figure 6.2 tend to be significant in both richer countries [$r(30) = .56, p < .001$] and poorer countries [$r(30) = -.26, p < .08$], whereas the simple slopes for the impact of income per head on the endorsement of a less autocratic and more democratic leadership culture is significant in harsher climates [$r(30) = .65, p < .001$], but not in temperate climates [$r(30) = .01$, n.s.].

14. Joint effect of colder winters, hotter summers, and income per head on autocratic versus democratic leadership ideals in 60 societies from 57 countries.

Predictors	B	B	B	B	B
Winters (W)	.25*	.37**	.25†	.12	.11
Summers (S)	−.19	−.23*	−.19	−.06	−.08
W × S			−.24	−.18	.08	.02
Income (I)			.27*	.26*	.24*
W × I				.35**	.42**
S × I				.22†	.21†
W × S × I					−.15
ΔR^2	.12*	.03	.08*	.12**	.01
Total R^2	.12*	.15**	.23**	.35***	.36***

$^\dagger p < .10.$ $^* p < .05.$ $^{**} p < .01.$ $^{***} p < .001.$

There was no multicollinearity (*VIFs* < 2.42), and there were no outliers (Cook's *Ds* < .30).

15. Cooperative teamwork was measured using five statements, including "The people in my work group are always willing to provide help in getting the work done," "People in my work group will gladly take on other people's responsibilities in an emergency," and "People in my work group are willing to make sacrifices to get the job done" (6-point scale; Cronbach's $\alpha = .83$).

16. Joint effect of demanding climate and income per head on cooperative teamwork in 53 countries (autocratic versus democratic leadership ideals were also controlled for).

Predictors	Leadership ideals uncontrolled for			Leadership ideals controlled for		
	B	B	B	B	B	B
Leadership				$.08^{***}$	$.08^{***}$	$.06^{*}$
Climate (C)	.01	.01	.00		−.01	−.01
Income (I)		.01	.01		−.01	−.01
C × I			$.08^{***}$			$.06^{*}$
ΔR^2	.00	.01	$.17^{***}$	$.18^{***}$	.01	$.07^{*}$
Total R^2	.00	.01	$.18^{***}$	$.18^{***}$	$.19^{***}$	$.26^{***}$

$^{\dagger}p < .10.$ $^{*}p < .05.$ $^{**}p < .01.$ $^{***}p < .001.$

Income (I) was the logged purchasing-power income per head in 1995 (source: United Nations Development Programme, 1998). There was no multicollinearity ($VIFs < 1.42$), and there were no outliers (Cook's $Ds < .33$).

17. For the results of a cross-level study of the egoistic and altruistic work motives of 13,584 individual volunteers nested within 33 nations, see the box "Habit and habitat of the good samaritan."

7

Organization

Just as the cheetah survives by speed, and hawks survive by their eyesight, humans survive by their ability to function in organizations.
Adapted from Johnson and Johnson, 1989, p. 3

"I am Evert Van de Vliert from Groot Donkelaar in Woudenberg in Utrecht in the Netherlands in Europe in the World." Every child discovers that each environment is nested inside a wider environment, like a set of Russian dolls. Why, then, do scholars disregard their childhood discovery by no longer unpeeling environments layer by layer before they reach the layer of climate? Potentially short-sighted insights are the result, also in the organizational sciences. My aim in this book is to present a longer sighted view of the so-far neglected impact of climate and financial compensation of climate on the survival function of work in organizations. In the preceding chapters, working for money or for achievement and endorsing autocratic or democratic organizational leadership have already been insightfully related to climate and cash, and to the inherent gratification of survival needs. Climato-economically anchored differences in how organizations are shaped would link up logically with such findings.

Globalization in the form of a worldwide tendency toward uniformization of culture in organizational settings is here to stay. Nonetheless, a growing number of cross-national differences in organizational structures and strategies is lining up before the doors of science, each ignorantly waiting to perhaps be declared a distant descendant of climate and cash. Trompenaars (1993, pp. 142–144), for example, gathered nonverbal data by showing managers from 39 countries a card with five triangles differing in steepness versus flatness. He asked the managers to think of the company they worked for in terms of these steeper and flatter "pine trees" and to pick the one that best represented their own company. A reanalysis of his data[1] revealed that the steepness of work organizations is indeed related to complex combinations of climate and wealth. The steepest organizations are found in poorer countries with temperate to demanding climates such as China, Ethiopia, Turkey, and Venezuela; the flattest organizations are found in richer countries with demanding climates in North America and Northern Europe.

These ecological markers of company steepness suggest that organizations, too, are modified in response to their climato-economic environments. Steeper organizations are usually more centralized and more formalized at the same time. In the section "Cultural Adaptations of Organizations," the adjustment of formalization and centralization to the contextual conditions of thermal climate and collective wealth is discussed. This is followed by reports of empirical research into the climato-economic niches of organizational structures and strategies, and a 116-nation illustration of the findings with regard to the occurrence of nepotism. The propositions at the end profess that bureaucratic, easygoing, and adhocratic organizations thrive in distinct regions around the globe.

CULTURAL ADAPTATIONS OF ORGANIZATIONS

Since the 1960s, steep versus flat organizations have been examined as variants of bureaucratic versus adhocratic constructions of task coordination (for overviews, see Burns & Stalker, 1966; Mintzberg, 1979; Morgan, 1986). Typical illustrations of bureaucratic organizations are McDonald's, a confectionery factory, a ministry, and a prison. They represent rigid constructions with much formalization, much centralization, and stable products for stable groups of customers (or clients, patients, students, or any other trade name for customer). Typical illustrations of adhocratic organizations are Google, a space agency, and an organizational consultancy firm. They represent flexible constructions with little formalization, little centralization, much training, and changing products for changing groups of customers. Every country abounds with bureaucratic and adhocratic organizations, and also a wide variety of mixtures and mutations. Highly similar skylines of steep and austere versus flat and ornate organizations are to be found everywhere.

This is not to say that basically the same bicycle factory is equally bureaucratic everywhere, nor that similar editorial offices of mass media outlets are equally adhocratic the world over. Rather, the above-mentioned cross-national differences in company steepness (Trompenaars, 1993) suggest that comparable bureaucratic organizations are more bureaucratic in some countries than in others, and that comparable adhocratic organizations are likewise more adhocratic in some countries than in others. In my search for a possible explanation of the underlying differences in formalization and centralization, the climato-economic perspective of cultural adaptations to national contexts has led to the following back-to-basics line of reasoning.

Climate-based survival needs have created the right conditions for the invention of money, the invention of work, and their innovative integration into paid work. Paid work is a superb form of cooperative exchange and the all-important building material of factories, institutions, and the like, except volunteer organizations. Money, work, and trading money for work are extremely important in any organization. So, for the overarching process of cultural adaptation, it may make little difference whether the work is primarily paid for in cash or in other resources such as experience and belongingness that can be converted into cash sooner or later.

Indeed, the existence of climato-economic niches of survival, easy-going, and self-expression cultures may well imply that all organizations are secretly penetrated by homey values and practices, leaving phantomlike cultural traces of climate and cash.

Reference to rigid versus flexible organizations as expressions of culture in the form of socially constructed realities introduces a building metaphor reminding us of the tenet of modern architectural theory that form follows function. We certainly find ourselves thinking about social constructions when we relate the forms of organization to the need-satisfying functioning of their members. Employees build and rebuild the bureaucratic or adhocratic organization in which they work to satisfy their daily needs for thermal comfort, nutrition, and health of themselves and their families. This continuous process of construing and constructing the bureaucratic or adhocratic organization is thought to shape vertical leader-follower coordination, horizontal subordinate-subordinate coordination, and diagonal subordinate-staff coordination.

As discussed below, survival cultures thriving in poor countries with demanding climates are thought to emphasize formalization, centralization, and stability, and are thus home to bureaucratic structures and strategies. By contrast, self-expression cultures thriving in rich countries with demanding climates are thought to emphasize flexibilization, decentralization, and change, and are thus home to adhocratic structures and strategies. Finally, as already mentioned, easygoing cultures thriving in temperate climates are expected to take up middle positions between these extremes, and are thus home to neither clear-cut bureaucratic nor clear-cut adhocratic structures and strategies.

Survival Cultivates Bureaucratic Organization

Inhabitants of poor countries with demanding climates are concerned with survival values and practices. It has been shown in the preceding chapters that they carry a heavy burden. They feel unhappy and unhealthy. Adults, working more for money than for achievement, deem it necessary to enlist their children in the struggle to survive as a family. They also encourage their children to behave egoistically. In general, people think it necessary to be very careful about trusting other people, with the consequence that they endorse autocratic rather than democratic leadership. The same people, with the same materialistic and egoistic lenses, and the same fundamental attitudes of dissatisfaction and distrust, are the architects and construction workers of organizations as systems of task coordination. They push and pull the organizational coordination in more bureaucratic and less adhocratic directions for obvious reasons to do with control.

To the extent that people work for money rather than achievement, there has to be more control of what they do in return for the money. Additionally, the more egoistic and autocratic the employees, the more control is needed to check whether individuals and groups subordinate their own interests to the general interest. On top of this, a more dissatisfied workforce will have to be controlled more because of its lower job commitment. Last but not least, members of a more distrustful workforce have a stronger inclination to spy on one another using control mechanisms. Taken together, *organization constructers* in survival cultures have an obsession with control and therefore ensure that a control mentality pervades the organization to be built or rebuilt. The key coordinating mechanisms of formalization and centralization come in handy as they are also key control mechanisms. More formalization ties the workers more securely to behavioral prescriptions that guide and control work activities and outputs. More centralization places the power of decision making and control in the hands of fewer people at the top. Appointing relatives to key positions, a form of nepotism, may function as a supplementary means of formalizing and centralizing control.

In short, survival cultures foster standardization and stability, with the consequence that more bureaucratic and less adhocratic organizations predominate in poorer societies in more demanding climates (for highly similar arguments, see Landes, 1998). Bureaucratic organizations have stable structural components and dynamic strategic components. Structurally, organizations in clearer survival cultures have more regulations, more stringent enforcement routines, and larger power differences between higher-ups and lower-downs. Strategically, these organizations are increasingly more internally oriented and increasingly less externally oriented. They have stronger process-product orientations finding expression in efficient and effective use of natural and financial resources, and human resources as tail-end Charlie. Managerially, organizations in clearer survival cultures rely more on patterns of authority in which bureaucratic structures are integrated with bureaucratic strategies and less on professional managers, often squeezing out employee interests.

Self-Expression Cultivates Adhocratic Organization

In demanding climates money makes the difference between self-protection worries and self-expression worries. Self-protection is a must for members of poor societies in demanding climates, self-expression for members of rich societies in demanding climates. In spite of their common prefix, self-protection is more selfish and less social than self-expression. From early childhood, inhabitants of richer countries with more demanding climates are given more encouragement to behave cooperatively, and apparently not in vain. As adults, they tend to trust rather than distrust other people and embrace democratic rather than autocratic leadership ideals. This cooperative stance is part of their overall motivation to do work that gives them a feeling of accomplishment[2] and is further associated with feelings of happiness[3] and health.[4] One of their cooperative, challenging, and omnipresent tasks is the creation of organizations with satisfactory patterns of mutual coordination.

Workers in survival cultures typically have an obsession with control; workers in self-expression cultures typically have an obsession with creation. And control and creation are not on friendly terms. Control aims to maintain established practices that creation strives to break away from. Joint creation, or cooperation, sacrifices control as the parties involved break away from their own interests and opinions in creating compromises and solutions. Compromising and problem solving are entrepreneurial operations because neither the necessary reciprocity in the negotiation partner's behavior nor the necessary innovative aspects of the mutual agreement can be one-sidedly controlled (Van de Vliert, 1997). Self-expression through a major individual achievement is not without risk, because of counteractive circumstances and the often insuperable difficulty of creatively building castles in the air. Workers in self-expression cultures do not avoid these challenges, they seek them.

Self-expressionists prefer to build organizations on pillars of creativity, self-development, trust, and cooperation. They push and pull the inevitable coordination in less bureaucratic and more adhocratic directions. Standardization of work and numerous other behavioral prescriptions make way for informal brainstorming, constant mutual adjustment, and occasional task rotation. Power equality is enhanced through decentralization so as to create optimal conditions for conjoint creativity and growth. A telling case in point is the finding reported in Chapter 6 that managers of organizations in self-expression cultures cheer team-oriented leadership to the echo. In a similar vein, market-based units, flexible networks of function-by-project cells, and temporary interdisciplinary teams of experts gain in popularity. In self-expression cultures, ad hoc is in vogue.

All this boils down to the expectation that members of richer societies in more demanding climates will construct less bureaucratic and more adhocratic organizations that emphasize self-expression at the expense of formalization and centralization. Structurally, organizations in clearer self-expression cultures have weaker systems of regulations and sanctions, and smaller power differences. Strategically, these organizations are increasingly less internally oriented and increasingly more externally oriented. They have stronger customer orientations as a result of targeting the expectations, preferences, and evaluations of their sellers and buyers. Managerially, more adhocratic organizations in more developed countries with more demanding climates rely less on bureaucratic authorities and more on professional managers who, in turn, rely more on subordinates as sources of information and as targets of delegation.

Easygoing Organizations

In terms of the building metaphor, easygoingness refers to architectural freedom for individuals, groups, and organizations. When constructing their own work environment, individuals tend to be free from the Scylla of self-protection worries and the Charybdis of self-expression worries. There is little reason for individual obsession with control or creation. Groups tend to be free from the Scylla of collective belittlement through formalization and centralization and the Charybdis of collective blame for missing opportunities and messing up in hectic situations. Neither an internal nor an external group orientation predominates. The total workforce of the organization tends to be free from the straitjacket of the bureaucratic template, on the one hand, and the strain of the adhocratic template, on the other. This niche in which there is no pushing and pulling of organizational coordination in clear-cut bureaucratic or clear-cut adhocratic directions is bound to be found in societies with easygoing cultures in temperate climates.

CLIMATO-ECONOMIC NICHES
OF ORGANIZATIONAL STRUCTURES

For the theory of cultural adaptations of organizations to climato-economic contexts to hold true, formalization and centralization have to move in tandem. Much formalization in conjunction with much centralization, representing bureaucratic organizational structures, should typify poorer societies in more demanding climates. Moderate formalization in conjunction with moderate centralization, representing easygoing organizational structures, should typify poor and rich societies in temperate climates. And little formalization in conjunction with little centralization, representing adhocratic organizational structures, should typify richer societies in more demanding climates. This set of predictions was tested by examining whether thermal climate and collective income can foretell the specified degrees of formalization and centralization.

An appropriate pair of indicators for exploring the typical degrees of formalization and centralization in a country's organizations is available from the worldwide GLOBE surveys (House et al., 2004).[5] The GLOBE group defined formalization or uncertainty avoidance as "the extent to which members of collectives seek orderliness, consistency, structure, formalized procedures, and laws to cover situations in their daily lives" (Sully de Luque & Javidan, 2004, p. 603). Centralization or power distance was "the degree to which members of an organization or society expect and agree that power should be shared unequally" (Carl et al., 2004, p. 537). Four sets of five questions were developed to tap formalization values, formalization practices, centralization values, and centralization practices. Here, the more general formalization and centralization *values* were used,[6] because their occurrence is less dependent on coincidental circumstances than is the occurrence of the more specific formalization and centralization *practices*.

The impact of climate on the cultural combination of formalization and centralization, broken down for poorer and richer countries,[7] is mapped out and illustrated with country positions in Figure 7.1. A close cousin of the familiar triangle of survival, easygoing, and self-expression cultures surfaced at a different angle, as if pressed down by an invisible hand. The upward-sloping trend line for the poorer countries indicates that more demanding climates tend to go

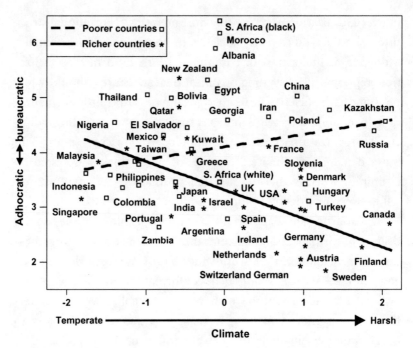

FIGURE 7.1. Effect of more demanding climate on adhocratic versus bureaucratic organizational structures, broken down for poorer and richer countries.

hand in hand with much more formalization and somewhat more centralization. By contrast, the downward-sloping trend line for the richer countries indicates that more demanding climates go hand in hand with less formalization and less centralization.[8] Thus, we find the most bureaucracy-minded societies in poorer countries with more demanding climates, such as China and Kazakhstan, in the upper right corner, and the most adhocracy-minded societies in richer countries with more demanding climates, including Austria and Finland, in the lower right corner.

After close scrutiny of Figure 7.1, critics may draw attention to religion as an alternative explanation of the cross-national differences in organizational structures. Islamic societies in Morocco,

Albania, Egypt, Iran, Kuwait, and Qatar have much higher degrees of cultural formalization and centralization than the Protestant and Roman Catholic societies in Sweden, Finland, Germany, Ireland, Spain, and Argentina. However, these religious differences cannot explain away the findings. When the analysis was repeated three times, with the national proportions of Muslims, Protestants, and Roman Catholics, respectively, controlled for, next to nothing happened.[9] The variation in the degree of bureaucracy accounted for by climate and wealth in concert decreased from 11% to 9% under the Islamic spotlight, from 11% to 7% under the Protestant spotlight, and from 11% to 9% under the Roman Catholic spotlight. This suggests that the cultural adaptation of organizational structures is not primarily dependent on religion.

Another rival explanation of the variation in organizational structures around the globe concentrates on the kind of work the economically active part of the population is involved in. Countries with higher percentages of employment in the industry sector have more bureaucratic organizations; countries with higher percentages of employment in the services sector have more adhocratic organizations. If the poorer societies in more demanding climates make their money mainly in the industry sector, more bureaucratic structures may be more appropriate; if the richer societies in more demanding climates make their money mainly in the services sector, more adhocratic structures may be more appropriate (Mintzberg, 1979). However, the impact of the economic sector cannot account for the observed climato-economic effects on the organizational structures that are prevalent in differing societal cultures.[10] These supplementary results, too, suggest that the model of bureaucratic, easygoing, and adhocratic adaptation of organizations has wide applicability.

To examine the extent to which the climatic extremes of cold and heat contributed to the results, the analysis was repeated also for the separate and joint effects of harsher winters and summers. These extra computations revealed that demanding cold and demanding heat are both important, but that colder winters bear much more responsibility for the findings than do hotter summers.[11] Precipitation and income inequality did not destroy or spoil the overall picture. Bureaucratic structures prevail in the ecological niches of survival cultures, intermediate bureaucratic-adhocratic structures in the ecological niches of easygoing cultures, and adhocratic structures in the ecological niches of self-expression cultures.

It is common knowledge that organizations have to function in, and adjust to, increasingly complex and dynamic environments. Each organization's environment is literally the world providing economic contexts, social contexts, technological contexts, and political contexts, all at local, national, and global levels. It is equally common, in our handbooks and classrooms, to completely ignore the relevance of the climatic context of organizations. Does this failure to recognize any climatic impact whatsoever reflect a more general scientific taboo? Do we perhaps share a hidden common interest in not admitting that nature imposes limits on our free will and freedom of action?

CLIMATO-ECONOMIC NICHES
OF ORGANIZATIONAL STRATEGIES

The pattern of decisions and actions workers take to achieve the organizational goals is their strategy. It normally includes the meta-strategy to gain competitive advantage and to outperform rivals by producing the same products at lower costs, better products, better service, and the like. Bureaucratic companies typically develop strategies to manufacture standard products such as Big Macs for mass markets or low-cost products such as tricycles or racing bikes for niche markets. The resulting bureaucratic policies separate strategy formulation from strategy implementation. Those policies highlight top-down planning and controlling, are primarily directed at the work environment inside the organization, and emphasize the reduction of the costs of production.

Adhocratic companies, by contrast, typically develop strategies to sell added-value products such as GSM phones to mass markets or to sell tailor-made products such as organizational advice to niche markets. The accompanying adhocratic policies integrate strategy formulation and implementation, highlight bottom-up innovation and change, and adjust their products to the work environment of customers and to new developments outside the organization. Although every country has bureaucratic as well as adhocratic organizations, the model of cultural adaptations of organizations predicts that bureaucratic strategies will thrive in poor countries with demanding climates, and adhocratic strategies in rich countries with demanding climates.

Research into worldwide differences in organizational strategies is rare, with one notable exception. The World Economic Forum in Geneva publishes an annual global competitiveness report based on surveys among top executives from randomly sampled companies in countries on all inhabited continents (with one respondent per firm). This executive opinion survey captures a broad array of factors, including company strategies dealing with the nature of competitive advantage, auditing, and accounting standards, capacity for innovation, human resource management, customer orientation, corporate social responsibility, and so forth. One edition of the survey (World Economic Forum, 2000) contained a forced-choice question that tapped adhocratic versus bureaucratic strategies.

In total, 4,022 executives from 59 countries indicated that the main strategy of their firm was based on one of the following five policies ranging from adhocratic differentiation of products to bureaucratic reduction of costs:

(a) differentiates our product from our competitors' based on service;

(b) differentiates our product from our competitors' based on
   product design or image;
(c) low cost based on product or process technology;
(d) low cost based on favorable costs of skilled workers;
(e) low cost based on low wages or natural resource availability.

An adhocratic-intermediate-bureaucratic strategy index was
constructed by adding the national percentages of firms that aimed
to achieve bureaucratic cost reduction through (d) or (e) and sub-
tracting the national percentages of firms that aimed to achieve
adhocratic product differentiation through (a) or (b).[12] This somewhat crude measure has the advantage of reflecting various strategies
and the disadvantage of being rather heterogeneous. Ample attention was therefore paid to the cross-national reliability,[13] equivalence,[14] and validity[15] of this strategy index before it was related to
the ecological framework of climate and wealth. Most important, the
occurrence of less adhocratic and thus more bureaucratic strategies
appeared to be related to more formalization and less externally
directed customer and market orientations.

The joint impact of climate and collective income on bureaucratic organizational operations was estimated twice—first without
taking into account the kind of business that is prevalent in each
country, then controlling for the size of the industry and services
sectors.[16] In addition, it was made certain that precipitation, income
inequality, religion, former communist rule, and a range of other
ambassadors of alternative explanations did not survive empirical
analysis. This time, yet another close cousin of the familiar triangle
of survival, easygoing, and self-expression cultures seemed to be
tilted by an invisible hand (see Figure 7.2). The upward slope for
poorer countries, here indicating increasing bureaucracy, is steeper
than usual. And the downward slope for richer countries, here indicating increasing adhocracy, is significantly different from a perfectly
horizontal line only if the service strategy [option (a)] is left out of

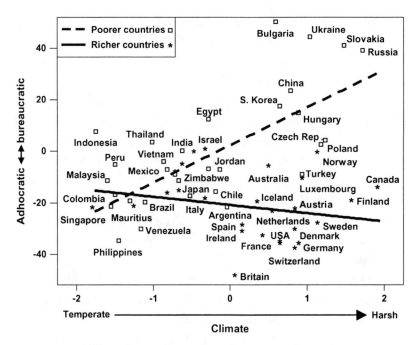

FIGURE 7.2. Effect of more demanding climate on adhocratic versus bureaucratic organizational strategies, broken down for poorer and richer countries.

consideration.[17] Hence, even though companies in richer countries with more demanding climates do not adopt more or better service strategies, there is considerable support for the proposed model of more and fewer bureaucratic adaptations of organizations to climato-economic niches.

Compared with Bulgaria, Ukraine, Slovakia, Russia, China, and South Korea in the upper right corner, Britain, Switzerland, Germany, France, the United States, and Denmark in the lower right corner employ fewer bureaucratic and more adhocratic strategies to make money. The countries named first have relatively large industry sectors, the countries named last relatively large services sectors. This raises the question of how the cultural adaptation unfolds. Is the niche combination of climatic demands and poverty more suitable for bureaucratic strategies, with more industrial work and less service work as a consequence? Or is this climato-economic niche more suitable for industrial work and less suitable for service work, with more bureaucratic strategies as a consequence? If an analysis of cross-sectional data can get us any closer to the truth, the results contain some clear answers. The climato-economic niches lead to more bureaucratic strategies or more adhocratic strategies first, which in turn lead to a larger industry sector or a larger services sector, respectively. And poorer peoples in countries with harsher winters, hotter summers, or both, evolve especially strong inclinations to push and pull organizational strategies in more bureaucratic directions.[18]

The findings that organizational structures and strategies are fine-tuned to climato-economic niches have numerous implications. Bureaucratic, easygoing, and adhocratic patterns of organization radiate into all elements and levels of collective and individual functioning. They affect the choice of key coordinating mechanisms, the importance of key parts of the organization, the flow of decision making, the specialization of jobs, the training and indoctrination of employees, and so on (Mintzberg, 1979). If we were to compare the bureaucratic templates of all McDonald's fast-food restaurants around the globe, we would find thousands of small easygoing adaptations in poor and rich countries with temperate climates, and thousands of small adhocratic adaptations in rich countries with demanding climates. And we would have to conclude that even the McDonaldization of the world (Ritzer, 2004) must obey the rules of climato-economics.

NEPOTISM: A 116-NATION ILLUSTRATION

Nepotism in the form of appointing relatives to key managerial positions is addressed here as a supplementary means of formalizing and centralizing control. Nepotism is also addressed because of its broad interdisciplinary relevance. Psychologists, sociologists, and economists can easily relate nepotism to discriminatory we-they thinking, individualism versus collectivism, global business competitiveness, and more. Additionally, nepotism appears to play a pivotal interdisciplinary role as both a social consequence and a social cause of a country's economic circumstances.

At first blush, favoritism shown to relatives by giving them influential leadership positions and organizational bureaucracy seem to have little in common. On closer consideration, however, both are born of an obsession with control, both place ultimate decision making in the hands of few people, and both tend to create large power differences between "haves" and "have-nots." No wonder family-member managers are prone to having bureaucratic rather than adhocratic identities—shunning innovation, professional management, and the empowerment of as many competent employees as possible.

In precapitalist and more feudal societies in which family businesses and privately held companies dominate, bureaucratic and nepotistic tendencies seem to be more common (Robertson, 2002; Trompenaars, 1993). In Chad, Tajikistan, and Timor-Leste, for example, organizations tend to be more often managed top-down by close-knit groups of families than elsewhere. Mirrorwise, in so-called modernized nations such as Denmark, Spain, and the United States, organizations seem to be relatively often led by democratic professionals chosen on the basis of their superior expertise. But organizational size seems to be a complicating issue. As a rule, smaller organizations have more family-member managers whereas larger organizations have more professional managers.

Given the complication of organizational size, a case for climato-economic niches of bureaucracy-minded nepotism can convincingly be made only if the following holds true. As an integral part of survival cultures, many relatives and few professionals manage both smaller and larger organizations in poor countries with demanding climates. Conversely, peoples enacting self-expression cultures in harsh-rich niches tend to appoint few relatives and many professionals to lead smaller as well as larger organizations. And moderate numbers of relatives and professionals manage any-size organizations in countries with temperate climates. Data provided by top executives of 10,932 firms from 116 nations[19] (World Economic Forum, 2005) allowed a test of these implications of the finding that bureaucratic, easygoing, and adhocratic organizations thrive in distinct regions around the globe. The sample was drawn from a master list of companies in each country, which most closely represented the spectrum of companies grouped by economic sector, geographical region, and size. The 116 nations sampled covered 94% of the world population and 98% of the gross world product.

The executives responded to the following 7-point statement. "Senior management positions in your country are usually held by" (1) = professional managers chosen based on superior qualification, (4) = neither professional managers nor relatives, (7) = relatives. This stimulus yielded reliable[20] and valid[21] information. In Azerbaijan, Bolivia, and Chad, senior-management positions are more likely to be held by relatives; in Britain, New Zealand, and the United States, they are more likely to be held by professionals. There was an impressive 40% overlap of reported increases in nepotism and factual decreases in the average size of the country's organizations.[22] In consequence, I ran conservative analyses in which the entire overlapping area was cut out, so that the impact of organizational size could no longer confound the impact of climate and wealth on nepotism.

The first analysis showed that the climato-economic niches of bureaucratic, easygoing, and adhocratic organizations are also the respective niches of relatives, neither relatives nor professionals, and professionals as senior managers. Controlling for industry sector and services sector strengthened rather than weakened this result.[23] Figure 7.3 contains 116 data points, 65 country labels, and 2 trend lines for poorer and richer countries. The trend lines mark off the expected triangle of degrees of nepotism. A combination of demanding climate and poverty pushes and pulls the occupancy of top positions toward nepotism (see China, Mongolia, and Kazakhstan in the upper right corner). In affluent countries, similarly demanding climates push and pull the occupancy of top positions away from nepotism (see Estonia, Canada, and Finland in the lower right corner). For peoples in temperate climates, such as the Indonesians, the Mauritians, and the Guyanese, collective wealth does not make much difference in the appointment or reappointment of senior managers, which completes another replica of the triangle of survival, easygoing, and self-expression cultures[24] (for an even more fundamental explanation of culture in terms of climate-related mortality salience, see the box "Mortals organizing mortals").

The present observation that nepotism peaks in poor countries with demanding climates complements the earlier observation reported in Chapter 5 that ethnocentrism in the form of rejecting foreigners, homosexuals, and people with AIDS also peaks in poor countries with demanding climates. Apparently, nepotism and ethnocentrism are two of a kind.[25] Nepotism represents the we-side of positive social discrimination, ethnocentrism the they-side of negative social discrimination. Together they support the overarching conclusion that we-they thinking thrives in typical harsh-poor climato-economic niches of survival cultures.

The case of China is particularly striking and intriguing. Right now, it is the only country in the world to combine strong nepotism, strong ethnocentrism, and strong sustained economic growth. As nepotism and ethnocentrism undermine mutual trust and harmony while underpinning mutual distrust and discord between in-groups and out-groups, they may well stand in the way of economic cooperation and progress. Consequently, unless

184   *Survival, Cooperation, and Organization*

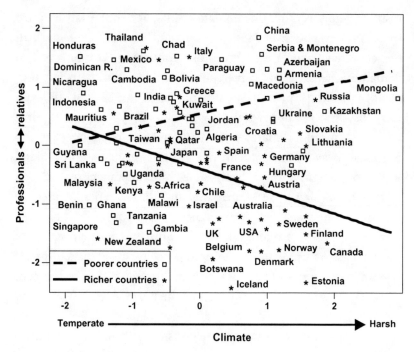

FIGURE 7.3 Effect of more demanding climate on nepotism (relatives rather than professionals as managers), broken down for poorer and richer countries.

Mortals organizing mortals

Living is tossing the coin of basic needs with its sides of death and survival. Nowhere will the death side land facing up more often than among the poor losing the battle against harsh climates. And nowhere will the survival side land facing up more often than among the rich successfully coping with harsh climates. In temperate climates where death is less of a threat and survival less of a challenge, the death-survival coin rolls out of sight.

From the basic perspective of needs for thermal comfort, nutrition, and health, mortality is more noticeable and important in some societies than in others. Mortality is maximally salient in poor societies in climates with bitter winters or scorching summers, moderately salient in temperate climates, and minimally salient in rich societies in taxing cold or hot climates. Thus, societies have different psychological distances from death, and it would be a miracle if the experience of nearness or remoteness of death were to be without consequence.

Research findings show that different distances from death lead people to organize life differently (Dechesne & Kruglanski, 2004; Solomon et al., 2004). Mortality salience enhances the quest for certainty and for knowledge that gives something to hold on to. Mortality salience also increases the inclination to favor *us* above *them*, members of the in-group above members of the out-group. Building on these findings, I got the futuristic brainwave that organizers with different distances from death construe and construct different organizations.

Greater mortality salience leads organizers to place greater emphasis on certainty-producing rules and standardization of objectives and processes. Consequently, templates of bureaucratic structures and strategies are highly prevalent among the poor in cold or hot regions. But practitioners build less rigid organizations in regions with temperate climates, and even more flexible organizations in rich cold or hot regions.

Greater mortality salience also leads organizers to have stronger preferences for recruiting and appointing relatives as managers, because relatives belong to *us*. So, relatives are popular as managers in poor countries with harsh climates whereas professional managers are popular in rich countries with harsh climates. In temperate climates, with moderate degrees of mortality salience, a country's organizations are managed by a more balanced representation of relatives and professionals.

In short, we all know that we must die. We also know that our future death influences our doings today. And sooner or later we'll discover that, deep down in their doings, organizers pick structures, strategies, and managers on the basis of their own distance from death. One day we'll realize organizers are spin doctors of Father Death.

China finds ways to fight nepotism and ethnocentrism and develop counterstrategies, its economic boom may be bound to level off and plateau or decline in the near future. In Serbia and Montenegro, and in other countries, nepotism and ethnocentrism are also pushing and pulling in directions that keep survival cultures in place.

Breakdowns of Figure 7.3 for precipitation and income inequality failed to yield supplementary information. But the breakdown of harsh climate for cold and hot seasons was very interesting indeed.[26] Visual inspection of these additional findings revealed that the upward nepotism trend for poorer countries is the result of colder winters only; the downward nepotism trend for richer countries is affected by both colder winters and hotter summers. In richer countries, (a) too little climatic stress from temperate winters and temperate summers increases nepotism, (b) optimal climatic stress from either extremely cold winters and temperate summers, or temperate winters and extremely hot summers, decreases nepotism, and (c) too much climatic stress from extremely cold winters and extremely hot summers increases nepotism.

In the studies reported in Chapters 3 and 4, the same breakdowns for too little and too much climatic stress led to exactly the same pattern of results for happiness, subjective health, and child labor in richer countries. Apparently, in addition to bringing out stark black-and-white contrasts in culture between poorer and richer countries, climatic demands add shades of white-gray nuances to culture in the richer group of countries. In richer countries, feelings of happiness and healthiness are strongest, and practices of child labor and nepotism are weakest, to the extent that either winters are very cold and summers temperate, or summers are very hot and winters temperate. It is hard to believe that this subtle pattern of research results is a false positive. Rather, climato-economics is an out-of-the-way gold-mine for social-science researchers and practitioners, who have yet to start a gold rush.

PROPOSITIONS

7.1. Bureaucratic structures and strategies thrive in poor societies in demanding climates.

7.2. Easygoing structures and strategies thrive in societies in temperate climates irrespective of their level of wealth.

7.3. Adhocratic structures and professional management thrive in rich societies in demanding climates.

RESEARCH NOTES

1. Joint effect of demanding climate and income per head on the steepness of companies in 39 countries.

Predictors	B	B	B
Climate (C)	-6.79^{***}	$-3.67^{\dagger}$	.61
Income (I)		-5.85^{**}	-2.82
C × I			-6.63^{***}
ΔR^2	$.28^{***}$	$.17^{***}$	$.16^{***}$
Total R^2	$.28^{***}$	$.45^{***}$	$.61^{***}$

$^{\dagger}p < .10.$ $^{*}p < .05.$ $^{**}p < .01.$ $^{***}p < .001.$

For this analysis, and for all other analyses reported in this chapter, demanding climate (C) was the sum of the absolute deviations from 22°C for the average lowest and highest temperatures in the coldest winter month (W) and for the average lowest and highest temperatures in the hottest summer month (S). Income (I) was the logged gross national product per head in 1985 (Source: *World Bank Atlas*, 1965–2002). There was no multicollinearity (*VIFs* < 2.59), and there were no outliers (Cook's *Ds* < .13).

2. With selfish versus cooperative enculturation from Chapter 6 controlled for, the joint effect of demanding climate and income per head on working for money versus working for achievement, reported in Chapter 4, decreased from 62% to 41% ($N = 37$; for the interaction terms ΔR^2 decreased from .16 to .11).

3. With selfish versus cooperative enculturation from Chapter 6 controlled for, the joint effect of demanding climate and income per head on happiness, reported in Chapter 3, decreased from 63% to 42% ($N = 74$; for the interaction terms ΔR^2 decreased from .17 to .10).

4. With selfish versus cooperative enculturation from Chapter 6 controlled for, the joint effect of demanding climate and income per head on subjective health, reported in Chapter 3, decreased from 44% to 26% ($N = 68$; for the interaction terms ΔR^2 decreased from .14 to .05).

5. Hofstede's (2001) indices of formalization (labeled *uncertainty avoidance*) and centralization (labeled *power distance*) were not used because formalization or uncertainty avoidance was questionably derived from the odd bedfellows of job stress, long-term commitment to the organization, and rule orientation.

6. Cultural formalization (uncertainty avoidance) and cultural centralization (power distance) were measured on 7-point response scales (source: House et al., 2004, pp. 745–747). After correction for response bias, cultural formalization ranged from 3.20 in the German-speaking part of Switzerland to 5.77 in Morocco ($M = 4.62$; $SD = .59$), and cultural centralization ranged from 2.21 in Colombia to 3.80 among the black section of the South African population ($M = 2.75$; $SD = .32$). Cross-culturally, the aggregatability ($ICC_1 = .38$ for formalization and .14 for centralization), internal consistency (Cronbach's $\alpha = .85$ for formalization and .74 for centralization), interrater reliability ($ICC_2 = .96$ for formalization and .88 for centralization), and construct validity ($r = .88$ for formalization and .60 for centralization) were all good (for details, see Hanges & Dickson, 2004; Gupta et al., 2004).

   It is difficult to examine whether formalization and centralization move in tandem. None of the common statistical techniques can be used to test an interaction effect of two independent variables (climate and wealth) on two interacting dependent variables (formalization and centralization). The problem was solved by combining formalization and centralization into a single dependent variable (for an alternative procedure leading to essentially the same results, see Van de Vliert, 2008a). First, formalization and centralization were both standardized. Second, an increment of 2.5 was added to get rid of negative values, so as to permit raising to the square. Third, applying the Pythagorean theorem, the square root was extracted of the sum of squared formalization and squared centralization (for this procedure, see Van de Vliert, Kluwer, & Lynn, 2000). The resulting dependent variable ranged from least bureaucratic and most adhocratic in Sweden (1.78) to most bureaucratic and least adhocratic in the black section of the South African population (6.45; $M = 3.66$; $SD = 1.03$).

7. Joint effect of demanding climate and income per head on adhocratic versus bureaucratic organizational structures in 61 societies from 58 countries.

Predictors	B	B	B
Climate (C)	$-.23^{\dagger}$	$-.10$	$-.11$
Income (I)		$-.49^{***}$	$-.45^{***}$
C × I			$-.37^{**}$
ΔR^2	$.05^{\dagger}$	$.21^{***}$	$.11^{**}$
Total R^2	$.05^{\dagger}$	$.26^{***}$	$.37^{***}$

$^{\dagger}p < .10.$ $^{*}p < .05.$ $^{**}p < .01.$ $^{*}p < .001.$

Income (I) was the logged purchasing-power income per head in 1995 (source: United Nations Development Programme, 1998). There was no multicollinearity ($VIFs < 1.09$), and there were no outliers (Cook's $Ds < .18$).

8. The simple slopes for the impact of the demandingness of climate on the degree of bureaucracy are marginally significant for poorer societies $[r(31) = .25, p < .10]$ and highly significant for richer societies $[r(30) = -.59, p < .001]$.

9. The variation in bureaucracy accounted for by the interaction terms of climate and income per head decreased from $\Delta R^2 = .11$ to $\Delta R^2 = .09$ when the national proportion of Muslims was controlled for, to $\Delta R^2 = .07$ when the proportion of Protestants was controlled for, and to $\Delta R^2 = .09$ when the proportion of Roman Catholics was controlled for.

10. Together, the national percentages of employment in the industry sector (source: Parker, 1997; $\Delta R^2 = .04$; $\beta = -.18$, n.s.) and in the services sector ($\Delta R^2 = .34$; $\beta = -.58, p < .001$) accounted for 37% of the variation in cultural formalization. Similarly, employment in the industry sector ($\Delta R^2 = .10$; $\beta = .32, p < .01$) and in the services sector ($\Delta R^2 = .06$; $\beta = -.25, p < .05$) accounted for 16% of the variation in cultural centralization. In combination with climate

and income per head, the employment percentages accounted for 28% of the variation in bureaucracy, while the interactive effect of climate and income per head decreased from $\Delta R^2 = .11$ to $\Delta R^2 = .05$ ($p < .05$).

11. Joint effect of colder winters, hotter summers, and income per head on adhocratic versus bureaucratic organizational structures in 61 societies from 58 countries.

Predictors	B	B	B	B	B
Winters (W)	.17	.18	.11	−.02	−.02
Summers (S)	−.29*	−.30†	−.10	.07	.07
W × S		.02	−.11	−.41*	−.42*
Income (I)			−.47***	−.46***	−.47***
W × I				−.46***	−.45**
S × I				−.20†	−.20†
W × S × I					−.03
ΔR^2	.11*	.00	.18***	.15***	.00
Total R^2	.11*	.11*	.29***	.44***	.44***

$^\dagger p < .10.$ $^* p < .05.$ $^{**} p < .01.$ $^{***} p < .001.$

There was no multicollinearity ($VIFs < 2.46$), and there were no outliers (Cook's $Ds < .36$).

12. Options a and b, about service, added-value product, and product image, represent more adhocratic strategies; options d and, e about low wages and natural resource availability, represent more bureaucratic strategies. Option c was left out of consideration because of its ambiguous mixture of emphasis on added-value products, low-cost products, or both, and emphasis on innovative process technology, cheap process technology, or both.

13. When Cornelius and Warner (2000) randomly dropped half of each country's sample of on average 68 firms, they obtained country scores virtually identical with those of the full sample, which reflects robust interobserver reliability. The correlation of the index of decreasing adhocratic and increasing bureaucratic strategies with its service option a was −.75 ($p < .001$), with its product-design option b was −.60 ($p < .001$), and with its low-cost and resource-availability options d and e was .68 ($p < .001$) and .71 ($p < .001$), respectively.

After 40 was added to get a more elegant distribution of negative and positive values, the index ranged from −49 in Britain and −39 in Switzerland to 50 in Bulgaria and 60 in Ecuador ($M = -9.54$; $SD = 22.66$).

14. The cross-national equivalence of the index was assessed using GLOBE's cultural values of uncertainty avoidance, power distance, performance orientation, future orientation, humane orientation, institutional collectivism, in-group collectivism, gender egalitarianism, assertiveness, autocratic leadership, self-protective leadership, autonomous leadership, humane leadership, team-oriented leadership, and charismatic leadership (source: House et al., 2004). Correlations were computed between the index and each of the 15 values. This was done separately for 16 poor countries with demanding climates, for 14 countries with temperate climates, and for 16 rich countries with demanding climates. Cronbach's alpha for the three sets of 15 correlations was .76, indicating that executives in different climato-economic niches conceptualize organizational strategies equivalently in terms of a broader nomological network of cultural values.

15. The construct validity of the index of decreasing adhocratic and increasing bureaucratic strategies is apparent from its associations with more "burdensome administrative regulations" [$r(59) = .27$, $p < .05$], more time spent on "dealing with government bureaucracy" [$r(59) = .44, p < .001$], less "willingness to delegate authority to subordinates" [$r(59) = -.44, p < .001$], less "attention paid to customer satisfaction" [$r(59) = -.44, p < .001$], and much less agreement with the statement that "competitive advantage of companies in international markets is due to unique products and processes" [$r(59) = -.58, p < .001$] (source of all validation criteria: World Economic Forum, 2000). Additionally, cultural formalization and cultural centralization from the preceding study were used to check the discriminative validity of the index. A measure of bureaucratic strategies should have more in common with the bureaucratic purposiveness and orderliness of formalized procedures than with the bureaucratic inequality among people with respect to power, authority, and status. In line with this argument, the index is positively related to formalization [$r(46) = .51, p < .001$] but not to centralization [$r(46) = .03$, n.s.].

16. Joint effect of demanding climate and income per head on adho-cratic versus bureaucratic organizational strategies in 58 countries (economic sector was also controlled for).

Predictors	Economic sector uncontrolled for			Economic sector controlled for		
	B	B	B	B	B	B
Industry				$-.12$	$.82^{***}$	$.42^{\dagger}$
Services				$-.67^{***}$	$.20$	$.03$
Climate (C)	$5.13^{\dagger}$	10.24^{***}	9.17^{***}	8.77^{**}	9.16^{***}	8.98^{***}
Income (I)		-14.13^{***}	-8.49^{***}		-20.53^{***}	-12.38^{**}
C × I			-9.50^{***}			-7.31^{**}
ΔR^2	$.05^{\dagger}$	$.41^{***}$	$.14^{***}$	$.26^{***}$	$.30^{***}$	$.06^{**}$
Total R^2	$.05^{\dagger}$	$.46^{***}$	$.60^{***}$	$.26^{***}$	$.56^{***}$	$.62^{***}$

$^{\dagger}p < .10.$ $^{*}p < .05.$ $^{**}p < .01.$ $^{***}p < .001.$

Income (I) was the logged purchasing-power income per head in 1999 (source: World Economic Forum, 2000). There was no multi-collinearity ($VIFs < 5.72$), and after removal of Ecuador there were no outliers (Cook's $Ds < .34$).

17. In Figure 7.2, the symbols for Belgium, Bolivia, Costa Rica, El Sal-vador, Greece, Hong Kong, New Zealand, Portugal, South Africa, and Taiwan have no symbol label. The simple slope for the impact of the demandingness of climate on adhocratic versus bureaucratic strategies is significant for poorer countries $[r(31) = .70, p < .001]$ but not for richer countries $[r(27) = -.21, \text{n.s.}]$. However, if option a is left out of the adhocratic versus bureaucratic strategy index, the simple slopes are significant for both poorer $[r(31) = .67, p < .001]$ and richer $[r(27) = -.45, p < .05]$ countries.

18. The simple slopes for the impact of the demandingness of climate on the use of bureaucratic strategies are significant for poor countries with colder winters $[r(28) = .64, p < .001]$ or hotter summers $[r(28) = .32, p < .05]$ but not for rich countries with colder winters $[r(30) = -.09, \text{n.s.}]$ or hotter summers $[r(30) = .08, \text{n.s.}]$.

19. Timor-Leste had to be left out of consideration because its income per head was unknown. For a breakdown of respondents by eco-nomic sector, firm size, and firm type, see Blanke and Loades (2005).

20. The test-retest reliability of the nepotism measure (ranging from 1 = *professional managers* to 7 = *relatives as managers*) is excellent. The same question led to almost identical cross-national patterns of responses in the preceding executive opinion surveys, one year earlier [2004, $r(101) = .95, p < .001$] and two years earlier [2003, $r(97) = .93, p < .001$].

21. The construct validity of the nepotism measure is apparent from its positive cross-national associations with the steepness of organizations [$r(38) = .58, p < .001$; source: Trompenaars, 1993], reliance on social norms, rules, and procedures [$r(60) = .68, p < .001$: source: House et al., 2004], and use of bureaucratic organizational strategies [$r(59) = .56, p < .001$; source: World Economic Forum, 2000].

22. A proxy of the average size of the country's organizations was available from the World Economic Forum (2005, pp. 218–219; number of employees < 101, 101–500, 501–5,000, 5,001–20,000, > 20,000). The cross-national correlation between nepotism and the size of the country's organizations was –.64 (< 101, .001). After organizational size was controlled for, the standardized residual of the dependent variable of who usually hold senior management positions ranged from –2.49 in Iceland, –2.28 in Estonia, and –1.88 in Botswana (professional managers) to 1.66 in Bangladesh, 1.71 in Thailand, and 1.89 in China (relatives).

23. Joint effect of demanding climate and income per head on nepotism in 116 countries (economic sector in 89 countries was also controlled for).

Predictors	Economic sector uncontrolled for			Economic sector controlled for		
	B	B	B	B	B	B
Industry				$-.02^{**}$	$-.01$	$-.02^{\dagger}$
Services				$-.02^{**}$	$-.01$	$-.01$
Climate (C)	$-.13$	$-.01$	$.03$	$-.13$	$-.09$	$.23^{\dagger}$
Income (I)		$-.39^{***}$	$-.20^{*}$		$-.25$	$-.05$
C × I			$-.42^{***}$			$-.57^{***}$
ΔR^2	$.02$	$.14^{***}$	$.13^{***}$	$.23^{***}$	$.01$	$.13^{***}$
Total R^2	$.02$	$.16^{***}$	$.29^{***}$	$.23^{***}$	$.24^{***}$	$.37^{***}$

$^{\dagger}p < .10.$ $^{*}p < .05.$ $^{**}p < .01.$ $^{***}p < .001.$

Income (I) was the logged purchasing-power income per head in 2002 (source: United Nations Development Programme, 2004). There was no multicollinearity ($VIFs < 4.25$), and there were no outliers (Cook's $Ds < .19$).

24. The simple slopes for the impact of the demandingness of climate on nepotism are significant for both poorer countries [$r(58) = .33$, $p < .01$] and richer countries [$r(58) = -.35, p < .01$].

25. Cross-nationally, nepotism is strongly related to ethnocentrism incorporated in the degree of survival rather than self-expression culture [$r(74) = .54, p < .001$].

26. Joint effect of colder winters, hotter summers, and income per head on nepotism in 116 countries.

Predictors	B	B	B	B	B
Winters (W)	$-.18^{\dagger}$	$-.22^{*}$	$-.07$	$.04$	$.05$
Summers (S)	$.13$	$.08$	$.07$	$.10$	$.05$
W $\times$ S		$.11$	$.05$	$-.06$	$.03$
Income (I)			$-.36^{***}$	$-.17^{\dagger}$	$-.11$
W $\times$ I				$-.43^{***}$	$-.50^{***}$
S $\times$ I				$-.03$	$-.11$
W $\times$ S $\times$ I					$.21^{*}$
ΔR^2	$.05^{\dagger}$	$.01$	$.10^{***}$	$.14^{***}$	$.03^{*}$
Total R^2	$.05^{\dagger}$	$.06^{\dagger}$	$.16^{***}$	$.30^{***}$	$.33^{***}$

$^{\dagger}p < .10$. $^{*}p < .05$. $^{**}p < .01$. $^{***}p < .001$.

There was no multicollinearity ($VIFs < 1.67$), and there were no outliers (Cook's $Ds < .15$).

PART FOUR

CONCLUSION

8

Bird's-Eye Views of Culture

The climato-economic conductor fine-tunes the world's cultural orchestra to the violins of life satisfaction.

This epigraph provides a one-line summary of the theme of this book. The conductor introduces causality, the orchestra diversity, and the violins universality. Causality, diversity, and universality are complex phenomena producing complex problems, certainly with regard to an already complex topic such as the origins of culture. To put the problems as simply as possible, it is easy to challenge climato-economic causation of culture, it is difficult to chart cultural diversity in an indisputable way, and it is impossible to demonstrate statistically the existence of universal needs arising from survival of cold and heat. Some explanatory remarks on each of these complications follow, first for climato-economic causality.

The central tenet of my theory is that climate and cash influence each other's impact on culture. A lot of evidence seems to support this idea. But factors other than climate and cash may also cause the results. Seasonal cycles and day-night cycles, for instance, may be responsible in whole or in part for the simultaneous occurrence of (a) harsh climate, poverty, and survival culture in Azerbaijan, Russia, and elsewhere; (b) temperate climate and easygoing culture in Ghana, Singapore, and elsewhere; and (c) harsh climate, affluence, and self-expression culture in Austria, the United States, and elsewhere. Certainly, rival explanations in terms of precipitation, income inequality, inflation rate, former communist rule, and the like have been ruled out. But no researcher ever will be able to trace, capture, and incorporate all alternative roots of culture. Origins of culture are inevitably hemmed in by question marks. The theory with the fewest question marks will eventually produce the most scientific progress.

The orchestra part of the epigraph concerns the diversity of culture. I have told many cohorts of students that culture is a kaleidoscope of values and practices reflected differently in each society on earth. Indeed, enough cultural dimensions exist to design a pack of cards for playing round games (for overviews of these dimensions, see Bond et al., 2004; Hofstede, 2001; House et al., 2004; Osland & Bird, 2000; Schwartz, 1994, 2004). Consequently, it is difficult to chart cultural diversity as it can be mapped in so many ways. For example, how are we to know that the contrast between survival culture in Pakistan and self-expression culture in Norway represents cultural diversity better than do the alternative contrasts of collectivism-individualism, masculinity-femininity, high-low dynamic externality, and high-low societal cynism? The choices made in the studies reported in the preceding chapters were based on the back-to-basics criterion of survivability of the human environment. Human values and practices are diverse because the local circumstances of human survival are diverse.

The epigraph ends with the violins of life satisfaction. They refer to the universal human drives to ceaselessly satisfy needs for thermal comfort, nutrition, and health in various cultural ways. The universality of the continuous production of life satisfaction is an axiom rather than a testable hypothesis because the currently available research techniques are unsuited for confirming universality.[1] This axiom of an all-pervasive hedonistic principle does not deny that cultures have many parents. It merely adds that cultures vary most fundamentally because different societies have to satisfy exactly the same survival needs daily in different climato-economic niches. The universal survival needs are thought to trigger the joint causal influence of colder-than-temperate or hotter-than temperate climate and cash as ready money or unready capital on the diverseness and richness of culture. This concluding chapter is, therefore, focused on the crucial conundrum of causality.

Following are three sections. Climato-economic causation of survival, easygoing, and self-expression cultures is successively viewed as absent, as theoretically interpretable, and as practically usable. The absence of causality in the first section boils down to a *conglomerate view of culture*, the theoretical interpretability in the second section to an *adaptational view of culture*, and the practical usability in the third section to a *strategic view of culture*. The concluding strategic view of culture comes back full circle to the model of cultural adaptation discussed in Chapter 1, with climate protection and the planned reduction of poverty seen as creators of culture. The research results reported in this book are not about global warming and hardly about economic decline. Nevertheless, the context-culture links found are bound to have implications for the cultural consequences of climate protection and poverty reduction in the long run.

CONGLOMERATE VIEW OF CULTURE

A conglomerate is a composite of climate, cash, and culture, in which the riddle of the chicken and the egg does not apply. This perspective assumes no causality whatsoever. A cultural conglomerate is simply the simultaneous occurrence of a certain climatic context, a certain economic context, and a certain cultural syndrome, which characterizes a society. An example is the co-occurrence of a harsh desert climate, poverty, and survival culture in and around the Central African Republic. In an opposite cultural corner, we find the Swiss conglomerate of a harsh mountain climate, wealth, and self-expression culture, in this case evidenced by the most innovative research and development institutions and activities internationally (World Economic Forum, 2006).

At first blush, the conglomerate view of culture discussed in this section resembles the ecocultural viewpoint that psychological human diversity is related to the climatic, economic, and sociopolitical contexts (Georgas & Berry, 1995; Georgas et al., 2004). On closer consideration, however, my conglomerate framework pits harsher climates against temperate climates, whereas the ecocultural framework pits cold climates against hot climates as core descriptors of the climate-culture alignment. By showing the importance of 22°C (ca. 72°F) as a point of reference for the survivability of climate, the empirical evidence presented in Chapter 3 through Chapter 7 thus leads me to favor the conglomerate viewpoint over the ecocultural viewpoint.

Cultures may traditionally be described as universalistic versus particularistic, individualistic versus collectivistic, horizontal versus vertical, feminine versus masculine, loose versus tight, and so on (Hofstede, 2001; Osland & Bird, 2000; Triandis, 1995; Trompenaars, 1993). But unlike the syndromes of survival, easygoing, and self-expression cultures, developed and contextualized in Chapter 5, none of these descriptive dimensions has ever been associated with embeddedness in conglomerates of climate and cash. The three main climate-cash-culture branches of my still-young tree of knowledge are represented by three columns in Figure 8.1. The keywords in the rows of this tabular overview represent three side branches, to wit, life and death (Chapters 2 and 3), typical relations between self and others (Chapters 6 and 7), and typical construals and constructions of work and organization (Chapters 4 and 7).

As shown in the second column of Figure 8.1, the conglomerate of harsh cold or hot climate, poverty, and survival culture is uniquely characterized by unhappiness, unhealthiness, selfish children, relatives as senior managers, autocratic leaders, much child labor, work for money, and bureaucratic organizational structures

Climatic context	Cold or hot	Temperate	Cold or hot
Economic context	Poor	Poor or rich	Rich
Cultural syndrome	Survival culture	Easygoing culture	Self-expression culture
Life and death			
Happiness	Unhappy	Happy	Happy
Subjective health	Unhealthy	Healthy	Healthy
Suicide	High suicide rates	Low suicide rates	High suicide rates
Self and others			
Child enculturation	Selfish children	More of a mix	Cooperative children
Nepotism	Relatives as managers	More of a mix	Professionals as managers
Leadership	Autocratic leaders	More of a mix	Democratic leaders
Work and organization			
Child labor	Much child labor	Little child labor	No child labor
Work motivation	Work for money	More of a mix	Work for achievement
Work organization	Bureaucratic organization	More of a mix	Adhocratic organization

FIGURE 8.1. Overview of three cultural conglomerates.

and strategies. An adequate candidate for the role of common denominator is lonely misery.

In striking contrast, the conglomerate of harsh cold or hot climate, richness, and self-expression culture in the last column of Figure 8.1 is characterized by happiness, healthiness, cooperative children, professionals as senior managers, democratic leaders, absence of child labor, work for achievement, and adhocratic organizational structures and strategies. The common factor here seems to be something like joint enjoyment.

Interestingly, the in-between conglomerate of temperate climate and easygoing culture comes with a neat in-between profile of characteristics for all bipolar dimensions, including selfish-cooperative, autocratic-democratic, and bureaucratic-adhocratic. The ratings for the unipolar dimensions of happiness and subjective health, however, are lower in the survival conglomerate than in the easygoing and self-expression conglomerates. This array of findings suggests that bipolar dimensions produce sharper pictures of cultural conglomerates than do unipolar dimensions. The reason may be obvious. Bipolar dimensions, made up of two unipolar dimensions linked together at a meaningful midpoint, contain more information.

The conglomerates in Figure 8.1 can best be seen as a descriptive theory of culture. Descriptive conglomerates have to be taken as seriously as geographic maps and astronomic charts. The survival conglomerate tells us where life is at stake, where self-interests carry the day, where children and adults work out of necessity, and where control systems prevail. The self-expression conglomerate, by contrast, tells us where life is extremely stressful for a suicidal minority but manageable for the majority, where cooperation carries the day, where children play while adults work for achievement, and where creative initiatives prevail. In between these two, the easygoing conglomerate tells us where people live a relatively happy-go-lucky life because survival constraints and self-expression constraints are both moderate.

In short, the descriptive conglomerates tell us where we can find and investigate three specific combinations of climatic context, economic context, and cultural syndrome. They represent a novel map of cultures around the globe. This chart has the great advantage that even bucketfuls of variables other than climate, cash, and culture cannot call into question the charted co-occurrence of climate, cash, and culture.

ADAPTATIONAL VIEW OF CULTURE

Three considerations, coupled with the respective components of climate, cash, and culture, are difficult to reconcile with a purely descriptive interpretation of the conglomerates. As for climate, it would be the first wonder of the world if humans, unlike plants and animals, were the one and only species on earth with so much

control over evolutionary processes that they have somehow contrived to wipe out their own climatic underpinnings. As for cash, it
would be a true miscarriage of science if economists, sociologists,
and psychologists were all mistaken in their firm belief that economic development and culture change influence each other (for
recent overviews, see Harrison & Huntington, 2000; House et al.,
2004; Inglehart & Welzel, 2005). As for culture, it would be a bizarre
jackpot hit if the similarities between all the context-culture links in
this book were to happen for no other reason than pure coincidence.

It is difficult to believe that humans have no climate-culture
code, that influences of economies on cultures rest on scientific
errors, and that the equivalence of climate-cash-culture pictures is
a chance hit. It is easier to focus through a climatic, an economic, or
a climato-economic lens of gradual adaptation of societies in the
direction of survival, easygoing, or self-expression cultures. Taking
these viewpoints, one at a time, the discussion in this section leads to
the insight that the salience of mortality has a crucial role to play as a
bridge between climato-economic niches and culture.

Climatic Roots?

From the very beginning of science, the psychosocial consequences
of climate have received notice. Many classic scientists tried in vain
to relate climate to culture, looking as they were for direct effects of
cold-hot contexts on collective values, beliefs, and practices. Similarly, in the 20th century, adherents of the "geographical school"
(Sorokin, 1928) also failed to find and explain straightforward climate-
culture links, with the consequence that their theories were eventually
rejected as crackpot ideas (Van de Vliert & Lindenberg, 2006).

Members of the geographical school of thought would have been
delighted to read the box in Chapter 1 about the increased use of
consonants in colder-region languages and the increased use of
vowels in hotter-region languages. At first sight, increases of suicide

in increasingly demanding climates also stand out as an illustration of cultural adaptation to climate as such. We have seen that colder winters and hotter summers come with higher suicide rates and with the mystery that this tendency is unaffected by wealth. On second thoughts, however, the foundations of the triangle of cultures presented in Chapter 5 may contain a clue to hidden climato-economic roots of suicide.

Suicide-prone members of more demanding cultures in harsher climates have more worries and constraints than do members of easygoing cultures in temperate climates. However, these worries and constraints evolved out of an obsession with control in poor peoples with survival cultures and out of an obsession with creation in rich peoples with self-expression cultures. Perhaps poor peoples with survival cultures run more risk of taking their own lives than poor peoples with easygoing cultures because of their greater obsession with control. By contrast, rich peoples with self-expression cultures may run more risk of taking their own lives than rich peoples with easygoing cultures because of their greater obsession with creation. In this vein, supplementary analyses revealed that colder winters and hotter summers accounted for 43% of the cross-national variation in suicide; for 29% directly, and for 14% through poverty-dependent and richness-dependent worries and constraints inherent in survival and self-expression cultures.[2] To a considerable extent, therefore, suicide rates may be seen as a manifestation of cultural adaptations to climato-economic niches.

This conclusion may shake up the field. Ever since the French sociologist Emile Durkheim (1897) published his pioneering comparative study of suicide in industrial societies, it has been taken for granted that external constraints act as a brake on suicide. In striking contrast, the results reported here suggest that, at least nowadays, external constraints drive suicide. Although the findings support Durkheim's general contention that less traditional societies have higher suicide rates, they reject his explanation that this is because less traditional societies have fewer norms, rules, and procedures. Less religious-traditional societies in more demanding climates appear to have evolved more suicide, even on top of the impact of colder winters and hotter summers, because of their stronger control-based rule orientation in survival cultures and stronger creation-based rule orientation in self-expression cultures.

Reflecting on the studies reported in Chapter 3 through 7 through a purely climatic lens, we do see suicidal and other cultural adaptations to climate, but we appear to painfully underestimate them. If we completely neglect the interaction between climate and the availability of money resources, the underestimation of the adaptation of survival, easygoing, and self-expression cultures to climate is 44% on average. Broken down for segments of culture, the underestimations of the adaptations to climate are 26% for matters of life and death, 53% for matters of self and others, and 58% for matters of work and organization.[3] Given this amount of interactive influence of climate and cash, it is not at all surprising that many generations of our scientific ancestors wearing purely climatic lenses ran into great trouble when trying to crack the climate-culture code.

Economic Roots?

Early modernization theorists, from Marx (1867) to Toffler (1970) and Bell (1973), have argued that industrialization and economic progress bring pervasive cultural shifts breaking away from religious-traditional values and practices. Employing cross-sectional and longitudinal studies, the World Values Surveys group has convincingly and repeatedly shown that this is the case. Economic development tends to push and pull societies from survival orientations toward self-expression orientations and also from religious-traditional orientations toward secular-rational orientations (Inglehart & Baker, 2000; Inglehart et al., 2004; Ingelhart & Welzel, 2005).

Conversely, as we saw in Chapter 5, in less than a decade the peoples of Estonia, Latvia, Lithuania, and Russia moved from self-expression orientations toward survival orientations with the collapse of the economic and sociopolitical systems of the Soviet Union in 1990–1991.

The research findings reported in this book show that the World Values Surveys researchers have an even more defensible claim than they think they have, because they are unaware of how climate strengthens their economy-drives-culture fortification. This unconscious narrow-mindedness regarding interactive economic effects conceals a good deal of cultural adaptations to the available money resources in circumstances of more demanding climates. The overly simple, purely economic lens appears to conceal 53% of cultural adaptations to poverty and wealth in the sphere of life and death, 60% of adaptations in the sphere of self and others, and 33% of adaptations in the sphere of work and organization.[3] These are huge numbers. It is, therefore, safe to conclude that climate reveals itself as the secret weapon of the economy-drives-culture camp in the continuing debates with the culture-drives-economy camp.

Climato-economic Roots

Gradual cultural adaptations to climato-economic niches have two faces. The first face is active if climate accounts for the largest portion of the variation in culture, with that impact fine-tuned to the available money resources. The second face is active if collective income accounts for the largest portion of the variation in culture, with that impact fine-tuned to the harshness of climate. The burgeoning theory of cultural adaptation would gain considerable validity if it could explain not only *why* climate and cash rock the cradle of culture, but also *when* climatic demands and *when* money resources take the lead in this process. This need to deepen our understanding brings us back to the basics of what makes climate and cash so influential as antecedents of culture.

The point of departure was that a more temperate climate is the only environmental condition that produces more thermal comfort, easier obtainability of food and water, and better health. Harsher climates endanger the satisfaction of survival needs, and we respond to these threats by building cultural elements of what we collectively value, believe, seek, avoid, and do. From this starting point it follows that the impact of climate on culture is greater to the extent that components of culture are more closely linked to the survival needs for thermal comfort, nutrition, and health. Happiness, subjective health, and suicide may be more sensitive to climatic conditions and less sensitive to economic conditions than other components of culture because of their closer connections with critical matters of life and death.

According to additional postulates in Chapters 3 and 4, money and work, and especially paid work, can make up for the adverse effects of harsh climates. To the extent that money and work do so, they in essence replace the influences of climatic conditions on culture by influences of economic conditions on culture. Compared with other components of culture, child labor, work motivation, and work organization may, therefore, be more sensitive to economic conditions and less sensitive to climatic conditions. The harshness and demands of climate may change the prevailing impact of cash only lightly for the worse or for the better.

The sizes of the estimates of the cultural adaptations to climato-economic demands and resources indicated that my intuition did not fail me.[3] Aspects of the life-and-death segment represented by happiness, subjective health, and suicide are related primarily to climate (29%), and secondarily to cash (9%) and to climate-cash complications (10%); aspects of the work-and-organization segment represented by child labor, work motivation, and work organization are related primarily to cash (30%), and secondarily to climate (10%) and to climate-cash complications (15%). In between these two, aspects of the typical relation between self and others represented by child enculturation, nepotism, and leadership are primarily related to neither climatic demands nor money resources. These observations of cultural adaptation allow the following refinements of the climato-economic theory of culture in the making.

Notwithstanding the fact that climate and cash influence each other's impact on culture, climate takes the lead in matters concerning life and death, whereas cash takes the lead in matters concerning work and organization. In hindsight, Figures 3.1 and 3.2 reflect that climate bears primary responsibility for the conclusions that threatening climatic demands and poverty decrease life satisfaction in survival cultures, and that challenging climatic demands and affluence increase life satisfaction in self-expression cultures. In Figures 4.1, 4.2, 7.1, and 7.2, however, cash is the bellwether of the findings that greater mismatches of climate and cash increase extrinsic work motives and bureaucratic organization in survival cultures, and that better matches of climate and cash increase intrinsic work motives and adhocratic organization in self-expression cultures.

In the present phase of theory building, a further breakdown of the climato-economic roots of culture for colder winters and hotter summers has little purpose as it relies so heavily on the convenience sampling of countries. Take the connection between heat, pauperism, and child labor. Hotter summers and levels of wealth are much more important in explaining child labor than are colder winters and levels of wealth, simply because child labor is overrepresented around the equator. Unfortunately, cold-temperate-hot sampling will always remain a problem as it can be argued that very cold climato-economic niches do not have equivalently hot counterparts.[4] The earth's present cold bias also forms a hindrance to badly needed research into qualitative differences between cultural adaptations to demandingly cold versus demandingly hot climato-economic niches.

The existence of cultural adaptations to climato-economic niches gives nuance to the notion that humankind has set itself on a path of irresistible and irreversible globalization, leading to the demise of local cultures and the birth of a homogeneous world culture. Beyond a shadow of a doubt, experiences such as enjoying foods and goods from foreign sources, fearing pandemics and terrorism, watching international happenings, surfing on the Web, communicating via the Internet, flying long distances, and using credit cards abroad embrace us everywhere (for details and discussions, see Lechner & Boli, 2005). But those common feelings and behaviors are more peripheral signs of convergence, which may blind us to three more central layers of understanding the specifics and particulars of local cultures.

The first more central layer of insight, less peripheral than globalization, emphasizes differential production of life satisfaction in distinct climato-economic niches. In the next more central layer of comprehension operate the universal needs for thermal comfort, nutrition, and health, unobtrusively using the cultural tool of money. Economic development is thought to transform the relation between harsher environments and harder work from controlling climatic threats to creating and meeting climatic challenges. And the core layer of explanation deals with the ultimate origin of culture – the survivability of the human habitat or, conversely, the ecological threat of death.

The Bridging Role of Mortality Salience

Coping with freezing or boiling weather conditions means, in essence, saving life by escaping death. This maxim is supported by the above quantitative information about the striking relevance of harsh and demanding climates for the life-and-death segment of culture. Bitter winters and scorching summers threaten the gratification of survival needs, produce health problems, stimulate suicidal behavior, and, in consequence, make mortality highly salient. In temperate climates mortality is less salient. Given that mortality salience enhances our quest for certainty and increases in-group favoritism in tandem with out-group discrimination (see the box "Mortals organizing mortals" on page 184), a moneyless world would have a neatly arranged culture map. We would find tighter, more nepotistic, more xenophobic—that is, more obsessive—cultures in regions with colder winters or hotter summers, but not in temperate climates.

Money makes a big difference, at least in harsh cold or hot climates. Without cash, the now peaceful Norwegians, Swedes, and Danes, who have always lived in cold climates, would still be the aggressive Vikings they once were. Mortality salience may help to improve understanding of why this is so (see Figure 8.2). Let's call the lower mortality salience in temperate climates *moderate* and the higher mortality salience in cold or hot climates *high*. People like the Vikings, living in harsh climates without money resources to reduce their high mortality salience, evolve cultural obsessions with survival and control. For both the poor and the rich in temperate climates, money is not of great consequence and will not drastically influence their moderate degrees of mortality salience, with relatively easygoing cultures as a result. Ready money and capital work their wonders on mortality salience and culture first and foremost in cold and hot climates.

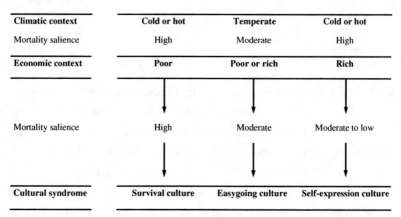

Climatic context	Cold or hot	Temperate	Cold or hot
Mortality salience	High	Moderate	High
Economic context	Poor	Poor or rich	Rich
Mortality salience	High	Moderate	Moderate to low
Cultural syndrome	Survival culture	Easygoing culture	Self-expression culture

FIGURE 8.2. The bridging role of mortality salience between climato-economic niches and cultures.

In harsh cold or hot areas, only rich people have both the climate-driven obsession with life and death and the financial means to turn conspicuousness of death inherent in climatic threats into conspicuousness of life inherent in climatic challenges. Money resources elicit control and, through it, even temporary illusions of immortality. Thus, affluence enables rich people in harsh cold or hot climates to turn their initially high degrees of mortality salience into moderate to low degrees of mortality salience and to sublimate obsessions with death and survival into obsessions with life and self-expression. In short, more climatic demands lead to stronger obsessions and the addition of more money resources to greater changes in directing these obsessions from death-avoiding control toward life-seeking creation.

Failing a cross-cultural measure of mortality salience, the proposed bridge between climato-economic niches and culture cannot be tested. It thus reflects conjecture at best and pure speculation at worst. Yet it is included without apology on the assumption that there is scientific "virtue in such things as speculation, armchair theorizing, aphorisms, overdetermined explanations, enlarged questions, complicated explanations, and journalism" (Weick, 1979, p. 41). Sooner or later, researchers or practitioners may be inspired by the as yet premature idea of mortality salience as an antecedent condition of culture. Alternatively, the bridging role of mortality salience may be unmasked as idle reverie. Neither future development, however, can take the edge off the present argument that it is easier to adopt a climato-economic lens of cultural adaptation than to believe that all climate-cash-culture pictures reported and discussed in the preceding chapters are equivalent chance hits.

STRATEGIC VIEW OF CULTURE

When I was sketching these bird's-eye views of culture, in June 2007, the annual summit of the Heads of State and Government of the

Group of Eight leading industrialized nations (G8) reached wide-ranging agreements on climate protection and poverty reduction. Apparently, world leaders see climate protection and poverty reduction as desirable strategic moves to avoid disastrous consequences of global warming and local poverty in the longer run. Viewed in this way, not as issues by themselves but as sources of future problems, global warming and local poverty are explicitly and intentionally treated as forerunners of cultural values and practices. In this respect, today's world leaders no doubt have the posthumous support of their predecessor, Winston Churchill, whose adage about the environment could easily be paraphrased as "If we can reshape global warming and local poverty, we can reshape cultures."

Legally binding international commitments to climate protection and poverty reduction can best be established within the framework of the United Nations. But even if the United Nations follows the Group of Eight, speaks with one voice, and makes climate protection and poverty reduction world priorities, effective implementation is not guaranteed. Climate protection may fail or succeed, as may poverty reduction. In combination, these two either-or scenarios confront our present world community with four scenarios for the future of culture change (see Figure 8.3). Viewed from a fear-and-flight perspective, these scenarios are possible destinies. Viewed from the face-and-fight perspective adopted here, they are possible options.

		Climate protection	
		No	Yes
Poverty reduction	No	*Creating survival cultures*	*Creating cultural stability*
	Yes	*Creating cultural uncertainty*	*Creating self-expression cultures*

FIGURE 8.3. Creating cultures through climate protection and poverty reduction.

Building on the research findings presented in this book, the cultural implications for each of the four cells in Figure 8.3 are as follows. If we choose to pursue neither climate protection nor poverty reduction, global warming will steadily push and pull self-expression cultures first toward easygoing cultures and then toward survival cultures. If we successfully seek poverty reduction only, step by step, we will produce cultural uncertainty, to wit, survival cultures if the problem of global warming proves overwhelming, but self-expression cultures if global warming is manageable. If we successfully strive for climate protection only, we will maintain stability of survival, easygoing, and self-expression cultures. Finally, if we effectively implement both climate protection and poverty reduction, we will gradually push and pull survival cultures first toward easygoing cultures and then toward self-expression cultures. These four prototyped world policies constitute both the very heart of the strategic view of culture and the final objectives from which our species has to make a principal and principled choice soon.

Creating Survival Cultures

Global warming and local poverty are worlds apart. Yet they have several things in common. Both top the list of the most vexing problems facing world citizens today. Both are money-swallowing black holes. Both suffer under diffusion of who must be held responsible; both foreshadow future danger. On closer scrutiny, it is in every country's interest to get other countries to clean up the mess, and it is in every generation's interest to wait and see, leading to delegation of the cleaning-up job to the following generation. These common characteristics of global warming and local poverty place premiums on inactivity and stalemate rather than exploration and settlement, increasing the likelihood of the following scenario.

While we pay lip service to policies of climate protection and poverty reduction, the livability zones on our planet shift toward higher latitudes, followed by plants and animals, leaving little room for survival for polar bears in the north and king penguins in the south. Thermal comfort becomes a scarcer resource in many heavily populated regions. Armies of perilous species of ticks, ants, bees, and mosquitoes are slowly but surely marching and flying toward the poles, carrying parasites and further endangering nutritional customs and health. Relatedly, global warming also undermines economic growth in tropical and temperate climes. Particularly painful is the widening mouth of the economic grand canyon alongside the equator – the world's main river of poverty. By pursuing neither climate protection nor poverty reduction in the short run, we are frustrating the gratification of many people's basic needs for thermal comfort, nutrition, and health in the long run.

If all analyses and figures reported in this book indeed provide evidence of cultural adaptation to climato-economic niches, global heating in conjunction with economic decline is bound to increase survival values and practices bit by bit. Survival switches will be thrown to the full "on" position in Africa soon; life will also get increasingly debilitating and exhausting in Central and South America, and in South Asia. Hotter summers helped by greater poverty will make the inhabitants of these regions unhappier, unhealthier, and more selfish and suicide-prone, and their leaders more autocratic. Greater poverty helped by hotter summers will increase these people's inclination to use child labor, to work merely for money, to appoint relatives as organizational managers, and to organize work in bureaucratic ways. Strong effects will also occur for the rejection of foreigners and other out-group members, which could easily spark social discrimination and ethnic clashes, as is already apparent today in several hot and poor spots in Africa. Global warming and local poverty have yet another thing in common after all: doing nothing is doing a lot.

Creating Cultural Uncertainty

Local poverty poses global threats and discomfort for all humans. Abject poverty is the eye of a hurricane of thirst, hunger, infectious diseases, insanitation, environmental pollution, infant mortality, repression, violence, and migrating hordes of displaced peoples. Even if the epidemics, conflicts, and refugees do not spread across the globe, films do, evoking feelings of despair and guilt in societies on all continents. According to the latest estimates, almost 1 billion people are living on the equivalent of less than $1 a day. Halving this share of people in such a parlous state is the first of the Millennium Development Goals to which 189 countries subscribed in September 2000. It is not only an important but also a feasible goal, as the world community has the finance, the human capacity, and the technology to remove this blight of misery from millions of lives (for appropriate strategies, see Collier, 2007).

From this vantage point in history, human suffering may loom larger and crazier from local poverty than from global warming, causing our leaders to give poverty reduction high priority over climate protection. Perhaps the recent agreements among the members of the G8 to stand by their commitment to increase the official development assistance for Africa from $25 billion to $50 billion a year and to provide an additional $60 billion a year to fight HIV/ AIDS, malaria, and tuberculosis may be interpreted as a sign of moving policies in that direction. Granted, $110 billion a year may seem a lot, but it is only a drop in the ocean. It is a drop of hope, though, that our leaders are beginning to develop the long-range vision and political will needed to apply their money resources to pulling the world's poor out of the pit of poverty where they seem irredeemably stuck.

The results of my climato-economic studies suggest that a one-sided focus on sharp poverty reduction seems great as long as global warming does not exceed an as-yet-unknown threshold level. Below that threshold of, let us say, an average of 2°C (3.6°F), financial aid, sociostructural assistance, and trade improvement can still create conditions for economic growth and for the compensation of global warming effects by turning climatic threats into climatic challenges. But what is the critical threshold level? And how much are we willing to gamble on a throw of the climate dice? "Predicting how much hotter a particular level of carbon dioxide will make the world is impossible. It's not just that the precise effect of greenhouse gases on temperature is unclear. It's also that warming has countless indirect effects. It may set off mechanisms that tend to cool things down (clouds which block out sunlight, for instance) or ones that heat the world further (by melting soils in which greenhouse gases are frozen, for instance). The system could right itself or spin out of control" (*The Economist*, September 9, 2006, p. 9).

The one-eyedness of agencies mesmerized by the aim of drastic poverty reduction creates climatic uncertainty and, through it, cultural uncertainty. This holds especially true for all the hot African countries with the lowest levels of human development, and for Haiti and Yemen. Below the unidentified critical level of global warming, banishing poverty in these countries pushes and pulls their cultures from survival orientations toward self-expression orientations. But beyond that critical level of warming it becomes virtually impossible to fight the poverty-producing impact of overheating. With too much heating, there seems to be no escape whatsoever from stronger survival tendencies in a variety of cultural characteristics, including unhappiness, unhealthiness, suicide, selfishness, nepotism, and xenophobia. A few degrees of overall overheating is all it takes to turn life upside down. Cultural orientations of easygoingness and self-expression will almost completely disappear like snow in the desert. Clearly, and unfortunately, taking one-sided action against poverty means taking climatic and thus cultural risks.

Creating Cultural Stability

By way of reaction to global warming and ultimate extinction, living creatures have two opposite options: they can change their context, or they can change themselves. Many plants and animals have already started to change their context through migration; others have started to adapt to the warmer environment. Likewise, farmers continuously adapt their agricultural practices to changes, including the current climate change (Reidsma, 2007). On an overarching scale, human societies, being reluctant to migrate, have begun to use their money resources to engage in geo-engineering to stabilize the climatic context. Step by step, larger parts of the world community are coming to see climatic stability as a value and climate protection as a corresponding practice. If this trend continues, the day may come when we give fighting a war against warming priority over poverty reduction in a desperate attempt to protect the earth's biodiversity, including our human cultures. Self-evidently, cultural stability will be much more difficult to achieve in those regions where climate change hits harder and faster.

The climate-culture links reported are unambiguous in their predictions that direct and indirect consequences of serious global warming may destroy entire cultures. The Inuit cultures of the indigenous peoples inhabiting the Arctic coasts of Alaska, the Northwest Territories, Nunavut, Québec, Labrador, Greenland, and Siberia are a clear case in point. Melting ice, rising seas, and the impact on the animals they rely on for food threaten their subsistence livelihoods and lifestyles. Migrating farther north may serve as a short-term solution, but sooner or later drastic adaptations to the warming environment seem inevitable.

In a similar vein and mood, Flannery (2005, p. 287) discusses the example of the sovereign atoll countries of Kiribati, Maldives, Marshall Islands, Tokelau, and Tuvalu – which among them support around half a million people. "Atolls are rings of coral reef that surround a lagoon, and scattered around the reef crest are islands and islets whose average height above sea level is a mere seven feet . . . . As a result of the destruction of the world's coral reefs, rising seas and the intensifying weather events already in train, it seems inevitable that those nations will be destroyed by climate change during the course of this century."

From a worldwide comparative perspective, the UN's Intergovernmental Panel on Climate Change (IPCC; www.ipcc.ch) predicts that global warming will have a graver effect on Africa than on any other continent. Drylands bordering the deserts may get drier, wetlands bordering the rainforests may get wetter, and rising seas may ravage the coastal areas of Egypt, the Gambia, the Gulf of Guinea, and Senegal. The fact alone that 600,000 square kilometers of cultivable African land may be ruined requires drastic measures to guarantee cultural stability. At the same time, non-Eskimos living closer to the polar icecaps in the northernmost territories will benefit hugely from a gently warmer climate because of the greater livability, the higher yields from agriculture, the easier exploitation of as yet undiscovered oil and gas reserves, and the heightened attractiveness for tourists. Thus, creating climatic and cultural stability will create winners and losers in differing ecological niches on earth. This raises unprecedented controversial questions about the fairness of our climato-economic interventions and distributions of culture, as illustrated in the box "Desert diets of sand and salt" on page 35 (for more on ethical aspects of climate change, see http://climate ethics.org).

Radical strategies exist to protect climate and, through it, the world's colorful collection of cultures. Action plans are in place to reduce the emissions of greenhouse gases by closing down coal-burning power plants, building more modern and alternative electricity generators, cutting electricity use, and making cleaner cars and engines. Economic tools include the implementation of carbon taxes or of cap-and-trade programs that let polluters buy and sell emissions credits or replant forests being lost. New technologies, such as producing biofuels and capturing carbon dioxide to store it underground or underseas, are being developed. But none of these strategies to stabilize climate and culture will gain momentum unless politicians and government officials around the globe get more serious about a packet of emergency meaures.

Even if an all-out war against warming is fought and won so that cultural stability is achieved, local poverty and survival cultures will remain a real problem. A difficulty with the current policies of climate protection is that cultural consequences are not modeled. My empirical observations point to two possible improvements in the models of predicting long-term consequences of global warming. The first improvement gives due honor to the biological laws of warm-bloodedness by incorporating a survivability optimum of about 22°C for climatic temperature into the model. The second improvement gives due honor to the amount of money a society has available for surviving bitter winters or scorching summers by including income per head as a complicating shared mold of culture. Climate models lacking such modifications cannot accurately predict and guide culture stability and change.

Creating Self-expression Cultures

If the climate-cash-culture triangles resulting from this project can be trusted, only intelligent combinations of climate management and poverty reduction can optimize the chances of successfully implementing self-expression cultures. Climate protection as such cannot fine-tune its impact on survival, easygoing, and self-expression cultures in poor and rich regions; poverty reduction as such cannot tailor culture to bearably warm and to unbearably hot circumstances. As briefly discussed below, only in carefully crafted mutual interactions can climate and cash manifest themselves in life satisfaction, concern for others, and functional dedication and flexibility.

Apart from politics, the Achilles' heel of such a plan of campaign is the scientific feasibility of climate change policies. The present insight into temperature oscillations, expressed with high confidence in February 2007 (www.ipcc.ch), is that current global warming is largely man-made rather than merely one of the cyclical warmings the earth goes through. This observational conclusion was generally received as bad news, but it is actually not that bad since it gives us some clear clues as to how to make a difference for future generations. To the extent that human activity rather than solar activity is to blame for global heating, we are in a better position to use money resources to overcome or mitigate the problem by reducing its detrimental effects. If we can boost global warming, we can also monitor climatic stability or even bring about global cooling if we desperately want that.

Time and again, I have registered that self-expression cultures thrive in rich societies in demanding cold or hot climates. This will end if global heating gets completely out of hand. Today's self-expression cultures will slide back into survival values and practices, and become extinct. To prevent this from happening, preliminary measures must be taken to keep global warming in check. Having an obsession with creating and being in possession of the necessary financial and technological means, the richer societies in harsher climates are well equipped to design reasonably effective interventions for climate management. At the very least, they can drastically restrict global warming to no more than 2°C, as the maximum limit that is possibly sustainable. In addition, these richer societies in harsher climates can use their wealth-based resources to implement international policies of climato-economic intervention to improve the fate of humankind. The following takes on climato-economic creation of foreign self-expression cultures prompt themselves.

Richer countries in temperate but warming climates, such as Malta and Singapore, need no help from abroad. They will spontaneously adapt to global warming by moving from easygoing toward self-expression values and practices. Similarly, poorer countries in cold but warming climates, including Mongolia and Kyrgyzstan, can perhaps also take care of themselves. Official development assistance may primarily be given to the remaining poorer countries with problematically warming climates, many of which are to be found within the equatorial radiation belt. As a rule of thumb, poorer countries may receive all kinds of support to the extent that their winters and summers deviate from mild temperatures around 22°C (for a listing of country scores on the winter index, the summer index, and the total climate index, see Appendix). Dealing with the intertwined problems of global warming and local poverty forms a litmus test for the usefulness and effectiveness of the cultural tool of money. It provides us with an opportunity to show migrating plants and animals that smart exchanges of money for goods and work are adequate alternative solutions to migration. It is a welcome opportunity, too, given that we spoiled the preceding one of the Little Ice Age, a period of modest cooling of the Northern Hemisphere that ended in the mid 19th century. More often than not, bitter winters reduced crop and livestock production, caused malnutrition and poverty, and weakened immunity to a variety of illnesses. As a consequence, the frequency of wars, raids, and riots increased all over Europe and Asia (Lamb, 1995; McGovern, 2000; Zhang et al., 2007).

Today's joint occurrence of global warming and local poverty is a unique second chance to prove that regions lacking water and food, and money, need not have to become hot spots for conflicts and other malice. All we need to do is start putting a small proportion of the world's financial resources into preventive and de-escalative action where necessary.

Within the scope of this passionate mission, and after a decade of intensive research, I wrote this book. It tells the fairy tale of how I embraced climate, how I conditioned climate with cash, and how I ended up with culture. Surprisingly, the frog of climate turned into the prince of culture.

RESEARCH NOTES

1. The universality of meeting survival needs represents a null hypothesis of no differences, which cannot be statistically confirmed.
2. Joint effect of colder winters, hotter summers, survival versus self-expression culture (S-SE), easygoing culture [(S-SE)^2], and religious-traditional versus secular-rational culture (RT-SR) on suicide rates in 75 countries.

Predictors	B	B	B	B	B
Winters (W)	4.70***		4.64***	3.77**	3.52***
Summers (S)	1.35†		1.24†	1.22	1.54*
W × S	2.13*		2.04*	1.87*	1.88*
W²	2.37**		2.36**	2.26**	2.06**
S-SE culture		−1.69*	−.32	−.59	1.54†
(S-SE)²		1.96**	.08	−.28	−.32
RT-SR culture				2.09*	2.91***
(RT-SR)²				.90	1.02
(S-SE) × (RT-SR)					−3.85***
ΔR²	.29***	.14**	.14**	.28***	.40***
Total R²	.29***	.14**	.43***	.48***	.60***

†$p < .10$. *$p < .05$. **$p < .01$. ***$p < .001$.

Missing values for S-SE and RT-SR culture were estimated on the basis of the logged purchasing-power income per head in 1995 (source: United Nations Development Programme, 1998) and the World Values Surveys' S-SE by RT-SR cultural zones (source: www.worldvaluessurvey.org). There was no multicollinearity (*VIFs* < 3.09), and there were no outliers (Cook's *Ds* < .15).

3. Joint effects of demanding climate and income per head on overall cultures and components of cultures (in percentages).

Climato-economic niche	Climate (C)	Income (I)	C × I
Survival/Self-expression			
Overall cultures	22	37	19
Life and death			
Happiness	28	18	17
Subjective health	23	7	14
Suicide	37	3	0
Self and others			
Child enculturation	16	10	12
Nepotism	6	10	17
Leadership	15	8	13
Work and organization			
Child labor	14	27	17
Work motivation	10	36	16
Organizational structures	11	18	15
Organizational strategies	7	37	10

Some percentages in this table differ from those presented in Chapters 3 to 7 as the present analyses were all modeled after the analyses for happiness and subjective health reported in Chapter 3. Predictors: Winters (W), Summers (S), W × S, Income (I), W × I, S × I, W × S × I.
Looking through a purely climatic lens, the underestimation of the adaptation of culture to climate is (C × I)/([C × I] + C). Looking through a purely economic lens, the underestimation of the adaptation of culture to income per head is (C × I) / ([C × I] + I).

4. World climates have a restriction of range on the hot side. With the survivability optimum of 22°C as a point of reference, the maximum average deviation from temperateness is much larger in the coldest winter month (22 °C minus 66 °C in Mongolia) than in the hottest summer month (22 °C plus 27 °C in Iraq and in Morocco's disputed territory of the Western Sahara).

Climate Indices

The research reported in this book was based on three indices of the harshness of a country's thermal climate, with 22°C (ca. 72°F) as a point of reference for temperate climate (for argumentation, see Chapter 2). The winter index is the sum of the absolute deviations from 22°C for the average lowest and highest temperatures in the coldest month. The summer index is the sum of the absolute deviations from 22°C for the average lowest and highest temperatures in the hottest month. The overall climate index is the sum of all four absolute deviations from 22°C. Three prototypical examples follow.

THE MOST EXTREME CASE ON THE COLD SIDE

In Mongolia, the lowest and highest temperatures in the coldest month are -44°C and 1°C; the lowest and highest temperatures in the hottest month are -6°C and 36°C.

Score for harshness of winters: $|22 - (-44)| + |22 - 1| = 87.$
Score for harshness of summers: $|22 - (-6)| + |22 - 36| = 42.$
Score for harshness of climate: $|22 - (-44)| + |22 - 1| +$
$|22 - (-6)| + |22 - 36| = 129.$

A PROTOTYPICAL CASE ON THE TEMPERATE SIDE

In Burundi, the lowest and highest temperatures in the coldest month are 17°C and 20°C; the lowest and highest temperatures in the hottest month are 28°C and 31°C.

Score for harshness of winters: $|22 - 17| + |22 - 20| = 7$.
Score for harshness of summers: $|22 - 28| + |22 - 31| = 15$.
Score for harshness of climate: $|22 - 17| + |22 - 20| +$
$$|22 - 28| + |22 - 31| = 22.$$

THE MOST EXTREME CASE ON THE HOT SIDE

In Sudan, the lowest and highest temperatures in the coldest month are 5°C and 19°C; the lowest and highest temperatures in the hottest month are 40°C and 48°C.

Score for harshness of winters: $|22 - 5| + |22 - 19| = 20$.
Score for harshness of summers: $|22 - 40| + |22 - 48| = 44$.
Score for harshness of climate: $|22 - 5| + |22 - 19| +$
$$|22 - 40| + |22 - 48| = 64.$$

Country	Winters	Summers	Total
All countries: Range	1–87	2–44	22–29
All countries: Median	25	25	51
All countries: Average	30	24	54
Afghanistan	54	26	80
Albania	41	21	62
Algeria	43	22	65
Andorra	57	23	80
Angola	9	21	30
Antigua and Barbuda	8	25	33
Argentina	44	21	65
Armenia	61	28	89
Australia	51	25	76
Austria	58	25	83
Azerbaijan	61	28	89
Bahamas	20	19	39
Bahrain	19	30	49
Bangladesh	17	27	44
Barbados	7	20	27
Belarus	71	30	101
Belgium	55	24	79
Belize	17	24	41

Benin	4	22	26
Bhutan	28	16	44
Bolivia	45	6	51
Bosnia and Herzegovina	59	21	80
Botswana	38	29	67
Brazil	16	27	43
Brunei	6	18	24
Bulgaria	57	21	78
Burkina Faso	16	42	58
Burma (Myanmar)	9	31	40
Burundi	7	15	22
Cambodia	8	31	39
Cameroon	13	23	36
Canada	78	27	105
Cape Verde	9	20	29
Central African Republic	12	28	40
Chad	17	38	55
Chile	42	20	62
China	52	30	82
Colombia	33	2	35
Comoros	3	19	22
Congo-Brazzaville	13	25	38
Congo-Kinshasa	13	25	38
Costa Rica	21	18	39
Côte d'Ivoire	9	23	32
Croatia	61	22	83
Cuba	14	24	38
Cyprus	35	22	57
Czech Republic	66	25	91
Denmark	60	23	83
Djibouti	6	37	43
Dominica	8	26	34
Dominican Republic	9	26	35
East Timor	4	26	30
Ecuador	40	12	52
Egypt	26	34	60
El Salvador	21	34	55
Equatorial Guinea	8	17	25
Eritrea	6	33	39
Estonia	72	26	98
Ethiopia	37	17	54
Fiji	12	25	37

(continued)

TABLE *(continued)*

Country	Winters	Summers	Total
Finland	72	26	98
France	50	25	75
Gabon	8	26	34
Gambia	16	30	46
Georgia	45	20	65
Germany	60	24	84
Ghana	8	26	34
Greece	34	22	56
Grenada	9	23	32
Guatemala	27	16	43
Guinea	6	23	29
Guinea-Bissau	10	34	44
Guyana	2	21	23
Haiti	8	28	36
Honduras	12	11	23
Hong Kong	22	18	40
Hungary	59	25	84
Iceland	60	13	73
India	23	30	53
Indonesia	4	26	30
Iran	50	25	75
Iraq	34	30	64
Ireland	53	16	69
Israel	36	23	59
Italy	38	21	59
Jamaica	10	25	35
Japan	36	16	52
Jordan	37	23	60
Kazakhstan	67	37	104
Kenya	28	13	41
Kiribati	4	25	29
Kuwait	25	30	55
Kyrgyzstan	71	26	97
Laos	19	29	48
Latvia	72	26	98
Lebanon	27	23	50
Lesotho	47	17	64
Liberia	11	19	30
Libya	26	30	56
Liechtenstein	60	23	83

Lithuania	72	26	98
Luxembourg	59	26	85
Macedonia	59	21	80
Madagascar	31	18	49
Malawi	32	18	50
Malaysia	5	28	33
Maldives	5	25	30
Mali	17	39	56
Malta	21	18	39
Marshall Islands	1	23	24
Mauritania	15	38	53
Mauritius	16	18	34
Mexico	38	11	49
Micronesia	1	23	24
Moldova	60	27	87
Monaco	31	15	46
Mongolia	87	42	129
Morocco	32	31	63
Mozambique	20	36	56
Namibia	39	17	56
Nauru	4	25	29
Nepal	28	16	44
Netherlands	58	19	77
New Zealand	41	12	53
Nicaragua	3	21	24
Niger	17	40	57
Nigeria	7	30	37
North Korea	37	32	69
Norway	66	23	89
Oman	15	34	49
Pakistan	31	28	59
Palau	6	27	33
Panama	6	26	32
Papua New Guinea	5	25	30
Paraguay	34	36	70
Peru	19	16	35
Philippines	8	28	36
Poland	66	24	90
Portugal	32	19	51
Qatar	20	33	53
Romania	68	25	93
Russia	71	30	101
Rwanda	18	7	25

(continued)

TABLE *(continued)*

Country	Winters	Summers	Total
Saint Kitts and Nevis	8	25	33
Saint Lucia	9	23	32
Saint Vincent and the Grenadines	9	23	32
Samoa	6	22	28
San Marino	38	21	59
São Tomé and Principe	11	20	31
Saudi Arabia	32	31	63
Senegal	11	34	45
Serbia and Montenegro	61	22	83
Seychelles	3	19	22
Sierra Leone	4	22	26
Singapore	4	25	29
Slovakia	67	29	96
Slovenia	61	22	83
Solomon Islands	4	25	29
Somalia	8	22	30
South Africa	39	24	63
South Korea	54	25	79
Spain	46	23	69
Sri Lanka	7	23	30
Sudan	20	44	64
Suriname	8	26	34
Swaziland	40	20	60
Sweden	64	25	89
Switzerland	60	23	83
Syria	37	24	61
Taiwan	25	24	49
Tajikistan	63	22	85
Tanzania	20	23	43
Thailand	11	34	45
Togo	8	26	34
Tonga	6	22	28
Trinidad and Tobago	17	29	46
Tunisia	34	29	63
Turkey	62	23	85
Turkmenistan	47	26	73
Tuvalu	4	25	29
Uganda	17	21	38
Ukraine	60	27	87
United Arab Emirates	20	33	53

United Kingdom	47	20	67
United States of America	59	20	79
Uruguay	40	25	65
Uzbekistan	47	26	73
Vanuatu	12	25	37
Venezuela	25	17	42
Vietnam	16	32	48
Yemen	5	28	33
Zambia	26	22	48
Zimbabwe	35	17	52

REFERENCES

Aschoff, J. (1981). Annual rhythms in man. In J. Aschoff (Ed.), *Handbook of behavioral neurobiology: Biological rhythms* (Vol. 4, pp. 475–487). New York: Plenum Press.

Bach, G. R., & Wyden, P. (1969). *The intimate enemy*. New York: Morrow.

Basabe, N., Paez, D., Valencia, J., Gonzalez, J. L., Rime, B., & Diener, E. (2002). Cultural dimensions, socioeconomic development, climate, and emotional hedonic level. *Cognition and Emotion, 16*, 103–125.

Bell, D. (1973). *The coming of post-industrial society*. New York: Basic Books.

Bierhoff, H. W. (2002). *Prosocial behaviour*. Hove, England: Psychology Press.

Bjorklund, D. F., & Kipp, K. (1996). Parental investment theory and gender differences in the evolution of inhibition mechanisms. *Psychological Bulletin, 120*, 163–188.

Blanke, J., & Loades, E. (2005). The executive opinion survey: An essential tool for measuring country competitiveness. In A. Lopez-Claros, M. E. Porter, & K. Schwab (Eds.), *The global competitiveness report 2005–2006* (pp. 213–223). New York: Palgrave MacMillan.

Bond, M. H., Leung, K., Au, A., Tong, K. K., Reimer de Carrasquel, S., et al. (2004). Cultural-level dimensions of social axioms and their correlates across 51 cultures. *Journal of Cross-Cultural Psychology, 35*, 548–570.

Bonta, B. D. (1997). Cooperation and competition in peaceful societies. *Psychological Bulletin, 121*, 299–320.

Boyd, R., & Richerson, P. J. (2005). *The origin of cultures*. New York: Oxford University Press.

Bronfenbrenner, U. (1979). *The ecology of human development: Experiments by nature and design*. Cambridge, MA: Harvard University Press.

Burns, T., & Stalker, G. M. (1966). *The management of innovation* (2nd ed.). London: Tavistock Publications.

Burroughs, W. J. (1997). *Does the weather really matter? The social implications of climate change.* Cambridge, UK: Cambridge University Press.

Buss, D. M. (2004). *Evolutionary psychology: The new science of the mind* (2nd ed.). Boston, MA: Allyn and Bacon.

Carl, D., Gupta, V., & Javidan, M. (2004). Power distance. In R. J. House, P. J. Hanges, M. Javidan, P. W. Dorfman, & V. Gupta (Eds.), *Culture, leadership, and organizations: The GLOBE study of 62 societies* (pp. 513–563). Thousand Oaks, CA: Sage.

Cheung, G. W., & Rensvold, R.B. (2000). Assessing extreme and acquiescence response sets in cross-cultural research using structural equations modeling. *Journal of Cross-Cultural Psychology, 31,* 187–212.

Clutton-Brock, , T. H. (1991). *The evolution of parental care.* Princeton, NJ: Princeton University Press.

Collier, P. (2007). *The bottom billion: Why the poorest countries are failing and what can be done about it.* New York: Oxford University Press.

Coltrane, S. (1988). Father-child relationships and the status of women: A cross-cultural study. *American Journal of Sociology, 93,* 1060–1095.

Cornelius, P., & Warner, A. M. (2000). The executive opinion survey. In World Economic Forum, *The global competitiveness report 2000* (pp. 92–98). New York: Oxford University Press.

Cronbach, L. J., & Furby, L. (1970). How we should measure "change"—or should we? *Psychological Bulletin, 74,* 68–80.

Dawkins, R. (1989). *The selfish gene* (2nd ed.). New York: Oxford University Press.

Dechesne, M., & Kruglanski, A. (2004). Terror's epistemic consequences: Existential threats and the quest for certainty and closure. In J. Greenberg, S. L. Koole, & T. Pyszczynski (Eds.), *Handbook of experimental existential psychology* (pp. 247–262). New York: Guilford Press.

Deutsch, M. (1973). *The resolution of conflict: Constructive and destructive processes.* New Haven, CT: Yale University Press.

Diamond, J. (2005). *Collapse: How societies choose to fail or survive.* London: Allen Lane.

Diener, E., Diener, M., & Diener, C. (1995). Factors predicting the subjective well-being of nations. *Journal of Personality and Social Psychology, 69,* 851–864.

Diener, E., & Oishi, S. (2000). Money and happiness: Income and subjective well-being across nations. In E. Diener & E. M. Suh (Eds.), *Culture and subjective well-being* (pp. 185–218). Cambridge, MA: MIT Press.

Diener, E., & Suh, E. M. (Eds.). *Culture and subjective well-being.* Cambridge, MA: MIT Press.

Ditlevsen, P. D., Svensmark, H., & Johnsen, S. (1996). Contrasting atmospheric and climate dynamics of the last-glacial and Holocene periods. *Nature*, **379**, 810–812.

Dogan, M. (1994). Use and misuse of statistics in comparative research. In M. Dogan & A. Kazancigil (Eds.), *Comparing nations*. Oxford, England: Blackwell.

Dorfman, P. W., Hanges, P. J., & Brodbeck, F. C. (2004). Leadership and cultural variation: The identification of culturally endorsed leadership profiles. In R. J. House, P. J. Hanges, M. Javidan, P. W. Dorfman, & V. Gupta (Eds.), *Culture, leadership, and organizations: The GLOBE study of 62 societies* (pp. 669–719). Thousand Oaks, CA: Sage.

Durkheim, E. (1897/1951). *Suicide: A study of sociology* (J. A. Spaulding & G. Simpson, Trans.). New York: Free Press.

England, P. (1992). *Comparable worth: Theories and evidence*. New York: Aldine de Gruyter.

Figart, D. M. (2000). Equal pay for equal work: The role of job evaluation in an evolving social norm. *Journal of Economic Issues*, **34**, 1–19

Fisher, S. (1986). *Stress and strategy*. London: Lawrence Erlbaum.

Flannery, T. (2005). *The weather makers: How man is changing the climate and what it means for life on earth*. New York: Atlantic Monthly Press.

Fought, J. G., Munroe, R. L., Fought, C. R., & Good, E. M. (2004). Sonority and climate in a world sample of languages: Findings and prospects. *Cross-Cultural Research*, **38**, 27–51.

Frank, R. H. (2005). Does money buy happiness? In F. A. Huppert, N. Baylis, & B. Keverne (Eds.), *The science of well-being* (pp. 461–473). New York: Oxford University Press.

Fredrickson, B. L. (2005). The broaden-and-build theory of positive emotions. In F. A. Huppert, N. Baylis, & B. Keverne (Eds.), *The science of well-being* (pp. 217–238). New York: Oxford University Press.

Fukuyama, F. (1995). *Trust: Social virtues and the creation of prosperity*. New York: Free Press.

Furnham, A., & Argyle, M. (1998). *The psychology of money*. London: Routledge.

Gardner, D. G., & Cummings, L. L. (1988). Activation theory and job design: Review and reconceptualization. In B. M. Staw & L. L. Cummings (Eds.), *Research in organizational behavior* (Vol. 10, pp. 81–122). Greenwich, CT: JAI Press.

Gaulin, S. J. C., & McBurney, D. H. (2001). *Psychology: An evolutionary approach*. Upper Saddle River, NJ: Prentice-Hall.

Gelfand, M. J., Nishii, L. H., & Raver, J. L. (2006). On the nature and importance of cultural tightness-looseness. *Journal of Applied Psychology*, **91**, 1225–1244.

Gelfand, M. J., & Brett, J. M. (Eds.). (2004). *The handbook of negotiation and culture*. Palo Alto, CA: Stanford University Press.

Georgas, J., & Berry, J. W. (1995). An ecocultural taxonomy for cross-cultural psychology. *Cross-Cultural Research*, **29**, 121–157.

Georgas, J., Van de Vijver, F. J. R., & Berry, J. W. (2004). The ecocultural framework, ecosocial indices, and psychological variables in cross-cultural research. *Journal of Cross-Cultural Psychology*, **35**, 74–96.

Golembiewski, R. T., Billingsley, K. R., & Yeager, S. (1976). Measuring change and persistence in human affairs: Types of change generated by OD designs. *Journal of Applied Behavioral Science*, **12**, 133–157.

Gunderson, M. (1994). *Comparable worth and gender discrimination: An international perspective*. Geneva, Switzerland: International Labour Office.

Gupta, V., Sully de Luque, M., & House, R. J. (2004). Multisource construct validity of GLOBE scales. In R. J. House, P. J. Hanges, M. Javidan, P. W. Dorfman, & V. Gupta (Eds.), *Culture, leadership, and organizations: The GLOBE study of 62 societies* (pp. 152–177). Thousand Oaks, CA: Sage.

Halman, L., Luijkx, R., & Van Zundert, M. (Eds.). (2005). *Atlas of European values*. Leiden, The Netherlands: Brill.

Hampden-Turner, C., & Trompenaars, F. (1993). *The seven cultures of capitalism*. New York: Doubleday.

Hanges, P. J., & Dickson, M. W. (2004). The development and validation of the GLOBE culture and leadership scales. In R. J. House, P. J. Hanges, M. Javidan, P. W. Dorfman, & V. Gupta (Eds.), *Culture, leadership, and organizations: The GLOBE study of 62 societies* (pp. 122–151). Thousand Oaks, CA: Sage.

Harrison, L. E., & Huntington, S. P. (Eds.). (2000). *Culture matters: How values shape human progress*. New York: Basic Books.

Helliwell, J. F., & Putnam, R. D. (2005). The social context of well-being. In F. A. Huppert, N. Baylis, & B. Keverne (Eds.), *The science of well-being* (pp. 435–459). New York: Oxford University Press.

Hewlett, B. S. (Ed.). (1992). *Father-child relations: Cultural and biosocial contexts*. New York: Aldine de Gruyter.

Hippocrates, C. (460 B.C./1977). The genuine works of Hippocrates (F. Adams, Trans.). In T. H. Benzinger (Ed.), *Temperature: Part I. Arts and concepts. Benchmark papers in human physiology, Vol. 10*. Stroudsburg, PA: Dowden, Hutchinson, & Ross.

Hofstede, G. (2001). *Culture's consequences: Comparing values, behaviors, institutions, and organizations across nations.* London: Sage.

Houghton, J. T., Ding, Y., Griggs, D. J., Noguer, M., Van der Linden, P. J., Dai, X., Maskell, K., & Johnson, C. A. (Eds.). (2001). *Climate change 2001: The scientific basis.* New York: Cambridge University Press.

House, R. J., Hanges, P. J., Javidan, M., Dorfman, P. W., & Gupta, V. (Eds.). (2004). *Culture, leadership, and organizations: The GLOBE study of 62 societies.* Thousand Oaks, CA: Sage.

Huntington, E. (1945). *Mainsprings of civilization.* New York: Wiley.

Huntington, S. P. (1996). *The clash of civilizations and the remaking of world order.* New York: Simon & Schuster.

Ingham, G. (2004). *The nature of money.* Cambridge, UK: Polity Press.

Inglehart, R. (1997). *Modernization and postmodernization: Cultural, economic, and political change in 43 societies.* Princeton, NJ: Princeton University Press.

Inglehart, R., & Baker, W. E. (2000). Modernization, cultural change, and the persistence of traditional values. *American Sociological Review, 65,* 19–51.

Inglehart, R., Basánez, M., Díez-Medrano, J., Halman, L., & Luijkx, R. (Eds.). (2004). *Human beliefs and values: A cross-cultural sourcebook based on the 1999–2002 values surveys.* Mexico: Siglo XXI Editores [also available from www.worldvaluessurvey.org].

Inglehart, R., Basánez, M., & Moreno, A. (1998). *Human values and beliefs: A cross-cultural sourcebook.* Ann Arbor: University of Michigan Press.

Inglehart, R., & Klingemann, H. D. (2000). Genes, culture, democracy, and happiness. In E. Diener & E. M. Suh (Eds.), *Culture and subjective well-being* (pp. 165–183). Cambridge, MA: MIT Press.

Inglehart, R., & Welzel, C. (2005). *Modernization, cultural change, and democracy.* New York: Cambridge University Press.

Inkeles, A. (1997). *National character: A psycho-social perspective.* New Brunswick, NJ: Transaction Publishers.

Intergovernmental Panel on Climate Change (IPCC): www.ipcc.ch.

Janssen, O. (2001). Fairness perceptions as a moderator in the curvilinear relationships between job demands, and job performance and job satisfaction. *Academy of Management Journal, 44,* 1039–1050.

Johnson, D. W., & Johnson, R. T. (1989). *Cooperation and competition: Theory and research.* Edina, MN: Interaction.

Kabasakal, H., & Bodur, M. (2004). Humane orientation in societies, organizations, and leader attributes. In R. J. House, P. J. Hanges, M. Javidan, P. W. Dorfman, & V. Gupta (Eds.), *Culture, leadership, and organizations: The GLOBE study of 62 societies* (pp. 564–601). Thousand Oaks, CA: Sage.

Kamarck, A. M. (1976). *The tropics and economic development.* Baltimore: Johns Hopkins University Press, published for the World Bank.

Kanazawa, S. (2006). Where do cultures come from? *Cross-Cultural Research,* 40, 152–176.

Kasser, T., & Ryan, R. M. (2001). Be careful what you wish for: Optimal functioning and the relative attainment of intrinsic and extrinsic goals. In P. Schmuck & K. M. Sheldon (Eds.), *Life goals and well-being: Towards a positive psychology of human striving* (pp. 116–131). Goettingen, Germany: Hogrefe & Huber.

Knight, C. (1991). *Blood relations: Menstruation and the origins of culture.* New Haven, CT: Yale University Press.

Krug, E. G., Dahlberg, L. L., Mercy, J. A., Zwi, A. B., & Lozano, R. (2002). *World report on violence and health.* Geneva, Switzerland: World Health Organization.

Kuhn, T. S. (1977). *The essential tension.* Chicago: University of Chicago Press.

Lamb, H. H. (1995). *Climate, history and the modern world.* London: Methuen.

Landes, D. S. (1998). *The wealth and poverty of nations: Why some are so rich and some so poor.* New York: Norton.

Lechner, F. J., & Boli, J. (2005). *World culture: Origins and consequences.* Malden, MA: Blackwell.

Lopez-Claros, A., Blanke, J., Drzeniek, M., Mia, I., & Zahidi, S. (2005). Policies and institutions underpinning economic growth: Results from the competitiveness indexes. In A. Lopez-Claros, M. E. Porter, & K. Schwab (Eds.), *The global competitveness report 2005–2006* (pp. 3–42). New York: Palgrave Macmillan.

Lynn, R. (1971). *Personality and national character.* Oxford, England: Pergamon Press.

Lynn, R. (1991). *The secret of the miracle economy: Different national attitudes to competitiveness and money.* Exeter, England: Social Affairs Unit.

Lyubomirsky, S., King, L., & Diener, E. (2005). The benefits of frequent positive affect: Does happiness lead to success? *Psychological Bulletin,* 131, 803–855.

Marx, K. (1867). *Das Kapital: Kritik der politischen Ökonomie,* Vol. 1. Hamburg, Germany: O. Meissner.

Maslow, A. H. (1943). A theory of human motivation. *Psychological Review,* 50, 370–396.

Maslow, A. H. (1954). *Motivation and personality* (2nd ed.). New York: Harper & Row.

McClelland, D. C. (1961). *The achieving society.* Princeton, NJ: Van Nostrand.

McGovern, T. H. (2000). The demise of Norse Greenland. In W. Fitzhugh & E. I. Ward (Eds.), *Vikings: The North Atlantic saga* (pp. 327–339). Washington, DC: Smithsonian Institution Press.

McMullin, E. (1983). Values in science. In P. D. Asquith & T. Nickles (Eds.), *Proceedings of the 1982 philosophy of science association* (Vol. 2, pp. 3–23). East Lansing, MI: Philosophy of Science Association.

Michael, R. T., Hartmann, H. I., & O'Farrell, B. (Eds.). (1989). *Pay equity: Empirical inquiries.* Washington, DC: National Academy Press.

Miller, E. M. (1994). Paternal provisioning versus mate seeking in human populations. *Personality and Individual Differences, 17,* 227–255.

Mintzberg, H. (1979). *The structuring of organizations: A synthesis of the research.* Englewood Cliffs, NJ: Prentice-Hall.

Mocca, P., Anthony, D., & Brazier, C. (Eds.). (2005). *The state of the world's children.* New York: UNICEF.

Montesquieu, C. d. S. (1748/1989). *L'esprit des lois (The spirit of the laws;* A. M. Cohler, B. C. Miller, & H. S. Stone, Trans.). New York: Cambridge University Press.

Morgan, G. (1986). *Images of organization.* Beverly Hills, CA: Sage.

Nolan, P., & Lenski, G. (1999). *Human societies: An introduction to macro-sociology* (8th ed.). New York: McGraw-Hill.

Oishi, S. (2000). Goals as cornerstones of subjective well-being: Linking individuals and cultures. In E. Diener & E. M. Suh (Eds.), *Culture and subjective well-being* (pp. 87–112). Cambridge, MA: MIT Press.

Osland, J. S., & Bird, A. (2000). Beyond sophisticated stereotyping: Cultural sensemaking in context. *Academy of Management Executive, 14,* 65–77.

Parker, P. M. (1995). *Climatic effects on individual, social, and economic behavior: A physioeconomic review of research across disciplines.* Westport, CT: Greenwood Press.

Parker, P. M. (1997). *National cultures of the world: A statistical reference.* Westport, CT: Greenwood Press.

Parker, P. M. (2000). *Physioeconomics: The basis for long-run economic growth.* Cambridge, MA: MIT Press.

Parsons, K. C. (1993). *Human thermal environments: The effects of hot, moderate and cold environments on human health, comfort and performance.* London: Taylor & Francis.

Rahim, M. A., & Blum, A. A. (1994). *Global perspectives on organizational conflict.* Westport, CT: Praeger.

Reidsma, P. (2007). *Adaptation to climate change: European agriculture.* Unpublished doctoral dissertation, Wageningen University, The Netherlands.

Richerson, P. J., & Boyd, R. (2005). *Not by genes alone: How culture transformed human evolution.* Chicago, IL: University of Chicago Press.

Ritzer, G. (2004). *The McDonaldization of society* (Rev. ed.). Thousand Oaks, CA: Pine Forge Press.

Robbins, M. C., De Walt, B. R., & Pelto, P. J. (1972). Climate and behavior: A biocultural study. *Journal of Cross-Cultural Psychology*, 3, 331–344.

Robertson, D. C. (2002). Business ethics across cultures. In M. J. Gannon & K. L. Newman (Eds.), *The Blackwell handbook of cross-cultural management* (pp. 361–392). Malden, MA: Blackwell.

Ronen, S., & Shenkar, O. (1985). Clustering countries on attitudinal dimensions: A review and synthesis. *Academy of Management Review*, 10, 435–454.

Ross, M. H. (1993). *The culture of conflict: Interpretations and interests in comparative perspective*. New Haven, CT: Yale University Press.

Sachs, J. (2000). Notes on a new sociology of economic development. In L. E. Harrison & S. P. Huntington (Eds.), *Culture matters: How values shape human progress* (pp. 29–43). New York: Basic Books.

Schneider, F. (2002). Size and measurement of the informal economy in 110 countries around the world. Retrieved March 27, 2003, from rru.worldbank.org/documents/paperslinks/informal_economy.pdf.

Scholander, P. F., Hock, R., Walters, V., Johnson, F., & Irving, L. (1950). Heat regulation in some arctic and tropical mammals and birds. *Biological Bulletin*, 99, 237–258.

Schroeder, D. A., Penner, L. A., Dovidio, J. F., & Piliavin, J. A. (1995). *The psychology of helping and altruism: Problems and puzzles*. New York: McGraw-Hill.

Schwartz, S. H. (1994). Beyond individualism/collectivism: New cultural dimensions of values. In U. Kim, H. C. Triandis, C. Kağitçibaşi, S. C. Choi, & G. Yoon (Eds.), *Individualism and collectivism: Theory, method, and applications* (pp. 85–119). Thousand Oaks, CA: Sage.

Schwartz, S. H. (1999). A theory of cultural values and some implications for work. *Applied Psychology: An International Review*, 48, 23–47.

Schwartz, S. H. (2004). Mapping and interpreting cultural differences around the world. In H. Vinken, J. Soeters, & P. Ester (Eds.), *Comparing cultures: Dimensions of culture in a comparative perspective* (pp. 43–73). Leiden, The Netherlands: Brill.

Singelis, T. M., Triandis, H. C., Bhawuk, D. S., & Gelfand, M. (1995). Horizontal and vertical dimensions of individualism and collectivism: A theoretical and measurement refinement. *Cross-Cultural Research*, 29, 240–275.

Smith, P. B., Bond, M. H., & Kağitçibaşi, C. (2006). *Understanding social psychology across cultures*. Thousand Oaks, CA: Sage.

Smith, P. B. (2004). Acquiescent response bias as an aspect of cultural communication style. *Journal of Cross-Cultural Psychology*, 35, 50–61.

Solomon, S., Greenberg, J., & Pyszczynski, T. (2004). The cultural animal: Twenty years of terror management theory and research. In J. Greenberg, S. L. Koole, & T. Pyszczynski (Eds.), *Handbook of experimental existential psychology* (pp. 13–34). New York: Guilford Press.

Sommers, P., & Moos, R. H. (1976). The weather and human behavior. In R. H. Moos (Ed.), *The human context: Environmental determinants of behavior* (pp. 73–107). New York: Wiley.

Sorokin, P. A. (1928). *Contemporary sociological theories.* New York: Harper and Brothers.

Sully de Luque, M., & Javidan, M. (2004). Uncertainty avoidance. In R. J. House, P. J. Hanges, M. Javidan, P. W. Dorfman, & V. Gupta (Eds.), *Culture, leadership, and organizations: The GLOBE study of 62 societies* (pp. 602–653). Thousand Oaks, CA: Sage.

Sullivan, M. J., III. (1991). *Measuring global values: The ranking of 162 countries.* New York: Greenwood.

Taylor, S. (1982). *Durkheim and the study of suicide.* London: Macmillan.

Theil, H., & Galvez, J. (1995). On latitude and affluence: The equatorial grand canyon. *Empirical Economics, 20,* 162–166.

Thierry, H. (1998). Motivation and satisfaction. In P. J. D. Drenth, H. Thierry, & C. J. de Wolff (Eds.), *Handbook of work and organizational psychology* (2nd ed., Vol. 4, pp. 253–289). Hove, England: Psychology Press.

Ting-Toomey, S., & Oetzel, J. G. (2001). *Managing intercultural conflict effectively.* Thousand Oaks, CA: Sage.

Tjosvold, D. (1991). *The conflict-positive organization: Stimulate diversity and create unity.* Reading, MA: Addison-Wesley.

Toffler, A. (1970). *Future shock.* New York: Random House.

Triandis, H. C. (1973). Work and nonwork: Intercultural perspectives. In M. D. Dunnette (Ed.), *Work and nonwork in the year 2001* (pp. 29–52). Monterey, CA: Brooks/Cole.

Triandis, H. C. (1995). *Individualism and collectivism.* Boulder, CO: Westview.

Triandis, H. C. (2000). Cultural syndromes and subjective well-being. In E. Diener & E. M. Suh (Eds.), *Culture and subjective well-being* (pp. 13–36). Cambridge, MA: MIT Press.

Triandis, H. C., & Gelfand, M. J. (1998). Converging measurement of horizontal and vertical individualism and collectivism. *Journal of Personality and Social Psychology, 74,* 118–128.

Trivers, R. L. (1972). Parental investment and sexual selection. In B. Campbell (Ed.), *Sexual selection and the descent of man* (pp. 136–179). Chicago: Aldine.

Trompenaars, F. (1993). *Riding the waves of culture: Understanding cultural diversity in business*. London: Nicholas Brealy.

United Nations Development Programme (1998–2005). *Human development report*. New York: Oxford University Press.

Van de Vliert, E. (1996). Interventions in conflicts. In M. J. Schabracq, J. A. M. Winnubst, & C. L. Cooper (Eds.), *Handbook of work and health psychology* (pp. 405–425). Chichester: Wiley.

Van de Vliert, E. (1997). *Complex interpersonal conflict behaviour: Theoretical frontiers*. Hove, England: Psychology Press.

Van de Vliert, E. (1998). Conflict and conflict management. In P. J. D. Drenth, H. Thierry, & C. J. de Wolff (Eds.), *Handbook of work and organizational psychology* (2nd ed., Vol. 3, pp. 351–376). Hove, England: Psychology Press.

Van de Vliert, E. (2003). Thermoclimate, culture, and poverty as country-level roots of workers' wages. *Journal of International Business Studies, 34*, 40–52.

Van de Vliert, E. (2006a). Autocratic leadership around the globe: Do climate and wealth drive leadership culture? *Journal of Cross-Cultural Psychology, 37*, 42–59.

Van de Vliert, E. (2006b). Climatic ecology of charismatic leadership ideals. *European Journal of Work and Organizational Psychology, 15*, 385–403.

Van de Vliert, E. (2007a). Climatoeconomic roots of survival versus self-expression cultures. *Journal of Cross-Cultural Psychology, 38*, 156–172.

Van de Vliert, E. (2007b). Climates create cultures. *Social and Personality Psychology Compass, 1*, 53–67.

Van de Vliert, E. (2008a). Climate, wealth, and organization. In P. B. Smith, M. F. Peterson, & D. C. Thomas (Eds.), *Handbook of cross-cultural management research* (pp. 333–350). Thousand Oaks, CA: Sage.

Van de Vliert, E. (2008b). Climato-economic niches of employee well-being. In S. Cartwright & C. L. Cooper (Eds.), *The Oxford handbook of organizational well being* (pp. 523–541). New York: Oxford University Press.

Van de Vliert, E., & Einarsen, S. (2008). Cultural construals of destructive versus constructive leadership in major world niches. *International Journal of Cross Cultural Management, 8*, 275–294.

Van de Vliert, E., Einarsen, S., Euwema, M. C., & Janssen, O. (2008). *Ecological limits to globalization of work, organization, and leadership culture*. Manuscript submitted for publication.

Van de Vliert, E., Huang, X., & Levine, R. V. (2004). National wealth and thermal climate as predictors of motives for volunteer work. *Journal of Cross-Cultural Psychology, 35*, 62–73.

Van de Vliert, E., Huang, X., & Parker, P. M. (2004). Do colder and hotter climates make richer societies more, but poorer societies less, happy and altruistic? *Journal of Environmental Psychology*, 24, 17–30.

Van de Vliert, E., & Janssen O. (2002). "Better than" performance motives as roots of satisfaction across more and less developed countries. *Journal of Cross-Cultural Psychology*, 33, 380–397.

Van de Vliert, E., Kluwer, E. S., & Lynn, R. (2000). Citizens of warmer countries are more competitive and poorer: Culture or chance? *Journal of Economic Psychology*, 21, 143–165.

Van de Vliert, E., & Lindenberg, S. (2006). Wealth, climate, and framing: Cross-national differences in solidarity. In D. Fetchenhauer, A. Flache, A. P. Buunk, & S. Lindenberg (Eds.), *Solidarity and prosocial behavior* (pp. 207–222). New York: Springer.

Van de Vliert, E., Schwartz, S. H., Huismans, S. E., Hofstede, G., & Daan, S. (1999). Temperature, cultural masculinity, and domestic political violence: A cross-national study. *Journal of Cross-Cultural Psychology*, 30, 291–314.

Van de Vliert, E., & Smith, P. B. (2004). Leader reliance on subordinates across nations that differ in development and climate. *Leadership Quarterly*, 15, 381–403.

Van de Vliert, E., & Van der Vegt, G. S. (2004). Women and wages world-wide: How the national proportion of working women brings underpayment into the organization. *Organization Studies*, 25, 969–986.

Van de Vliert, E., & Van der Vegt, G. S, & Janssen, O. (in press). Prosocial to egoistic enculturation of our children: A climatoeconomic contextualization. *Negotiation and Conflict Management Research*.

Van de Vliert, E., & Van Yperen, N. W. (1996). Why cross-national differences in role overload? Don't overlook ambient temperature. *Academy of Management Journal*, 39, 986–1004.

Van de Vliert, E., Van Yperen, N. W., & Thierry, H. (2008). Are wages more important for employees in poorer countries with harsher climates? *Journal of Organizational Behavior*, 29, 79–94.

Veenhoven, R. (2000). Freedom and happiness: A comparative study in forty-four nations in the early 1990s. In E. Diener & E. M. Suh (Eds.), *Culture and subjective well-being* (pp. 257–288). Cambridge, MA: MIT Press.

Veenhoven, R. (2005). World database of happiness: www.eur.nl/fsw/research/veenhoven.

Weber, M. (1904/1958). *The protestant ethic and the spirit of capitalism* (T. Parsons, Trans.). New York: Charles Scribner's Sons.

Weick, K. E. (1979). *The social psychology of organizing* (2nd ed.). Reading, MA: Addison-Wesley.

Whiten, A., Horner, V., & Marshall-Pescini, S. (2003). Cultural panthro-
pology. *Evolutionary Anthropology*, 12, 92–105.
Williamson, P., & Moss, R. (1993). Degrees of national wealth. *Nature*, 362,
782.
World Economic Forum (1999–2006). *The global competitiveness report.*
Geneva, Switzerland: World Economic Forum.
World Bank Atlas (1965–2002). Washington, DC: World Bank.
Yukl, G. (2002). *Leadership in organizations* (5th ed.). Upper Saddle River,
NJ: Prentice-Hall.
Zhang, D. D., Zhang, J., Lee, H. F., & He, Y. (2007). Climate change
and war frequency in eastern China over the last millennium. *Human
Ecology*, 35, 403–414.

INDEX

Afghanistan, 226
Africa, 35, 36, 37, 63, 71, 90, 91, 93, 113,
    214, 215, 216, 218
Albania, 72, 73, 175, 226
Algeria, 150, 226
Amish people, 25
Andorra, 226
Angola, 226
Antigua and Barbuda, 226
Argentina, 87, 175, 226
Argyle, M., 18
Armenia, 23, 48, 58, 101, 226
Aschoff, J., 16
Australia, 20, 26, 40, 101, 116, 226
Austria, 23, 86, 156, 174, 197, 226
authority, 12, 19, 25, 170
Azerbaijan, 101, 182, 197, 226

Bach, G. R., 148
Bahamas, 226
Bahrain, 93, 226
Baker, W. E., 19, 26, 115, 120, 124, 205
Bangladesh, 86, 87, 226
Barbados, 118, 119, 226
Basabe, N., 45
Belarus, 43, 47, 51, 57, 63, 103, 150, 226
Belgium, 226
Belize, 226
Bell, D., 120, 205
Benin, 227
Berry, J. W., 200
Bhutan, 227

Bierhoff, H. W., 137
Bird, A., 198, 200
Bjorklund, D. F., 142
Blum, A. A., 153
Bodur, M., 137
Boli, J., 209
Bolivia, 37, 182, 227
Bond, M. H., 198
Bonta, B. D., 144
Bosnia and Herzegovina, 85, 95,
    227
Botswana, 59, 227
Boyd, R., 5, 142, 149
Brazil, 47, 71, 75, 86, 101, 147, 227
Brett, J. M., 153
Britain. See United Kingdom
Bronfenbrenner, U., 151
Brunei, 227
Bulgaria, 72, 179, 227
Burkina Faso, 36, 227
Burma, 227
Burns, T., 166
Burroughs, W. J., 31, 142
Burundi, 34, 35, 36, 96, 225, 227
Buss, D. M., 5

Cambodia, 227
Cameroon, 40, 96, 227
Canada, 23, 34, 40, 85, 101, 125, 183,
    227
Cape Verde, 227
capital. See money

Index

Carl, D., 173
cash. *See* money
Central African Republic, 63, 85, 98, 199, 227
Central America, 12, 90, 113, 118, 119, 214
Chad, 36, 57, 63, 98, 181, 182, 227
Cheung, G. W., 75
child enculturation, 148–153
  climato-economic niches of, 150–153, 159, 201
child labor, 85, 92–97, 207
  climato-economic niches of, 92–97, 103–104, 105, 124, 200, 201, 208
  infant mortality and, 91–92, 97–98
Chile, 22, 227
China, 20, 26, 40, 44, 147, 156, 166, 174, 179, 183, 227
climate protection, 199, 212
  strategies of, 213–221
climate-culture research, 5–6, 7–16
  prediction model, 24–27, 197–198, 219
climate-income causation, 58–60
climate-income compensation, 4, 22, 58, 60–61
  match, 62, 146, 152, 208
  overmatch, 64, 75
  undermatch, 64, 75, 145, 208
climatic context, 7–16, 31–32, 35–36, 199, 201. *See also* climato-economic context
  cold-hot lens, 11–12, 13–14, 203
  cold-temperate-hot lens, 11, 12–16, 67
  computing indices, 225–226
  humidity, 9, 33, 43
  precipitation, 9–10, 33, 41, 43, 47, 59, 96–97, 101, 150, 176, 178, 186
  seasonal variation, 16, 32–33, 68
  summer index, 34, 221, 225, 226–231
  winter index, 34, 221, 225, 226–231
climatic determinism, 32
climatic survival, 119, 138, 139, 140–141
  basic needs and, 17, 139, 140, 214
  climatic resources, 4, 38
  fairness in Africa, 35–36
  genetic survival and, 5, 6, 137, 139, 142–145
  thermal stress, 35, 62, 73–75, 77, 95, 146, 186
climato-economic context, 7, 22–27, 58, 73, 84, 121, 172
  change and stability, 26, 127–130, 217, 218
  threats and challenges, 61–64, 89, 146, 186, 208, 209, 211, 216
Clutton-Brock, T. H., 142
cold. *See* climatic context
Collier, P., 215
Colombia, 48, 71, 227
Coltrane, S., 143
communist rule, 44–45, 71, 128, 178, 198. *See also* rival predictors
Comoros, 34, 36, 95, 96, 227
competition, 11, 36, 86–87, 141, 143, 144, 153, 177
  competitive advantage, 176, 177
conflict, 21, 44, 119, 215, 221. *See also* competition, cooperation, violence
  climato-economic niches of, 145–159
  conflict management, 148–149
Congo, 57, 227
cooperation, 4, 15, 137, 138–145, 167, 170, 171, 202. *See also* child enculturation, leadership
  climato-economic niches of, 145–159, 201
Costa Rica, 227
Côte d'Ivoire, 227
Croatia, 227
Cronbach, L. J., 122
Cuba, 227
cultural adaptation, 8, 10, 13–14, 15, 22, 23–24, 27, 50, 67, 77, 88, 119, 122, 138, 142, 152, 166–172, 175, 202–209. *See also* culture change
  assimilation, 23
  integration, 23, 24
  separation, 23

cultural obsession, 172, 204
 climato-economic niches of, 204,
  210, 211
 control, 169, 170, 181
 creation, 170–171, 220
cultural segments, 200
 climato-economic niches of, 208
 life and death, 200, 201, 205, 206,
  207, 208
 self and others, 200, 201, 205,
  206, 207
 work and organization, 200, 201, 205,
  206, 208
cultural syndrome, 5, 113, 201. *See also*
 easygoing culture, self-expression
 culture, survival culture
 definition, 4, 115
 measurement, 122, 123–124
cultural tightness-looseness, 119, 200
cultural transmission, 4, 5, 113, 137, 149
 compromising, 141, 148, 171
 fair fighting, 148
 problem solving, 141, 148, 171
 walk-away negotiating, 148, 149
culture change, 19, 26, 130
 climato-economic niches of, 127–130,
  215–216
 illusion of, 127
culture perspective, 5–7, 115–119
 adaptational view, 202–211
 conglomerate view, 199–202
 strategic view, 72, 98, 102–103, 211–221
culture-drives-economy camp, 120–121,
 206
Cummings, L. L., 64
Cyprus, 227
Czech Republic, 23, 227

Dawkins, R., 5
Dechesne, M., 185
demands-resources model, 62, 68,
 70, 145
 application, 62, 64, 75
democracy. *See* leadership

Denmark, 66, 70, 86, 150, 156, 179,
 181, 227
Deutsch, M., 141
Diamond, J., 5, 31
Diener, E., 40, 67, 71
discrimination, 181, 183, 210, 214, 216
 climato-economic niches of, 145,
  180–186
 ethnocentrism, 183–186, 210
 nepotism, 183–186, 210
Ditlevsen, P. D., 142
Djibouti, 227
Dogan, M., 60
Dominica, 227
Dominican Republic, 101, 118, 227
Dorfman, P. W., 154
Durkheim, E., 46, 48, 204

East Asia, 12, 20, 90, 113
East Timor. *See* Timor-Leste
easygoing culture, 117–120
 climato-economic niches of, 121–126,
  131, 153–159, 172–187, 201–202
 spontaneous change, 127–130
 strategic creation, 213
ecocultural framework, 200
ecology. *See* climato-economic context
economic context, 7, 16–22, 120, 199,
 201, 210. *See also* climato-economic
 context
 economic decline, 26, 77, 122, 128, 130,
  199, 214
 economic growth, 19, 20, 26, 120, 122,
  128–129, 183, 214, 216
 income inequality, 71, 77, 97, 101, 150,
  176, 178, 186, 198
 income per head, 19, 22, 25, 45, 57,
  58–60
 informal economy, 60, 101
 purchasing power parity, 17, 68, 103
economy-drives-culture camp, 120–121,
 206
Ecuador, 227
Egypt, 20, 66, 87, 175, 218, 227

Einarsen, S., 6
El Salvador, 42, 66, 227
England, P., 103
equatorial grand canyon, 57, 59, 214
Equatorial Guinea, 227
Eritrea, 227
Estonia, 43, 51, 70, 128, 183, 206, 227
Ethiopia, 57, 166, 227
ethnocentrism. *See* discrimination
evolution. *See* human evolution
expatriates, 23–24, 86–87

fauna, 4, 7, 14, 24, 31, 37, 38, 59, 214, 217
Figart, D. M., 102
Fiji, 227
Finland, 103, 156, 174, 175, 183, 228
Fisher, S., 64
Flannery, T., 217
flora, 4, 7, 10, 14, 24, 31, 37, 38, 59, 214, 217
Fought, J. G., 12, 13
France, 66, 179, 228
Frank, R. H., 71
Fredrickson, B. L., 114
Fukuyama, F., 120
Furby, L., 122
Furnham, A., 18

Gabon, 228
Galvez, J., 57
Gambia, 218, 228
Gardner, D. G., 64
Gaulin, S. J. C., 139
Gelfand, M. J., 120, 123, 153
gender, 77, 91
    inequality, 15–16, 143, 144–145
    mother-father investments, 16, 142–144
    son-daughter preference, 5
genetic survival, 138, 139
    climatic survival and, 5, 6, 137, 139,
        142–145
geographic location, 34, 115. *See also*
    rival predictors
    latitude, 6, 11, 45, 48, 101, 140, 214
    longitude, 101

geographical school, 6, 203
Georgas, J., 32, 200
Georgia, 66, 101, 150, 228
Germany, 66, 87, 99, 175, 179, 228
Ghana, 126, 197, 228
global warming, 5, 25, 199, 211–214,
    217–221. *See also* climate protection
globalization, 6, 165, 209
GLOBE project, 9–10, 144, 154, 158, 173
Golembiewski, R. T., 122
Greece, 70, 85, 86, 228
Greenland Norse. *See* Vikings
Grenada, 228
Group of Eight (G8), 212
Guatemala, 228
Guinea, 218, 228
Guinea-Bissau, 97, 98, 228
Gunderson, M., 103
Guyana, 95, 183, 228

habitat, 6, 25, 146, 209. *See also*
    climato-economic context
Haiti, 118, 228
Halman, L., 22, 120
Hampden-Turner, C., 120
happiness, 32, 39, 40–46, 48, 201. *See also*
    life satisfaction
    climato-economic niches of, 65–72,
        77, 200, 201, 207, 214
    health and, 76
    price of, 65–67
Harrison, L. E., 120, 203
health, 10, 46, 48, 62. *See also* life
    satisfaction
    climato-economic niches of, 72–77,
        114, 121, 200, 201, 207, 214
    subjective, 65, 77, 124, 201
    tropical diseases, 15, 59
heat. *See* climatic context
Helliwell, J. F., 72, 75
helping, 51, 146, 147, 153
Hewlett, B. S., 142
Hippocrates, C., 6, 8
Hofstede, G., 5, 11, 86, 88, 99, 158, 198, 200

homeostasis, 13, 18
  homeostatic goods, 18–19
  homeostatic needs, 37, 38, 39, 52, 61,
    78, 105, 198, 207, 209
  homeostatic utility, 22
Homo habilis, 43
Honduras, 31, 228
Hong Kong, 228
Houghton, J. T., 10
House, R. J., 9, 26, 158, 173, 198, 203
Huang, X., 62, 65, 67, 147
Human Development Index, 45, 58–59
human evolution, 13, 32, 37, 43, 113, 142,
    143, 203
Hungary, 75, 86, 228
Huntington, E., 6, 32
Huntington, S. P., 120, 203

Iceland, 70, 228
income inequality. *See* economic
    context; *see* rival predictors
income per head. *See* economic context
India, 20, 87, 228
individualism-collectivism, 40, 115, 123,
    181, 198
Indonesia, 15, 20, 73, 138, 183, 228
Ingham, G., 18
Inglehart, R., 19, 21, 26, 40, 63, 73, 85,
    99, 115, 120, 122, 124, 130, 138, 149,
    203, 205
Inkeles, A., 40
Intergovernmental Panel on Climate
    Change (IPCC), 10, 218
Inuit, 217
Iran, 37, 66, 73, 175, 228
Iraq, 87, 228
Ireland, 175, 228
Israel, 20, 228
Italy, 15, 228

Jamaica, 90, 95, 99, 118, 228
Janssen, O., 40, 64, 87, 150
Japan, 15, 20, 48, 66, 86, 99, 228
Javidan, M., 9, 173

Johnson, D. W., 141, 165
Johnson, R. T., 141, 165
Jordan, 73, 228

Kabasakal, H., 137
Kamarck, A. M., 59
Kanazawa, S., 5
Kasser, T., 84
Kazakhstan, 23, 33, 47, 51, 156, 174, 183,
    228
Kenya, 228
Kipp, K., 142
Kiribati, 217, 228
Klingemann, H. D., 40
Kluwer, E. S., 11
Knight, C., 5
Krug, E. G., 46, 48, 50, 51, 76, 77
Kruglanski, A., 185
Kuhn, T. S., 43
Kuwait, 175, 228
Kyrgyzstan, 221, 228

Lamb, H. H., 221
Landes, D. S., 120, 170
language, 12, 16
    consonants, 12–14, 203
    vowels, 12–14, 203
Laos, 228
Latvia, 43, 51, 128, 206, 228
leadership, 153
    climato-economic niches of, 26,
        153–159, 200, 201, 214
    autocratic, 113, 154, 155, 156, 157, 158,
        159, 169, 170
    democratic, 22, 113, 138, 154, 155, 156,
        157, 158, 159, 169, 170, 181
Lebanon, 228
Lechner, F. J., 209
Lenski, G., 5, 37
Lesotho, 36, 93, 228
Levine, R. V., 62, 147
Liberia, 228
Libya, 228
Liechtenstein, 228

life expectancy, 20, 39, 45, 48
life satisfaction, 39–41, 50, 52, 65, 70, 78,
  87, 104, 197, 198, 208, 209
  climato-economic niches of, 65–78
Lindenberg, S., 203
Lithuania, 43, 51, 86, 128, 206, 229
Little Ice Age, 221
livability, 3, 4, 35, 58, 152, 214. *See also*
  climatic survival
  desert regions, 17, 31, 36, 44, 96,
    199, 218
  polar regions, 17, 31, 214, 218
Lopez-Claros, A., 123
Luxembourg, 229
Lynn, R., 11, 46, 86
Lyubomirsky, S., 114

Macedonia, 73, 101, 229
Madagascar, 229
Malawi, 93, 229
Malaysia, 156, 229
Maldives, 217, 229
Mali, 36, 57, 229
Malta, 85, 220, 229
Marshall Islands, 33, 217, 229
Marx, K., 120, 205
masculinity-femininity, 113, 115, 198, 200
Maslow, A. H., 84, 88, 100
Mauritania, 229
Mauritius, 183, 229
Maya, 31
McBurney, D. H., 139
McClelland, D. C., 120
McGovern, T. H., 221
McMullin, E., 43
Mexico, 87, 229
Michael, R. T., 102
Micronesia, 229
Middle East, 20, 37, 87, 90
Millennium Development Goals, 98, 215
Miller, E. M., 142
Mintzberg, H., 166, 175, 180
Mocca, P., 90
modernization, 89, 181, 205

Moldova, 48, 63, 95, 101, 116, 125,
  138, 229
Monaco, 229
money, 4
  as means of exchange, 17–18, 22, 139
  as standard of value, 18–19
  functions of, 4, 7, 17, 60–61, 62, 221
  origins of, 16–17, 58
  ready (cash), 19, 199, 210
  unready (capital), 19, 199, 210
Mongolia, 34, 85, 95, 183, 221,
  225, 229
Montesquieu, C. d. S., 6, 22, 24, 71
Moos, R. H., 32
Morgan, G., 166
Morocco, 86, 174, 229
mortality salience, 183, 184–185. *See also*
  rival predictors
  bridging role of, 209–211
Moss, R., 57
motivating power parity, 103
Mozambique, 66, 229

Namibia, 229
national level of analysis, 10, 33–34
Nauru, 229
needs. *See* climatic survival
Nepal, 20, 229
nepotism. *See* discrimination
Netherlands, 116, 150, 229
New Zealand, 182, 229
Nicaragua, 229
Niger, 35, 57, 90, 98, 229
Nigeria, 36, 42, 63, 71, 99, 103, 229
Nolan, P., 5, 37
North America, 11, 113, 151, 166
North Korea, 20, 229
Northern Europe. *See* Scandinavia
Norway, 15, 26, 66, 85, 101, 147, 198,
  210, 229

Oetzel, J. G., 153
Oishi, S., 40, 71
Oman, 229

organizational structures and
    strategies, 4
    climato-economic niches of, 165–166,
      173–180, 187, 201, 207, 208
    adhocratic, 166–172
    bureaucratic, 166–170
    impact of mortality, 184–185
Osland, J. S., 198, 200

Pakistan, 63, 66, 198, 229
Palau, 229
Panama, 40, 47, 229
Papua New Guinea, 229
Paraguay, 229
parental investment, 5, 15–16, 142–144
Parker, P. M., 8, 18, 57, 65, 67
Parsons, K. C., 33
Peru, 229
Philippines, 20, 47, 151, 229
Plato, 71
Poland, 229
Portugal, 70, 73, 150, 229
poverty line, 57, 63
poverty reduction, 71, 212, 213–221
power distance, 26, 115, 170, 173, 181
precipitation. *See* climatic context;
    See rival predictors
Putnam, R. D., 72, 75

Qatar, 175, 229

Rahim, M. A., 153
rain. *See* climatic context
Reidsma, P., 217
religion, 16, 21, 119, 146, 175. *See also* rival
    predictors
    Buddhism, 20
    Christianity, 20, 175
    Islam, 20, 174, 175
    secularization, 19, 20, 22, 118, 119, 130,
      205
Rensvold, R. B., 75
research notes, 52–56, 78–83, 105–110,
    131–136, 159–164, 187–194, 222–223

Richerson, P. J., 5, 142, 149
Ritzer, G., 180
rival predictors, 43, 202
    atmospheric pressure, 43
    communist rule, 44–45, 47–48, 178
    country size, 44
    day-night cycles, 45, 197
    economic sector, 175, 179–180, 182–183
    geographic latitude, 45–46, 48, 101
    history, 102
    humidity, 43
    income inequality, 71, 97, 101, 150, 176,
      178, 186
    infant mortality, 97–98
    inflation rate, 101
    informal economy, 101
    mortality salience, 184–185
    obsession with rules, 204
    organizational size, 181–182
    performance-related pay, 101
    precipitation, 43, 47, 96–97, 101, 150,
      176, 178, 186
    religiosity, 102, 118, 119, 175, 178
    response bias, 75
    sampling bias, 126, 208
    traditionality, 118, 119
    wind, 43
Robbins, M. C., 119
Robertson, D. C., 181
Romania, 150, 229
Ross, M. H., 153
Russia, 43, 47, 51, 57, 75, 116, 125, 128, 156,
    179, 197, 206, 229
Rwanda, 229
Ryan, R. M., 84

Sachs, J., 38
Saint Kitts and Nevis, 230
Saint Lucia, 230
Saint Vincent and the Grenadines, 230
Samoa, 230
San Marino, 230
São Tomé and Principe, 230
Saudi Arabia, 230

Scandinavia, 11, 26, 51, 87, 113, 141,
147, 166
Schneider, F., 60
Scholander, P. F., 14
Schroeder, D. A., 137
Schwartz, S. H., 5, 15, 32, 34, 198
self-expression culture, 115–116
climato-economic niches of, 121,
124–126, 153–159, 172–187, 199–202
spontaneous change, 127–129
strategic creation, 219–221
selfishness, 5, 137–138, 146, 169, 170
climato-economic niches of, 145–153,
159, 200, 201, 214, 216
Senegal, 218, 230
Serbia and Montenegro, 186, 230
Seychelles, 34, 36, 230
Sierra Leone, 96, 230
Singapore, 42, 70, 101, 126, 150, 151, 197,
220, 230
Singelis, T. M., 123
Slovakia, 70, 86, 179, 230
Slovenia, 230
Smith, P. B., 5, 34, 75, 157, 158
snow. *See* climatic context
Solomon Islands, 230
Solomon, S., 185
Somalia, 57, 66, 95, 230
Sommers, P., 32
Sorokin, P. A., 6
South Africa, 23, 59, 71, 230
South America, 71, 87, 91, 113, 214
South Korea, 20, 73, 99, 103, 179, 230
Soviet successor states, 26, 44, 57, 68
Spain, 22, 73, 138, 175, 181, 230
Sri Lanka, 20, 230
Stalker, G. M., 166
Sudan, 36, 57, 66, 226, 230
Suh, E. M., 40
suicide, 32, 41, 49
climato-economic niches of, 46–49,
76–77, 203–204
obsession and, 204–205
reduction of, 50–51

religiosity and, 204–205
Sullivan, M. J., 144
Sully de Luque, M., 9, 173
Suriname, 230
survival culture, 115–116
climato-economic niches of, 121–126,
130, 152–153, 169–170, 176–187,
198–202
spontaneous change, 127–130
strategic creation, 213–214
Swaziland, 230
Sweden, 15, 40, 99, 116, 126, 147, 150,
175, 230
Switzerland, 66, 75, 85, 87, 101, 179, 230
Syria, 37, 230

Taiwan, 75, 99, 103, 230
Tajikistan, 58, 63, 85, 181, 230
Tanzania, 42, 43, 72, 85, 101, 230
Taylor, S., 46
temperature. *See* climatic context
Thailand, 15, 47, 230
Theil, H., 57
thermoneutral zone, 14, 37
thermoregulation, 13–14
Thierry, H., 84, 100, 102
Timor-Leste, 181, 227
Ting-Toomey, S., 153
Tjosvold, D., 141
Toffler, A., 205
Togo, 95, 98, 230
Tonga, 230
Triandis, H. C., 5, 72, 75, 99, 115
123, 200
Trinidad and Tobago, 93, 230
Trivers, R. L., 142
Trompenaars, F., 120, 166, 167, 181, 200
Tunisia, 230
Turkey, 20, 86, 166, 230
Turkmenistan, 230
Tuvalu, 217, 230

Uganda, 230
Ukraine, 43, 57, 63, 103, 116, 179, 230

uncertainty avoidance, 9, 26, 115, 118, 173
United Arab Emirates, 230
United Kingdom, 66, 85, 179, 182, 231
United Nations Development
    Programme, 59, 90, 93, 98, 120, 144
United States, 44, 63, 66, 101, 179, 181,
    182, 197, 231
Uruguay, 23, 73, 231
Uzbekistan, 63, 231

Van der Vegt, G. S., 102, 150
Van Yperen, N. W., 7, 100, 102, 140, 141
Vanuatu, 231
Veenhoven, R., 39, 40, 41, 71
Venezuela, 72, 87, 166, 231
Vietnam, 42, 85, 231
Vikings, 26, 31, 50, 141, 210
violence, 36, 48–49, 57, 118, 214, 215, 221

warm-blooded species, 12, 14, 17, 33,
    60, 219
wealth. *See* economic context
weather, 8, 14, 22, 39, 137, 140
Weber, M., 120
Weick, K. E., 211
Welzel, C., 21, 63, 115, 120, 130, 203,
    205
Whiten, A., 4

Williamson, P., 57
work, 4, 15, 84, 85–86. *See also* child
    labor
    climato-economic niches of, 101–105,
        114, 121, 124, 200, 201, 202
    extrinsic-intrinsic motives, 84–89, 99,
        100–101, 207
    paid, 18, 51, 88, 143–145, 166–167
    unpaid, 60, 143–145, 146, 147,
        166–167
World Economic Forum, 25, 123, 177, 182
World Values Surveys, 19, 22, 73, 99,
    115, 119, 120, 122, 124, 130, 149, 152,
    205, 206
world-oriented policies
    creating cultural stability, 217–219
    creating cultural uncertainty, 215–216
    creating self-expression cultures,
        219–221
    creating survival cultures, 213–214
Wyden, P., 148

Yemen, 216, 231
Yukl, G., 153

Zambia, 93, 95, 156, 231
Zhang, D. D., 221
Zimbabwe, 71, 73, 231

LaVergne, TN USA
29 March 2010
177449LV00002B/25/P